D0902637

Government Spending
and Income Distribution
in Latin America

Ricardo Hausmann and Roberto Rigobón
Editors
IESA, Venezuela

Published by the Inter-American Development Bank
Distributed by The Johns Hopkins University Press

Washington, D.C.
1993

The views and opinions expressed in this publication are those of the authors and do not necessarily reflect the official position of the Inter-American Development Bank.

Government Spending and Income Distribution in Latin America

© Copyright 1993 by the Inter-American Development Bank
1300 New York Avenue, N.W.
Washington, D.C. 20577

Distributed by
The Johns Hopkins University Press
2715 North Charles Street
Baltimore, Maryland 21218-4319

Library of Congress Catalog Card Number: 93-079315
ISBN: 0-940602-65-2

AUTHORS

Briceño, Arturo
Economist, Researcher at the Analysis for Development Group (GRADE), Peru.

Escobal, Javier
Economist, Researcher at the Analysis for Development Group (GRADE), Peru.

González, Rosa Amelia
Researcher at the Institute of Advanced Studies in Management (IESA), Venezuela.

Hausmann, Ricardo
Minister, Central Planning and Coordination Office of the Presidency (CORDIPLAN), Venezuela

Larrañaga, Osvaldo
Economist, Researcher at the Latin American Institute for Economic and Social Development (ILADES), Chile.

Márquez, Gustavo
Economist, Associate Professor of Economics at the Institute of Advanced Studies in Management (IESA), Venezuela.

Mujica, Patricio
Economist, Researcher at the Latin American Institute for Economic and Social Development (ILADES), Chile.

Mukherjee, Joyita
Economist, Associate Researcher at the Institute of Advanced Studies in Management (IESA), Venezuela.

Navarro, Juan Carlos
Economist, Associate Researcher at the Institute of Advanced Studies in Management (IESA), Venezuela.

Pascó Font, Alberto
Economist, Researcher at the Analysis for Development Group (GRADE), Peru.

Palacios, Roberto
Economist, Associate Researcher at the Institute of Advanced Studies in Management (IESA), Venezuela.

Rathe, Magdalena
Economist, ECOCARIBE Researcher, Dominican Republic.

Rigobón, Roberto
Economist, Associate Researcher at the Institute of Advanced Studies in Management (IESA), Venezuela.

Rodríguez, José
Economist, Visiting Researcher at the Analysis for Development Group (GRADE), Peru.

Santana, Isidoro
Economist, ECOCARIBE Researcher, Dominican Republic.

FOREWORD

This is the second book of a series published under the Centers for Research in Applied Economics Project sponsored by the Inter-American Development Bank. In keeping with the centers' objective of addressing the major economic and social problems affecting Latin America and the Caribbean, this volume examines the effects of public spending, taxation, and price policies on the distribution of income.

External shocks, high levels of inflation, and inefficiently managed state enterprises have in many cases led to a resurgence of government deficits. Along these lines, this study examines the discrepancies between government revenues and spending by focusing great attention on the impact of mechanisms that governments in Latin America have used to make resource transfers. These venues for collecting and spending revenues—namely the tax system, public health care, education, pension funds, and direct subsidies to productive sectors—merit close attention in order to ascertain whether governments are adopting adequate spending priorities and having a positive impact on equity and efficiency.

The book establishes parameters by which it will determine and evaluate whether a mechanism is progressive or regressive. In order to classify a program as progressive in the cases analyzed, per capita transfers to the lower-income strata of the population had to be greater in absolute terms than those received by the higher-income strata, or the transfer had to account for a greater proportion of the lower-income strata total income in relation to the higher-income. The study also clearly defines that an ideal transfer, from a distributional standpoint, should be both focused and transparent. Following these guidelines, the book examines tax collection and the other basic spending programs described above in Peru, Venezuela, the Dominican Republic, and Chile.

A review of government revenue and spending mechanisms instituted in these countries reveals that mechanisms that seek to transfer resources to the lower-income segments of the population often lack focus and, therefore, often are regressive. Given that some of these programs have proven to be progressive in relative terms, however, the authors have not recommended eliminating subsidies completely. Eliminating them would further exacerbate the poverty of the lower-income groups and prevent the government from attaining its objective of greater efficiency and more equitable income distribution. The authors' principal recommendation revolves around the need to design focused and transparent transfer mechanisms, a strategy which would rule out price controls and sectoral subsidies.

Nohra Rey de Marulanda, Manager
Economic and Social Development Department

CONTENTS

CHAPTER ONE

GOVERNMENT SPENDING AND INCOME DISTRIBUTION

Ricardo Hausmann[1]
Roberto Rigobón

In the 1980s, Latin American countries sustained external shocks that lowered their real income and impaired the ability of governments to generate revenues. Added to this problem were the demands of the poorest segments of the population for increased assistance through social spending or targeted subsidies.

Governments were confronted with deficits that forced them to revise existing programs or apply new measures to assist the lowest income groups. These measures affected both the generation of revenues and government spending, and are analyzed below.

The objective of this chapter is to provide a comparison of the national programs of Chile, the Dominican Republic, Peru, and Venezuela. First, certain criteria are defined to establish a common theoretical framework. Second, the differences and similarities in the various programs are highlighted, distinguishing between the types of measures implemented. Finally, relevant policy recommendations are given for all countries of the region that are experiencing the same popular demands and similar restrictions in their ability to respond.

[1] This chapter was produced under the direction of Gustavo Márquez. The first phase was coordinated by Ricardo Hausmann, who left the project as a result of his appointment as Minister of CORDIPLAN. I would like to thank Raquel Benbunam, Rosa Amelia González, Janet Kelly, and Juan Carlos Navarro for their invaluable comments and assistance.

What Constitutes an Effective Distribution Program?

What are the characteristics of a transfer aimed at improving the distribution of income? The first question addressed below is how to determine whether a program is progressive or regressive. The second is how the distribution of income affects inflation and unemployment. Third, the characteristics of an ideal distribution program are presented.

Progressive vs. Regressive

A transfer or spending program is considered progressive when the quantity of resources distributed to the lower income groups is greater, in absolute terms, than the amount distributed to the higher income groups. This is the most commonly used definition of progressivity. In this section, we will expand on this concept by giving two definitions of progressivity, one in absolute terms and the other in relative terms.

Let's assume that society has a linear utility function; i.e., the marginal utility of a dollar is constant across the income spectrum. If, in this case, the utility of the lower income groups is to be increased, then the transfer to this level must be larger than the transfer to the higher income level. This is the traditional definition of progressivity in absolute terms, and, as can be clearly seen, it is the result of assuming one type of utility function for society. On the other hand, if we assume that society's utility function is not linear but rather has decreasing returns to scale, then the marginal utility of each dollar decreases with the level of income. In the specific case of a CRRA[2] utility function, the marginal utility of a fixed percentage of income is constant; i.e., $100 for a person with an income of $1,000 has the same utility as $10 for a person whose income is $100.

Given this perspective, if a progressive transfer is to be made, the amount distributed to the lower income groups must necessarily represent a larger proportion of their income than in the case of a transfer to the higher income groups. Although the absolute amount distributed to the lower levels is less, it represents a larger contribution in proportion to the income.[3] Thus, a program is considered progressive if it is less regressive than the distribution of income; programs fulfilling this condition will be defined as progressive in relative terms.

The first definition of progressivity is more restrictive than the second; when it is satisfied, there is always relative progressivity. If a transfer in absolute terms is greater for the lower income level, it will also be so in relative terms.

---

[2] Constant Relative Risk Aversion (CRRA)—utility functions with a constant relative risk aversion coefficient.
[3] See A. Dixit, 1990.

It is difficult to argue for or against either of these definitions. The basic difference between them is the utility function assumed for society, despite the fact that the aim of both is to improve the welfare of the lower income groups. Both definitions will be used in this paper, and it will be indicated when a subsidy is progressive in absolute terms and when it is progressive in relative terms.

Inflation and Unemployment and their Effects on Income Distribution

In this section we will analyze the impact that inflation and unemployment can have on income distribution. Inflation can be interpreted as a restriction that a government encounters when it embarks on a spending program, while unemployment is the restriction it encounters when an adjustment program is implemented.

The restrictions operate as follows: When governments incur deficits that are not sustainable in the long term, they cause inflation, which will wipe out improvements made in the distribution of income. And if the macroeconomic adjustment required causes a high rate of unemployment (as it did in Chile and Peru), inequity in the distribution of income will increase. In the national studies, the effects of inflation and unemployment on the distribution of income will be indicated more or less specifically, but they all tend to intensify the regressive effect of both inflation and unemployment.

Inflation

The impact of inflation on income distribution can be analyzed from two different perspectives. The first concerns the effects of inflation when there are different marginal propensities to consume and when the consumption pattern of groups reacts differently to inflation. The second perspective is the effect of inflation on the value of the assets of different social groups.

If inflation is viewed as a tax on consumption, groups that have a greater marginal propensity to consume will be more affected than those that don't. Lower income groups have a greater marginal propensity to consume than higher income groups; therefore, inflation will have a greater impact on the former. Moreover, the basket of consumer goods of the lower income groups—consisting primarily of food—will be more affected due to the fact that inflation has a greater impact on perishable consumer goods. Goods consumed by these groups are more sensitive to inflation than those consumed by higher income groups.

All the conclusions that can be drawn regarding consumption indicate that inflation has a negative effect on income distribution, with the lower income groups being further impoverished as a result. However, analyzing the problem from the perspective of income leaves no doubt that real wages have affected income distribution, which has declined in recent years.

By dividing capital into two types—fixed assets and human capital—it can be assumed that the value of the former increases more than the latter in inflationary periods. The price of fixed assets increases with the real interest rate, which may or may not be positive during inflationary periods. The price of human capital is the real wage, which normally falls with inflation. Assuming that distribution of the types of capital varies across the income spectrum, the group whose income depends more on human capital will be more affected by inflation.

Higher income groups generally own fixed assets and, therefore, the decline in real wages caused by inflation affects their income less, while it affects the income of poorer families more. Moreover, the problem is not that the latter have only human capital, but rather that the little capital they have is highly specific, which makes mobility in the labor market more difficult. In other words, the lower income groups acquire human capital through their work experience (learning by doing) and this is so specific that their knowledge has no value in other sectors. For example, a worker with five years experience in the textile industry will be hired in the construction industry as an apprentice, or at least not at a level commensurate with five years of experience.

Inflation through the pattern of consumption, the marginal propensity to consume, the exclusive reliance on human capital and the specificity thereof are more damaging to lower income groups; the effect of inflation could therefore be considered regressive in absolute terms.

Unemployment

If each social group is not proportionally represented among the ranks of the unemployed, then the public measures affecting unemployment will have distributive effects. Recent evidence demonstrates that the composition of the unemployed changed in the 1980s, with lower income groups accounting for a growing percentage.

Economic theories that explain unemployment—both voluntary and involuntary[4]—predict that the group with the least mobility will be more represented among the unemployed.

The search models indicate that unemployment is the result of a search process that people undertake to obtain a reservation wage, and that the frictions of the labor market prevent full employment. These frictions increase with the lack of labor mobility; therefore,

---

[4]   Involuntary unemployment is explained by the theory of efficiency wages, while voluntary unemployment is based on the search theory. See Weiss (1991), Blanchard and Fisher (1989), Sargent (1987) and Lindbeck and Snower (1988) for a more detailed discussion.

lower income groups, with specific human capital, will spend more time looking for a job.

According to the theory of efficiency wages, unemployment is used as a mechanism to correct the behavior of workers. The size of correction required is proportional to the level of idleness among workers and the cost of unemployment, the latter being affected by the frictions of the labor market. Assuming that all workers require the same incentive to make an effort (all have the same level of idleness, regardless of income level), unemployment will exist in those groups where the costs and frictions are greater.

Both theories predict that unemployment will be most pronounced among groups with the greatest frictions, i.e., the lower income groups. An increase in unemployment will reduce the average family income of the lower socioeconomic groups. The Chilean study was the only one that analyzed the relationship between unemployment and income distribution, corroborating the conclusions set forth here.

Inflation, Unemployment and Fiscal Accounts

Inflation and unemployment stem from the fiscal management of governments and, from the distributive viewpoint, can be interpreted as restrictions the state encounters when it wants to implement a transfer program or system.

Inflation limits the financing or deficit a government can incur to justify a social spending program, which, if it is not sustainable, will cause inflation. Moreover, if the objective is to improve foreign sector accounts, macroeconomic adjustment will cause a certain level of unemployment, which will require additional funds to cope with the needs of the most affected groups, making the adjustment inadequate.

Awareness of these effects adds a new dimension to the problem of distribution. The resources allocated to address it will always be restricted by inflation and unemployment, making it essential that social spending be as efficient as possible. Otherwise, the restrictive mechanisms (inflation or unemployment) will wipe out any distributive benefits gained. Following is an analysis of the characteristics of an ideal transfer of resources consistent with the restrictions.

Characteristics of an Ideal Transfer Program

In this section the characteristics of an ideal transfer program and of an ideal transfer system are analyzed. The difference between the two is the length of time required. The first involves transfers with a relatively short useful life, while the second is permanent. For example, a direct allowance to poor mothers is a type of transfer program and the social security system is a transfer system.

A resource transfer program can be considered ideal if, given a definition of progressivity (relative or absolute), it is efficient, effective, progressive, focused, and the fiscal deficit it generates is sustainable. On the other hand, a transfer system is ideal if it is efficient, effective, progressive, general, and it produces no long-term deficit; in other words, if it is fully financed.

In both cases the transfer must be efficient, effective and progressive, obviously desirable characteristics. Efficiency means that the distortion caused by the program must be minimal and that the transfer of resources must involve the lowest possible cost. Effectiveness means that the program achieves its goal, which is generally progressivity.

A transfer program must be focused, so that the resources reach the target groups. In contrast, a transfer system must be general, to ensure its political viability in the long term. In this sense, a focused transfer is less likely to endure than a general transfer, since the former depends on the political will of its promoters, while the latter always has a collective character that guarantees its survival. A focused transfer program is like a subsidy to the group that receives the resources and a tax on the rest of society, which means that in the long term there will be incentives or pressures to abolish it. A general transfer system does not represent a tax on any specific group and therefore is not attacked by various segments of society.

The national studies found that the best way to focus resources is through public spending and not through the tax system. This is the direct consequence of the fact that expenditures are easier to allocate to target groups than to set aside for specific taxpayers.

Both the transfer program and the transfer system require financing. In the former case, a certain fiscal deficit sustainable over the life of the program is permissible. If the deficit is not sustainable, an adjustment will be necessary, which will cause inflation or unemployment, with the distributive consequences analyzed above. In the latter case, the restriction is greater due to the fact that the useful life of a transfer system is much longer; a small deficit today can become an unmanageable deficit in the future. Therefore, transfer systems cannot generate deficits and must be fully financed. The national studies show that there are numerous transfer systems that had a deficit for many years, so that these systems had or will have to be reformed in order to continue functioning.

If it is essential that a program continue functioning despite a lack of resources, the level of services offered will deteriorate as efforts are made to reduce demand; public health and education programs that discriminate through poor quality and old-age pensions that provide negative real interest rates are examples of this phenomenon. To avoid the negative effects of inflation, transfer programs and transfer systems must be viable in the long term.

In conclusion, governments must collect taxes in the least distorting manner possible through a tax system that is flexible and permits adapting revenue to needs. Distribution must be achieved through social spending, which must be efficient, effective and progressive; the deficit it generates must be sustainable in the long term and focused or general, as required.

Comparative Study on Distribution Programs

The regional studies looked at various mechanisms used by Latin American governments to transfer resources to society: the tax system, public health expenditures, social insurance and education funds, direct subsidies to productive sectors (such as agricultural and housing subsidies), price system controls and, finally, direct transfers to specific sectors of the population. Table 1.1 indicates the distribution of the policies analyzed in the national studies.

In the following section the most important conclusions of the regional studies are presented, grouped according to the concepts listed in Table 1.1. The similarities and differences are stressed, leaving their description to the respective regional studies.

Table 1.1 Policies Analyzed by Country

	Chile	Dominican Republic	Peru	Venezuela
Tax system		1		
Social spending	2	1	1	2
Subsidies		1	1	
Prices			1	2
Direct transfer	1			

Distributive Effects of a Tax System

The distributive impact of the Dominican Republic's tax system was measured, as well as the percentage of the tax burden on the average income of each socioeconomic level. This, by definition, is a measure of relative and not absolute progressivity. The work indicates there is a certain degree of relative progressivity in the tax system; in other words, lower income groups pay a lower proportion of their income than that paid by higher income groups.

Analyzing the characteristics of the system, we find that its progressivity results from taxes on fuels, communications, income, and net worth. This means the tax rate for higher income groups increases with the tax on the goods they consume.

Nevertheless, the study of the Dominican Republic shows that the results of redistributing income through the tax system are less effective than those obtained through spending on housing and health, indicating that taxation is not necessarily the best way to redistribute income.

Social Spending on Education, Health Care, Social Insurance and Old-Age Pension Funds

In this section, a comparison is made of the results obtained in the regional studies of spending on education, health care and retirement and social insurance funds.

Education

Education spending was analyzed for Chile, Peru and Venezuela. In Chile, only expenditures on higher education were studied. In the following, a distinction will be made between spending on basic education (elementary and secondary) and higher education. The three studies reveal that spending on basic education is progressive in absolute terms and that spending on higher education is regressive in absolute terms, but progressive in relative terms.

The progressivity of basic education expenditures and the regressivity in absolute terms of higher education expenditures can be explained. We will assume that there are two basic education systems in a society: one private, of high quality and expensive, and the other public, of lower quality but free of charge. The assumption is also made that there is only one higher education system, which is public and free of charge, but whose capacity is limited and entrance to which is consequently competitive.

General resources are scarce, and using them for higher education tends to lower the quality of basic public education. Students in the latter system are not as well prepared and, consequently, are less likely to enter the higher education system. The students in basic private education are the ones who pursue a higher education, making the spending on that system regressive in absolute terms. Higher income groups can pay for basic private education and will study in private schools and universities, while the lower income groups will have to content themselves with public schools. This problem is exacerbated when it is impossible to cut spending on higher education because it is progressive in relative terms and the groups who use the system are generally able to exert a great deal of political pressure.

For example, the Chilean study mentions a reform that could not be implemented in its entirety, but which points in the following direction: public spending on higher education should be devoted to strengthening and promoting research, granting loans to students economically disadvantaged, and transferring resources to universities on the basis of their ability to attract the best students. The aim of the reform was to compensate for one of the market failures of the higher education system: limited or nonexistent access to the credit market.

This market failure exists because the only assets students have to guarantee a loan is their human capital, which will be manifested in the future in the form of greater productivity. But the only guarantee that a student can give is human capital, which is intangible and, therefore, difficult to collect. If a loan is granted, some students will find countless excuses for not paying it back. The banks are therefore forced to charge a higher interest rate, reflecting the likelihood that students will not pay, which creates a negative selection problem, so that students who intend to pay the loan find that the interest rate is too high and consequently leave the system. The only ones who remain in the system are the ones least likely to pay. The banks raise the interest rate even higher and the market disappears because of the lack of guarantees.

The government may intervene, based on the assumption that it will be easier for it to do so, or that it will have ways of exerting pressure to collect the loans. The Chilean reform is aimed at solving this problem. It also creates the right incentives so that universities try to attract the best students as a way of obtaining more funds.

The reform also calls for the state to grant financing for research and development. In this case, the problem may be that there are no clear patent laws and, consequently, no incentives to invest in research and development. The reform was not approved or carried out in its entirety due to pressures from the interest groups that blocked privatization of the educational system.

Health Care

Health care expenditures were studied with respect to the Dominican Republic and Venezuela. In both cases social spending on health care was found to be progressive in absolute terms, but the inability to satisfy demand caused the system to collapse, harming users through the poor quality of care. This effect is known in the literature as discrimination through quality.

In the Dominican Republic, the flaws in the system are so serious that the lower income groups have no choice but to seek help from the private health care system.

The problem of health care spending has not been solved[5] and there are many scenarios that address it. As the Venezuelan example shows, the solution is to separate the provision of medical care from payment, leaving the private sector in charge of the former and the state as an insurance company responsible for payment. In this context, the government must provide the right incentives in the medical sector to guarantee high quality care.

The way the British system operates is a good illustration. The salaries of doctors who belong to the health care service are paid by the government, based on the number of patients the doctor sees. The patient selects the doctor of his choice and can change whenever he likes. All medical consultations and services (laboratory, X-rays, CAT scans, etc.) are ordered by the assigned doctor and the patient cannot go to another doctor unless he requests a change.

The incentives for a doctor to keep his patients as healthy as possible are built into the system. By keeping his patients healthy, the doctor is able to care for more patients. Unnecessary consultations and tests

---

are eliminated. The best doctor will keep his patients healthier and will have more patients and, consequently, more income. This way of creating incentives guarantees the quality of the health care system. The state collects payments, processes requests for a change of physician, and pays salaries and the cost of medical tests.

Social Insurance and Old-Age Pension Funds

The subject of the Chilean study was the reform of the social insurance system, which was found to be regressive in absolute terms. The study indicates this is the result of the regressive effect of the system's fixed fee, which is justified by the fixed costs the administrators incur in managing the individual accounts. However, the system is indeed regressive, since the fixed fee represents a larger percentage among lower income groups. Although the fee is justified by the fixed costs of the Pension Fund Administrators, it is unclear, from an economic viewpoint, why this price discrimination exists. Therefore, it would be important to identify the market failure (if there is one) and to justify government intervention, not necessarily through a subsidy but rather through regulation and control.

Another very important contribution of the study is measuring the progressivity of the system with respect to coverage, it being shown that, despite an increase in coverage in recent years, more than 30 percent of the work force remains outside the system. The state's efforts should be focused on expanding this coverage while removing obstacles that keep people out of the system. The study explains that this limitation exists because of the fixed fees or the sale of weak instruments by the Pension Fund Administrators. We strongly recommended that these subjects be studied in depth, since it would provide a better understanding and a means of more specifically defining the market failure responsible for the workers' indifference and what the state can do to lessen its impact.

It is important to realize there are also progressive aspects within the system. First, although deficiencies exist in the credit market and small investors may have no access to certain financial instruments, they do have access through the Pension Fund Administrators. The increase in efficiency works more to the benefit of lower income groups.

Second, the minimum return guaranteed by the state is more valuable to those with smaller deposits in the system. Viewed from the perspective of the options theory, the guarantee can be interpreted as an implicit put the government has given. The greater the value of the put, the greater the transfer from the state. The option is on the funds deposited, with a term of validity equal to the retirement period and an exercise price equal to the guarantee provided by the state. According to the options theory, the smaller the value of the asset optioned, the greater the value of the put. In other words, the smaller the deposits, the greater the value of the option and, consequently, the greater the transfer.

Old-age pensions studied in Venezuela were found to be transfers from workers to the state, since the pension received is much smaller than the contributions made plus the interest earned. The system can be viewed as a tax, which is rather far from its original objective of being social security.

To determine whether the transfer is progressive or regressive, an analysis was made of pensions received and contributions made. First, the pensions were calculated on the basis of a given wage that is the same for all contributors. Pensions represent a larger proportion of the income of less advantaged groups, which gives the system a progressive character.

Second, contributions made by workers have regressive characteristics in relative terms since they are calculated as a percentage of the wage, but limited to a maximum. The result is that lower income groups contribute a larger proportion of their wages than higher income groups. It is difficult to separate the two effects and to reach a conclusion about the progressivity or regressivity of the system.

It is interesting to compare the situations of Chile and Venezuela. The former is a privately managed individual capitalization system, while the latter is part contributory and part collectively capitalized; it could be described as a publicly managed, hybrid system. The difference in effectiveness in achieving social goals is obvious. The problem is that there are no incentives in Venezuela to invest the funds as efficiently as possible, resulting in negative real interest rates.

Subsidies to Specific Productive Sectors

This section examines the agricultural subsidy in Peru and the housing purchase subsidy in the Dominican Republic.

In Peru there are three transfer mechanisms: the minimum sales price guarantee, subsidies for agricultural inputs such as fertilizers and pesticides, and soft loans to producers. Subsidies are granted primarily for rice, cotton and yellow corn, which are produced for the most part by high-income farmers. Consequently, the transfer of resources is regressive in absolute terms, since it is more favorable to wealthier farmers.

The rule is to set the guaranteed price 20 to 40 percent higher than the average production cost. With this type of rule, negative selection problems arise since no account is taken of quality or of soil conditions. By ranking farmers according to their production costs, small farmers are placed within the range of the highest average costs and large farmers within the range of lowest average costs. Although the guaranteed price is based on the average, the actual result is that a tax is collected from small farmers and a subsidy is granted to large farmers. The study stresses that the transfer occurred to and from the agricultural sector.

Moreover, the price to the consumer was not much less than the shadow price, which shows that the transfer of resources from the state to the agricultural sector did not result in greater social welfare.

In the case of housing in the Dominican Republic, the state concentrated its efforts on increasing the housing supply and subsidizing mortgage credits. In both cases, the market failure justifying government intervention is unclear. The housing supply increased by only one percent, while funds were diverted to mortgage credits.

It is important to note that a simple model shows that every subsidy to the housing sector will be transferred to the builder and not to the consumer. It can be assumed that the supply curve is inelastic in the short term and that attempts to lower the price cause increases in demand, which in turn generate upward pressure within the sector, offsetting the subsidy.

The study shows that in absolute terms the subsidy is regressive, but in relative terms it is progressive. In absolute terms, the poorest 40 percent receive 16 percent of the subsidy, while the richest 10 percent receive 21 percent of the benefits.

Price Controls

In this section we will examine fuel in Peru and the prices of electricity and fuel in Venezuela. It should be noted that in all three instances, the government grants implicit subsidies in an attempt to modify relative prices.

The subsidies can be very large, as in the case of fuel in both Peru and Venezuela, where the subsidy represents 4 percent and 2.3 percent of GDP, respectively. The tax in Peru on this type of product was also analyzed.

All three studies describe price system controls beset by serious focalization problems, resulting in the diversion of government funds from their original objective. The equilibrium ends up being regressive in absolute terms but progressive in relative terms. This explains why, when the government wants to lift controls, numerous social problems ensue.[6]

Price controls have serious fiscal implications since the subsidy is granted implicitly, leaving the precise amount granted unclear. In the case of fuel in both Peru and Venezuela, the subsidy is granted through the state petroleum enterprise. There is no discussion of the size of the outlay and, in addition, it is difficult to determine its scope. The justification given is that it keeps costs down, especially the price of public transportation. In both cases, however, the transfer to the transportation sector is less than 10 percent of the total subsidy.

In the case of electricity, two types of transfers were studied, the electrical rate subsidy and the "theft" subsidy, which results from illegal connections. The former is regressive in absolute terms and is the result of greater electrical consumption by the higher income groups. The "theft" subsidy goes to the lower income groups and, therefore, it is found that this transfer is progressive in absolute terms. The subsidy as a whole is not regressive in absolute terms and is therefore progressive in relative terms.

---

[6] So much so that in Venezuela, after the coup attempt, price controls were announced on five products, including gasoline and electricity.

The results may suggest that the solution is to allow a greater degree of theft in order to improve distribution. However, the study indicates that the rate subsidy should be decreased and that the theft should be curbed. If a transfer to the lower income groups is the objective, it should not be achieved by rewarding an illegal activity.

Direct Transfer

Finally, the direct transfer system in Chile targets households and directs funds to them based on their socioeconomic level. It should be noted that all households receive some type of transfer, which is similar to a lump-sum transfer, the least distorting of all transfers. The study shows that the system is efficient and effective in absolute terms.

One of the conclusions to be drawn from the Chilean study is that societies must invest in the implementation of a direct transfer system that will permit the efficient eradication of inequalities.

The Trap in the System

In the 1980s, Latin America sustained multiple external shocks that reduced its real income. Unemployment and inflation rose and the situation of lower income groups worsened. They sought greater resources at a time when Latin American governments had external deficits and extremely rigid tax systems. Increased fiscal deficits and high rates of inflation resulted.

To solve the problems of external imbalance, processes of adjustment and trade liberalization were set in motion which eroded government revenues from customs, so that the adjustment required to achieve external balance was even greater. Unemployment rose, worsening the situation of lower income groups and increasing the pressure on governments to effect transfers.

In the regional studies, particular emphasis is given to the deterioration of the distribution of income in recent decades.

The question is: How can Latin American governments satisfy the demand for transfers? Because the current social system, the health care system, the educational system, etc. were (or are) inefficient, getting resources to the most needy groups through these systems was (and is) difficult, if not impossible. Except for Chile, there is no direct transfer system.

Governments, forced to take a nontraditional approach, ended up changing the tax system, changing the relative prices of certain products, and granting direct subsidies to productive sectors. All of these transfer systems were aimed at solving the short-term problem of the neediest groups, but they did not solve the basic problem, which is the productive capacity of these sectors. Moreover, in Peru, spending on education was cut so that more money could be allocated for these programs.

All of the measures attempted have efficiency and focalization problems and, in the final analysis, are generally regressive in absolute terms but progressive in relative terms, so that it is almost impossible to abolish them without creating another social ill. This is why this section is called the trap in the system. Governments fall into a trap created by the lack of an efficient social system and the development of alternative transfer mechanisms, which also prove to be inefficient but which, in relative terms, are important for the lower income groups and cannot be eliminated. It would be more productive from the social viewpoint if an investment were made in a direct transfer system, like the one in Chile, and if subsidies and price controls were replaced by direct transfers.

It should be noted that each instance of government intervention mentioned above addresses the income problem without reflecting any concern for the long-term problem, which is the formation of human capital. Moreover, in certain cases, short-term pressures have worked against such a formation.

The final recommendation to emerge from the studies is that governments generate revenue as efficiently as possible, with a flexible tax system to provide for the collection of taxes and the attainment of distributive objectives through public spending. The methods of distribution must permit a high degree of efficiency and progressivity. Price system controls and sectoral subsidies lack these qualifications and, consequently, their use must be kept to a minimum. Transfers must address both the short-term problem, through a direct transfer program, and the long-term problem, through the transfer system, i.e., public spending on health care and education.

While reading the studies, it is important to bear in mind that these measures were designed to deal with very serious problems and, unfortunately, the original objective was ultimately lost from view.

Bibliography

Atkinson, A., and J. Stiglitz. 1980. *Lectures on Public Economics*. New York: McGraw-Hill.

Blanchard, O., and S. Fischer. 1989. *Optimization in Economic Theory*. 2d ed. New York: Oxford University Press.

Figueroa, A. 1992. Gestión pública y distribución de ingresos: tres estudios de caso para la economía peruana. Paper prepared for the Program for the Network of Centers for Economic Research, Inter-American Development Bank.

González, R., G. Márquez, J. C. Navarro, and R. Rigobón. 1992. Gasto fiscal y distribución del ingreso en Venezuela. Paper prepared for the Program for the Network of Centers for Economic Research, Inter-American Development Bank.

Lindbeck, A., and D.J. Snower. 1988. *The Insider-Outsider Theory of Employment and Unemployment*. Cambridge, MA: The MIT Press.

Mujica, R., and J. Larrañaga. 1992. *Políticas sociales y distribución del ingreso en Chile*. Paper prepared for the Program for the Network of Centers for Economic Research, Inter-American Development Bank.

Santana, I. 1992. El impacto distributivo de la gestión fiscal en la República Dominicana. Paper prepared for the Program for the Network of Centers for Economic Research, Inter-American Development Bank.

Sargent, T. 1987. *Dynamic Macroeconomics Theory*. Cambridge, MA: Harvard University Press.

Stiglitz, J. 1988. *Economics of the Public Sector*. 2d ed. New York: W.W. Norton & Company.

Stokey, N., and R. Lucas. 1989. *Recursive Methods in Economic Dynamics*. Cambridge, MA: Harvard University Press.

Weiss, A. 1991. *Efficiency Wages: Models of Unemployment, Layoffs, and Wage Dispersion*. Oxford: Clarendon Press.

CHAPTER TWO

SOCIAL POLICIES AND INCOME DISTRIBUTION IN CHILE

Patricio Mujica
Osvaldo Larrañaga[1]

Introduction

The trend of Latin American economies in the 1980s largely reflected the process of forced adjustment initiated by the external financing crisis that erupted in mid-1982. This process was itself a consequence of the need to correct imbalances accumulated in the 1970s and exacerbated in the early 1980s by the deterioration of the region's terms of trade, the rise in international interest rates, and the abrupt halt in the flow of external financing.

While the performance of Latin American economies was deeply affected by external conditions, the nature of the adjustment process, the costs involved, and their redistributive impact were determined by the policies implemented in the period before and after the crisis.

Studying the Chilean experience is interesting because Chile instituted economic and social reforms before the external financing crisis affected most Latin American countries. These reforms significantly altered the country's productive structure as well as the state's role in the promotion of growth and social justice. The reforms implemented in the latter half of the 1970s created the initial conditions of the crisis and, in this way, determined the size of both the initial imbalance and the adjustment required. The policies implemented later were responsible for

[1] The authors are grateful for the efficient assistance of Francisco Bernasconi.

the specific content of the adjustment process, the nature of the costs involved, and their distributive impact.

The military government that took office in Chile in mid-1973 launched a series of economic reforms structured to drastically alter the pre-existing development pattern. The new strategy was based on the liberalization of domestic and foreign markets and a reduction of the public sector. Today, it is believed that an important component of the vitality of the Chilean economy originated in the economic reforms introduced in the second half of the 1970s. No such consensus exists, however, when evaluating the redistributive impact of the social reforms. The reforms of the educational system, social security, health and nutrition programs, and the housing sector sparked a lengthy debate which has been given added impetus by legislative proposals created to finance the current government's social programs.

The purpose of this study is twofold: first, an attempt is made to evaluate the redistributive impact of several Chilean government social programs. Second, two social policy reforms are evaluated: the social security reform and the reform of financing higher education.

The rest of the chapter is organized as follows: in the second section, which follows, major events are reviewed that have shaped social spending trends and income distribution. A quantitative analysis is presented of the redistributive impact of some of the most important government social programs. The third section examines the impact of social security reform on the social services system, its coverage, and the social security deficit. The fourth section evaluates the reform of the higher education system, emphasizing the relationship between equity and the policies governing the financing of higher education. The conclusions are summarized in the fifth section.

Social Policy and Income Distribution

The purpose of this section is to examine the distributive impact of social policies applied in Chile in the last 15 years. The first part of this section reviews the major events that have shaped the trend of economic variables during that period. In the second part, the social policy of the period is evaluated in terms of the effectiveness of social spending, the changes in its composition, and its distributive impact. Finally, there is a summary of the most important social policy lessons to be learned from the Chilean experience.

Major Events

A description follows of changes in employment, wages and income distribution in Chile in the last 20 years. In this subsection, the impact of economic reforms and stabilization policies on unemployment is discussed as well as the close relationship between unemployment and the distributive situation.

Unemployment

Table 2.1 summarizes employment trends in the 1970-1989 period, distinguishing two subperiods. The 1974-1983 period is characterized by persistent, high unemployment. The average open unemployment rate for this period was 14.3 percent of the labor force. This figure contrasts sharply with the average unemployment rate for the 1966-1970 period, which was only 5 percent.

The next period, from 1984-1989, was characterized by a sharp upturn in employment. The unemployment rate fell steadily throughout this period until reaching 8.6 percent in 1989, a drop of approximately 54 percent from the 1983 rate.

Table 2.1. Employment and Unemployment 1970-1989

					Unemployment Rate[**]	
Year	Work force[*]	Employment[*]	Emergency[*] plans (a)	Open unemployment[*]	(c)	(d)
1970	2890.4	2719.9		170.5	5.9	5.9
1971	2963.1	2808.2		154.9	5.2	5.2
1972	2955.7	2836.0		119.7	4.0	4.0
1973	2923.8	2784.3		139.5	4.8	4.8
1974	3059.6	2780.3		279.3	9.1	9.1
1975	3104.8	2558.3	60.6	485.9	15.7	17.6
1976	3279.8	2560.4	172.0	547.4	16.7	21.9
1977	3335.2	2703.8	187.7	443.7	13.3	18.9
1978	3496.1	2867.3	145.8	483.0	13.8	18.0
1979	3546.5	2932.8	133.9	479.8	13.5	17.3
1980	3654.6	3035.6	190.7	428.3	11.7	16.9
1981	3757.9	3190.6	175.6	391.7	10.4	15.1
1982	3793.8	2803.1	247.1	743.6	19.6	26.1
1983	3962.5	2720.3	502.8	739.4	18.7	31.3
1984	4022.8	3031.1	336.3	655.4	16.3	24.7
1985	4122.7	3216.1	324.3	582.2	14.1	22.0
1986	4219.7	3488.7	221.4	509.6	12.1	17.3
1987	4383.9	3775.6	124.1	484.2	11.0	13.9
1988	4504.2	4009.2	33.9	461.1	10.2	11.0
1989	4552.2	4159.0	(b)	393.2	8.6	8.6

Sources: Jadresic (1986); CIEPLAN (1989).
Notes:
(a) Minimum Employment Plan (PEM) and Heads of Household Employment Program (POJH).
(b) These programs were abolished in 1989.
(c) Open unemployment rate (not including PEM and POJH).
(d) Unemployment rate including PEM and POJH.

[*] Thousands.
[**] Percentage.

Table 2.2. Unemployment Rate by Age and Income Level in November 1990 (Percentages)

Decile	15-19	20-24	25-44	45-54	55-64	65+	Total
1	34.5	38.8	24.6	22.3	21.9	28.0	27.3
2	23.1	22.4	9.9	12.6	14.9	14.2	13.3
3	21.6	19.5	6.9	7.2	6.3	16.5	10.1
4	17.4	14.0	7.4	6.8	9.0	12.6	9.4
5	13.9	12.5	5.2	5.2	5.0	12.7	7.2
6	14.3	4.5	5.3	3.1	3.2	5.6	5.5
7	7.9	6.3	4.0	1.1	3.5	7.7	4.1
8	3.4	6.6	2.7	2.2	1.3	2.7	3.1
9	7.1	3.2	1.8	1.6	0.6	0.5	1.8
10	2.8	6.8	1.2	0.4	0.0	1.4	1.4
Total	17.7	13.3	6.5	5.0	4.9	2.5	7.7

Source: Author's calculations, based on CASEN 1990.

In addition to the efficiency problem caused by the underutilization of labor, the persistence of unemployment in Chile raises other questions about the nature of the relationship between unemployment and income distribution. In Table 2.2 distribution and unemployment are summarized by age group and income decile, based on information provided by the Socioeconomic Profile Survey (CASEN) conducted by MIDEPLAN in November 1990.

As seen in Table 2.2, the unemployment rate is invariably higher for age groups in the lower income levels. With an average unemployment rate slightly below 8 percent, the unemployment rate in the first decile is always above 20 percent in each age category and reaches 35 percent in the youngest age group. This situation contrasts sharply with the highest decile, where unemployment figures are consistently below the average rate of unemployment. In this group, with the exception of those under 24 years of age, whose rate of unemployment is about 5 percent on average, the unemployment rate is less than 1.5 percent and for many is practically nil. However, the evidence summarized in Table 2.2 indicates that there are pronounced differences in the distribution of unemployment rates by age group. Generally, the groups most affected are young. The figures show that the rate of unemployment for those under 24 years of age is higher than average and that the poorest young people are hit hardest by unemployment.

Real Wages

Table 2.3 shows the trend of principal wage indicators in the 1970-1989 period. As indicated in the table, the decline in purchasing power of workers earning the minimum wage as well as those whose wages

Table 2.3. Real Wages, Minimum Income and Family Allowance
(1970 = 100)

Year	Real wages	Minimum income	Family allowance
1970	100.0	100.0	100.0
1974	65.1	100.6	104.8
1975	62.9	99.3	100.8
1976	64.8	99.9	93.6
1977	71.5	102.6	87.2
1978	76.0	116.2	84.8
1979	82.3	112.6	82.0
1980	89.4	112.7	82.2
1981	97.4	117.9	81.6
1982	97.7	116.6	80.0
1983	87.0	91.6	64.1
1984	87.1	80.1	63.2
1985	83.2	74.6	55.1
1986	84.9	69.6	46.0
1987	84.7	64.0	38.4
1988	90.3	66.4	33.4
1989	92.0	73.8	29.2

Source: Arellano (1987), Cortázar (1983), Superintendency of Social Security.

are determined by the minimum wage is even greater than that of workers with average wages. The minimum wage's loss of purchasing power in the 1970-1989 period was more than 25 percent, and between 1982 and 1989 it was approximately 37 percent. These figures indicate that the loss of purchasing power of low-income workers was greater than the national average.

Distribution

Table 2.4 shows the change in the distributive situation in greater Santiago in the 1970-1987 period, based on the Gini coefficients of family income. As seen in the table, income distribution deteriorated significantly between 1974 and 1984. After 1974, the Gini coefficient increased and continued doing so until the 1977-1979 period. In 1979, however, income distribution resumed its steady decline.

The deterioration of income during 1974-1989 is reflected in the distribution of family income. Table 2.5 shows the distribution of household consumption by quintile in greater Santiago for 1969, 1978 and 1988. The figures indicate a steady decline for the first three quintiles, in terms of both aggregate consumption and share of total consumption. The trend of family expenditures in the highest quintile follows a completely opposite pattern, increasing its share in total consumption from 44.5 percent in 1969 to 54.6 percent in 1988.

Table 2.4. Gini Coefficient of Family Income Distribution in Greater Santiago
(1964-1987)

Year	Gini coefficient
1964	0.4620
1970	0.5009
1973	0.4500
1974	0.4499
1975	0.4712
1976	0.5380
1977	0.5260
1978	0.5197
1979	0.5179
1980	0.5257
1981	0.5215
1982	0.5391
1983	0.5420
1984	0.5550
1985	0.5320
1986	0.5390
1987	0.5310

Source: World Bank (1990).

Table 2.5. Distribution of Household Consumption by Quintile of Income for 1969, 1978 and 1988
(December 1990 pesos)

Quintile	1969	%	1978	%	1988	%
I	47,513	7.6	32,820	5.2	27,654	4.4
II	73,937	11.8	58,827	9.3	51,893	8.2
III	97,781	15.6	86,058	13.6	79,998	12.7
IV	128,901	20.6	132,666	21.0	127,244	20.1
V	278,939	44.5	322,720	51.0	344,930	54.6
Total	125,414	100.0	126,618	100.0	126,344	100.0

Source: INE, Family Budget Survey.

Social Spending and Income Distribution

Evidence indicates that income distribution has deteriorated in Chile in the last 15 years. The assumption of power by the military government in 1973 coincided with the initiation of economic and social reforms that drastically altered the existing pattern of development.

Some of the questions that naturally arise in studying Chile's recent history concern the role of social policy during this period. To what extent did state intervention allay regressive effects on income distribution of successive external shocks and on the stabilization and adjust-ment policies implemented in the last 15 years? Was the level of social spending in recent years sufficient to meet social needs? Was social spend-ing properly allocated?

The focus of the following analysis is the trend of social spending and the impact it has had on income distribution.

The Trend of Social Spending

One controversial subject in the debate on social policy is the measure-ment of social spending. The traditional and most widely-used concept of social spending is public social spending. This concept takes a broad view of the state's social action, which includes both government sup-port for specific social programs as well as expenditures of various pub-lic institutions—centralized and decentralized—that fulfill social functions. An alternative way to define the concept of social spending, and the one upon which the official figures for social spending in Chile are based, is state social spending. This includes only state subsidies granted to social programs while excluding the portion financed by the beneficiaries. In addition, this concept of social spending includes only activities in the centralized public sector.

Table 2.6 shows the trend of per capita social spending in Chile in the 1974-1988 period, using the two indicators discussed above, public social spending and state social spending. After an initial decline between 1974 and 1976 of approximately 20 percent, social spending began to re-cover in 1977, culminating in 1982 with a cumulative increase for the 1974-1982 period of approximately 40 percent. During this period, the aggregate growth of public and state spending was similar, despite a few differences in the trajectory of the two variables. In 1983, while public social spending began a decline that bottomed out in 1987 and then re-covered slightly in 1988, the trend of state social spending followed a more erratic pattern of ups and downs, with an aggregate growth of 29 percent for the 1974-1988 period. The aggregate growth of public social spending, however, was 14 percent for the same period.

An examination of composition by sector of social spending reveals that regardless of the definition used, the sector where the greatest growth occurred in the 1974-1988 period was social security. This sector includes all expenditures on pensions and social welfare, as well as disbursements made to reduce the impact of economic conditions on income.

The recovery of social spending between 1977 and 1982 basically reflects the growth of pensions and the creation of social programs and subsidies in response to the spread of unemployment caused by external shocks and government policies. The growth of pensions was basically a response to demographic factors and not to an increase in the average value of pensions. The social security sector also deter-mined the trend of social spending in the 1983-1988 period. The de-cline of social spending in this period essentially reflects the reduction in social security expenditures.

Table 2.6. Per Capita Social Spending 1974-1989
(1974 = 100)

Public social spending [1]

Year	Education	Health	Soc. sec	Housing	Others	Total
1974	100	100	100	100	100	100
1975	79	77	102	57	31	84
1976	85	72	101	42	80	82
1977	99	78	115	47	158	94
1978	104	87	138	44	135	104
1979	114	85	154	55	164	115
1980	111	95	160	55	166	119
1981	115	86	186	54	137	129
1982	117	91	214	38	106	138
1983	99	72	199	32	162	123
1984	95	76	198	37	142	124
1985	95	73	181	51	136	119
1986	89	72	175	47	142	114
1987	79	71	172	52	138	111
1988	82	80	173	58	144	114

State spending [2]

Year	Education	Health	Soc. sec	Housing	Others	Total
1974	100	100	100	100	100	100
1975	74	71	119	40	109	80
1976	74	59	121	35	171	79
1977	88	67	139	37	144	90
1978	88	68	154	28	139	92
1979	90	64	142	31	130	89
1980	94	81	186	34	128	105
1981	111	84	282	32	136	135
1982	111	78	329	11	63	141
1983	94	63	336	21	48	135
1984	95	62	364	33	37	143
1985	91	54	358	36	20	139
1986	90	50	361	36	57	139
1987	81	48	325	42	85	129
1988	75	49	320	58	99	129

Source: [1] Ffrench-Davis and Raczynski (1990).   [2] Central Bank of Chile, monthly newsletter.

A conclusion from this examination of changes in social spending is that the social policy of the period was oriented toward compensating for income losses caused by the economic slowdown. The counterpart of this bias in social resource allocation was a cutback in financing of programs aimed at promoting equal opportunities among social sectors and increasing the productive capacity of lower income groups.

Distribution of Social Spending

For the purpose of determining the specificity and distributional effectiveness of Chile's social policy, the distribution of state aid to social programs among the various sectors of the population is examined below.
Table 2.7 shows the distribution of state spending on monetary allowances by decile of per capita family income. The size of each monetary
allowance is taken from the CASEN survey of November, 1990.

Monetary allowances are a cash supplement granted to families by
the state. They include family allowances, welfare pensions, unemployment compensation, and a one-time family allowance. Also included in
this category are programs designed specifically to compensate for the
impact of economic conditions on income. As shown in Table 2.7, despite the fact that the monetary allowances tend to be concentrated in
the lower deciles, their distribution within the poorest groups is not consistent with the objective of satisfying the needs of lower income groups.
In fact, the poorest 10 percent of households receives, on average, an
amount that is approximately 40 percent lower than that of the second
and third deciles. Generally, the lowest decile receives a contribution
that in absolute terms is less than or roughly equal to that received by
households comprising the poorest 70 percent of the population. The
only program that is consistent with the objective of assigning top priority to the poorest groups is the one-time family allowance. The figures
on the distribution of monetary allowances indicate that a sharper focus
is needed, especially regarding lower income groups.

The other component of Chilean social policy consists of programs that provide nonmonetary allowances, their main purpose being to overcome the long-term restrictions that affect income levels
of the poorest groups. Table 2.8 shows the distribution of government spending on education, health and housing programs, based on
the findings of Haindl (1989). In most cases, nonmonetary allowances,
with the exception of health care, follow a pattern similar to that of
monetary allowances. In housing, for example, the distribution by
decile is relatively uniform. In education, however, the high percentage of social spending received by the higher deciles is not consistent with the stated objective of social policy to focus government
spending on the neediest sectors.

The Redistributive Impact of Social Spending

In evaluating the redistributive impact of monetary allowances, Table
2.9 compares the distribution by decile of autonomous and monetary
income, based on CASEN 1990 data. Monetary income is total income
received, less social contributions and income tax. Autonomous income
is monetary income less monetary allowances provided by the state.

As shown in Table 2.9, monetary allowances have a positive impact
on income distribution. By comparing the distribution of autonomous
income and monetary income, it is clear that monetary allowances in-

Table 2.7. Distribution of Monetary Allowances in 1990
(Percentage per decile)

Decile	Family allowance	Unemployment compensation	One-time family allowance	Welfare pension	Total
1	5.86	10.53	32.64	13.70	10.70
2	13.09	9.19	21.54	16.42	14.57
3	14.48	11.13	15.53	13.33	14.30
4	12.15	5.84	11.54	14.08	12.18
5	12.61	36.45	7.14	13.30	12.86
6	10.15	1.19	5.70	11.37	9.49
7	9.96	19.08	2.55	8.47	9.09
8	7.84	4.41	1.90	4.80	6.47
9	7.25	1.28	0.94	2.22	5.41
1 0	6.62	0.90	0.51	2.32	4.93
Total	100.00	100.00	100.00	100.00	100.00

Source: Author's calculations, based on CASEN 1990.

Table 2.8. Distribution of Nonmonetary Allowances

Decile	Education	Health	Housing
1	12.99	22.76	13.51
2	13.24	17.06	10.58
3	10.52	15.59	12.51
4	9.06	11.41	11.68
5	9.16	10.00	10.31
6	8.38	6.97	9.48
7	7.79	5.84	10.00
8	10.43	4.47	9.58
9	11.32	3.95	6.77
10	7.12	1.96	5.58
Total	100.00	100.00	100.00

Source: Haindl (1989).

crease the share of the seven lowest deciles. In particular, the poorest 10 percent received 1.3 percent of total autonomous income in 1990 and received 1.42 percent of total monetary income, which represents an increase in the share of the lowest decile of approximately 9.2 percent.

The quantitative impact of programs that provide monetary allowances on the level of autonomous income for each decile is shown in Table 2.10. The impact of monetary allowances decreases as the level of income increases. For households in the poorest 10 percent of the population, monetary allowances increase income by approximately 11 percent. In contrast, monetary allowances increase incomes in the highest decile by only about 0.2 percent.

Table 2.9. Distribution of Autonomous and Monetary Income in 1990
(Percentage per decile)

Decile	Autonomous income	Cumulated	Monetary income	Cumulated
1	1.30	1.30	1.42	1.42
2	2.97	4.27	3.12	4.54
3	3.92	8.19	4.06	8.60
4	4.85	13.04	4.95	13.55
5	5.81	18.85	5.91	19.46
6	7.10	25.95	7.13	26.59
7	8.60	34.55	8.61	35.20
8	10.53	45.08	10.47	45.67
9	15.16	60.24	15.03	60.67
10	39.76	100.00	39.30	100.00
Gini		0.4691		0.4687

Source: Author's calculations, based on CASEN 1990.

Table 2.10. Autonomous Income Adjusted for Monetary Allowances

Decile	Autonomous income	Unemployment compensation	Family allowance	Welfare pension	One-Time family allowance	Total
1	100.00	0.38	4.15	2.43	4.31	11.26
2	100.00	0.15	4.05	1.27	1.24	6.72
3	100.00	0.13	3.40	0.78	0.68	4.99
4	100.00	0.06	2.30	0.67	0.41	3.43
5	100.00	0.30	1.99	0.53	0.21	3.02
6	100.00	0.01	1.31	0.37	0.14	1.83
7	100.00	0.10	1.06	0.23	0.05	1.44
8	100.00	0.02	0.68	0.10	0.03	0.84
9	100.00	0.00	0.44	0.03	0.01	0.49
10	100.00	0.00	0.15	0.01	0.00	0.17

Source: Author's calculations, based on CASEN 1990.

The impact of nonmonetary allowances on autonomous income is summarized in Table 2.11.[2] As in the case of monetary allowances, the relative weight of nonmonetary allowances decreases as household income increases. The overall effects of the health, housing and education programs nearly double the income of households in the poorest 10 percent of the population. The impact on the highest decile, though, is only 1.3 percent.

---

[2] The quantitative impact of nonmonetary allowances on autonomous income is calculated on the basis of Table 2.9 and the share of the various sectors in state social spending in 1990.

Table 2.11. Autonomous Income Adjusted for Nonmonetary Allowances

Decile	Autonomous income	Education	Health	Housing
1	100.0	54.0	27.9	14.7
2	100.0	24.1	9.2	5.0
3	100.0	14.5	6.3	4.5
4	100.0	10.1	3.7	3.4
5	100.0	8.5	2.7	2.5
6	100.0	6.4	1.6	1.9
7	100.0	4.9	1.1	1.6
8	100.0	5.3	0.7	1.3
9	100.0	4.0	0.4	0.6
10	100.0	1.0	0.1	0.2

Source: Author's calculations, based on CASEN 1990.

These results indicate that social policy in Chile has a significant impact on the income of the poorest households and that the effect on high-income households is insignificant. Nevertheless, there is still much to be done to improve the distributive effectiveness of social policy.

Final Considerations

The Chilean experience in the last 20 years is rich in lessons and has significant implications for the design of social policy. In the following section we will examine some of these implications.

The evidence presented shows the close relationship between economic cycles and the distributive situation. During recessions, unemployment is concentrated in low-income sectors and the drop in wages tends to be accentuated in the case of less-skilled workers. From the perspective of formulating social policy, the implications of this situation are twofold. First, in recessionary periods an effort must be made to adjust the focus of social spending. Second, the close relationship in the short term between radical stabilization policies and economic slowdown suggests the necessity of supplementing these policies with social spending policies that are more tightly focused on the lower income groups.

Finally, the Chilean experience suggests that to be effective, social policy must be comprehensive. Diffusion of the concept of refocusing was one of the main contributions of the military government in the field of social policy. Nevertheless, the concept of refocusing as it pertained to the former government's social policy was based on income deficits. Consequently, the social network was oriented more toward elimination of deficits and did nothing to help people develop skills that would allow them to permanently overcome the problem of insufficient income. An effective social policy requires the empowerment of individuals based on a broader refocusing concept. The comprehensiveness of social policy implies that it must make some direct or indirect contribution to economic growth.

Social Security Reform

In the early 1980s, one of the most ambitious and radical reforms of a social security system in recent history was initiated in Chile. This reform changed the traditional distribution system administered by the state into an individual capitalization system administered by private social security institutions.

The main objective of this section is to examine the reform of the Chilean social security system focusing on its impact on the level of services, the system's coverage, and the social security deficit.

The first part of this section discusses the structure of the social security system prior to 1981, the social reform itself, and the main features of the current system. The second part examines the principal results of the new system regarding pensions, coverage, and the social deficit. Finally, the main lessons of the Chilean social security reform are discussed.

Organization of the Chilean Social Security System

The history of social security in Chile dates back to the 1920s. The system developed through gradual incorporation of economic and social sectors. Thus, in 1924 the Workers Insurance Fund was established, financed with contributions from beneficiaries, and by the state. Later, this organization evolved into the Social Security Service, created by law in 1952. In 1925 the Public Employees and Journalists Fund and the Private Employees Fund were created. The last sectors to join the system were the rural sectors, which gained access to social security between 1965 and 1970.

In November 1980 the government ordered a reform of the social security system beginning May 1981, resulting in significant changes.

Structure of the Old System

Prior to May 1981, the date on which Decree-Law 3,500 on social security reform was enforced, there were about 30 institutions in Chile that provided social security services for their affiliates.

All workers who joined the old system were covered against the same risks, but with considerable differences in quality of services, requirements for benefit eligibility, and coverage of services.

The old social security system in Chile was organized as a distribution system and benefits received were not related to compulsory savings made by workers during their active life.

Pension funds collected income in the form of contributions and distributed it among social security funds, while social security income was used to pay current benefits. The result was a redistribution of income generated from active and inactive workers as well as workers in different income levels.

Content of the Reform

The social security reform of 1981 drastically changed the pension system. The new system, like the one before it, is compulsory for all salaried employees and includes old-age, disability, and survivors' pensions. The new system also includes protection against work-related accidents, health and maternity benefits, unemployment insurance, and family allowances. Severance pay, however, was eliminated. Self-employed individuals have the option of joining the new system on terms similar to those of salaried employees.

A key element of the new system is that, unlike the old distribution system, benefits are directly related to the contributions made by affiliates during their active life. The affiliates' periodic contributions are deposited in individual accounts, which together make up the pension fund. The growth of the fund depends on the amount of contributions and investment income generated. The larger the amount in an affiliate's individual account, the larger the pension received at retirement.

The system is administered by private organizations known as Pension Fund Administrators (PFAs), which collect a commission for their services and are prohibited from engaging in any other activity. Their primary responsibility is to provide affiliates with disability and survivors' coverage and to invest the pension funds. This investment process regulated by the state requires the PFA pension funds to be kept legally and economically separate.

Results of the Reform

Pensions

Table 2.12 shows the trend of pensions in the 1970-1989 period. The index of real wages is included for comparative purposes. As indicated in the table, after a sudden drop in the first half of the 1970s, pensions began to recover in 1976 and grew uninterruptedly until 1984. In 1985 they declined sharply (-9.9 percent) but recovered again in 1986 and 1987.

The cumulative reduction of average pensions in 1970-1987 was 12 percent. Most of the decline was due to deterioration that occurred between 1970 and 1975 (approximately 50 percent).

After the downturn in the first half of the 1970s, minimum pensions recovered quickly in 1976 and remained above the 1970 level throughout the 1978-1984 period. In 1985 they declined again, until stabilizing at levels in the 1970 range.

Table 2.12. Trend of Pensions, 1970-1989
(1970 = 100)

	Average	Pensions		Real wages
		Minimum	Welfare	
1970	100.0	100.0		100.0
1974	51.3	84.7	(a)	65.1
1975	50.2	81.1	100.0	62.9
1976	52.3	85.6	121.3	64.8
1977	55.1	93.6	121.0	71.5
1978	62.1	100.5	116.5	76.0
1979	72.1	107.1	112.0	82.3
1980	74.3	109.3	152.6	89.4
1981	78.0	111.5	170.1	97.4
1982	83.5	111.5	181.5	97.7
1983	83.2	107.0	171.5	87.0
1984	89.7	111.6	181.1	87.1
1985	80.8	100.8	159.4	83.2
1986	82.7	101.5	156.9	84.9
1987	88.1	98.1	128.4	84.7
1988		100.5	135.0	90.3
1989		102.2	142.4	92.0

Sources: French-Davis and Raczynski (1990), Arellano (1990).
Note: (a) 1975 = 100.

Despite the fact that the number of individuals receiving pensions in the new system is still small, it is helpful to examine the composition of the pensions granted by the PFAs to evaluate their growth potential. This information, summarized in Table 2.13, presents the amount paid in pensions by the PFAs in each category of the social security system. The figures show that old-age pensions represent a small percentage of taxable income. Nevertheless, these figures do not reflect the long-term, break-even point of the new system's pensions, but are instead determined mainly by the value of the recognition bond granted to workers who transfer to the new system.

Tables 2.14 and 2.15 show the results of simulating the growth of pensions granted by PFAs, in normal circumstances, for taxable incomes at retirement. The simulations assume a contribution rate of 10 percent, a fixed monthly commission of 400 pesos, and an annual pension fund return of 5 percent. It is further assumed that wages increase in real terms by 2 percent a year until the age of 50, and then remain constant from that point on.

The results show a considerable difference in pensions, depending on how old the affiliate is when contributions begin. They also suggest that the redistributive impact of the fixed commissions collected by the PFAs is not insignificant. Pensions as a percentage of

Table 2.13. Average Amount of Pensions Paid by PFAs
(Thousands of December 1990 pesos)

	1981	1982	1983	1984	1985	1986	1987	1988	1989	1990
Average taxable income	-	89.8	77.5	70.3	64.3	71.5	67.3	72.8	81.2	84.4
Old-age pensions	-	-	20.5	22.7	21.9	25.8	26.7	32.7	37.4	39.4
Scheduled retirements	-	-	20.5	22.5	19.7	20.5	18.2	20.9	26.1	24.1
Life income	-	-	5.9	59.7	59.4	52.3	49.3	56.2	56.2	59.6
Disability pensions	n.a.	93.8	83.0	68.8	63.6	63.0	62.3	65.2	65.2	63.9
Survivors' pensions										
Widow	n.a.	34.6	32.2	27.9	26.7	26.9	26.2	27.4	28.5	27.8
Orphan	n.a.	9.9	9.0	7.8	7.5	7.8	7.6	8.0	9.2	9.5
Others	n.a.	n.a.	9.2	15.8	14.5	14.6	16.4	15.3	15.8	16.8
Total		30.9	29.9	25.9	25.5	26.9	27.7	30.5	32.9	33.2

Source: Iglesias and Acuña (1991).

Table 2.14. Projected Pensions Under the New Social Security System
(Affiliate starts contributing at 18 years of age)

Taxable income ($)					Projected pension (% taxable income)	
Starting	At retirement	Unmarried affiliate	Married affiliate		Unmarried affiliate	Married affiliate
33,000	62,190	73,539	61,341		118.2	98.6
60,000	113,072	139,633	116,472		123.5	103.0
120,000	226,145	286,510	238,986		126.7	105.7
180,000	339,217	433,388	361,500		127.8	106.6
240,000	452,290	580,265	484,014		128.3	107.0

Source: Author's calculations.

Table 2.15. Projected Pensions Under the New Social Security System
(Affiliate starts contributing at 24 years of age)

Taxable income ($)					Projected pension (% taxable income)	
Starting	At retirement	Unmarried affiliate	Married affiliate		Unmarried affiliate	Married affiliate
33,000	55,223	50,902	42,459		92.2	76.9
60,000	100,405	96,812	80,753		96.4	80.4
120,000	200,810	198,833	165,852		99.0	82.6
180,000	301,215	300,854	250,951		99.9	83.3
240,000	401,620	402,876	336,051		100.3	83.7

Source: Author's calculations.

taxable income are invariably smaller for lower income levels, indicating their lesser profitability resulting from contributors having to pay a fixed commission, regardless of the amount of taxable income.

The fixed commission on periodic contributions is a controversial aspect of the new system. Since the commission is deducted from the cumulative balance, the reduction in profitability is proportionately larger for affiliates with smaller incomes and fewer years as contributors. The solution involves efficiency and incentives that transcend the redistributive problem. To the extent that the administration of individual accounts involves fixed costs unrelated to the amount of taxable income, eliminating the fixed commission could discourage PFA efforts to include low-income workers in the system. However, retaining it might be a factor in the low coverage of the system among self-employed workers with low incomes. The existence of externalities associated with coverage expansion may be reason enough for the state to subsidize the costs of joining the new system, especially in cases where the fixed commission represents a significant portion of the taxable income.

The social security deficit originated, first, in revenues lost by the old system when a large percentage of contributors transferred to the new system. The state's assumption of this deficit turned the social security deficit into a fiscal problem severely restricting formulation of macroeconomic policy. Second, the state assumed responsibility in the new system for contributions accumulated in the old system by affiliates who transferred.

Table 2.16 shows the trend of the social security deficit from 1981 to 1990. In this period, the social security deficit increased four times, with much of this growth occurring in 1982 as a result of the massive transfer of contributors from the old distribution system to the new individual capitalization system.

The table also shows that the largest component of the social security deficit is the operating deficit. The operating deficit is defined as the difference between contributions received and disbursements made to pay pensions. Its considerable impact on the social security deficit reflects the volume of revenues lost by the old system from the wholesale transfer of contributors to the PFAs following the social security reform.

Table 2.17 projects the social security deficit. According to this projection, the social security deficit will continue growing until the year 2000, at which point it will decrease until reaching a value slightly below 1 percent of PGB (Gross Geographic Product).

Coverage

The growth of coverage, based on the number of affiliates in the old system, is summarized in Table 2.18 for the 1960-1980 period. As indi-

Table 2.16. Trend of the Social Security Deficit, 1981-1990
(Billions of December 1990 pesos)

Year	Operating deficit	Recognition bonds	Social security deficit	Deficit as a percentage of PGB
1981	87.438	396.000	87.834	1.2
1982	207.403	5.588	212.990	3.2
1983	231.375	10.878	242.253	3.7
1984	244.750	13.201	257.951	3.9
1985	234.626	16.515	251.141	3.6
1986	251.915	23.563	275.478	3.7
1987	267.374	29.894	297.268	3.8
1988	272.933	32.466	305.400	3.4
1989	n.a.	n.a.	312.830 (a)	3.3 (b)
1990	n.a.	n.a.	325.737 (a)	3.4 (b)

Source: Iglesias and Acuña (1991).
Notes: (a) Projected deficit.
        (b) Calculated on the basis of the projected deficit.

Table 2.17. Projected Social Security Deficit
(Millions of December 1990 pesos)

Year	Deficit	% GDP	Year	Deficit	% PGB
1990	325,737	3.4	2003	388,413	2.5
1991	338,643	3.4	2004	381,093	2.3
1992	351,650	3.4	2005	373,216	2.2
1993	364,025	3.4	2006	352,798	2.0
1994	375,872	3.4	2007	342,674	1.9
1995	383,854	3.3	2008	331,694	1.7
1996	390,155	3.3	2009	319,993	1.6
1997	395,198	3.2	2010	304,174	1.5
1998	397,859	3.1	2011	286,516	1.3
1999	398,334	3.0	2012	268,580	1.2
2000	399,229	2.9	2013	250,491	1.1
2001	397,515	2.7	2014	232,232	1.0
2002	393,922	2.6	2015	213,770	0.9

Source: Iglesias and Acuña (1991).

Table 2.18. Coverage of the Old Social Security System
(Percentages)

Year	Contributors/ labor force	Active/ employed	Year	Contributors/ labor force	Active/ employed
1960	69	75	1971	74	79
1961	60	65	1972	75	78
1962	61	66	1973	79	83
1963	61	66	1974	78	83
1964	68	73	1975	74	86
1965	69	74	1976	74	83
1966	71	75	1977	73	79
1967	72	76	1978	68	76
1968	n.a.	74	1979	68	75
1969	n.a.	76	1980	64	71
1970	73	77			

Source: Superintendency of Social Security and MIDEPLAN.

cated, coverage expanded steadily until the mid-1970s, reaching its maximum values as a percentage of the labor force and of the employed population in 1973 and 1976, respectively. In the latter half of the 1970s this trend was reversed, with a gradual decline until 1980, just before the social security reform. In 1980, the system's coverage as a percentage of the labor force was 64 percent.

To measure the impact of the reform on the system's coverage, it is necessary, from 1981 on, to take into account both affiliates of the new system and contributors to the old system. This information is presented in Table 2.19.

Table 2.19. Coverage of the Social Security System
(Thousands of persons)

	1985	1986	1987	1988	1989	1990
Labor force	4,018.7	4,270.0	4,354.4	4,551.6	4,675.0	4,728.0
Affiliates:						
New system	2,283.8	2,591.5	2,890.3	3,183.0	3,470.8	3,739.5
Old system	454.4	442.4	434.7	423.1	413.4	403.8
Inactive accounts	450.0	517.4	590.1	663.9	740.8	859.8
Noncontributing retirees	8.8	12.8	20.9	29.6	40.2	54.2
Affiliates (a)	2,279.4	2,503.7	2,714.0	2,912.6	3,103.2	3,229.3
Affiliates (a) as a percentage						
of labor force	56.72	58.63	62.33	63.99	66.38	68.30

Source: Iglesias and Acuña (1991).
Note: (a) Affiliates in both systems, net of inactive accounts and noncontributing retirees.

Table 2.20. Distribution of Employed Workers Without Social Security
(Thousands of persons in November 1990)

Category	Number (a) of persons	Percentages of total	by category
Employer	44.5	3.13	40.10
Self-employed	679.7	47.96	68.96
Laborer/office worker	521.0	36.76	18.09
Domestic service	113.2	7.98	55.83
Nonremunerated family member	58.8	4.17	80.91
Total	1,417.2	100.00	33.01

Source: Author's calculations, based on CASEN 1990.
Note: (a) Statistical projections, based on CASEN 1990.

The figures indicate steady growth in social security coverage. Between 1985 and 1990, coverage expanded from 56.7 percent of the labor force to 68.3 percent. This means that approximately a third of the labor force is not included in the social security system

Table 2.20 shows the distribution of noncovered employed workers by occupational category. According to the table, most noncovered workers are self-employed. The table also indicates that among self-employed workers, only 30 percent are covered far below average.

Table 2.21 shows the distribution of affiliation by sector of economic activity. The sector with the largest number of nonaffiliates is agriculture, suggesting a large percentage of informal employment.

To examine the distributive implications of the system's incomplete coverage, the socioeconomic composition of those not affiliated with any social security system is analyzed below.

Table 2.22 groups nonaffiliates according to level of per capita family income. The results indicate that nonaffiliates are distributed

Table 2.21. Distribution of Affiliates by Economic Activity
(Percentages in November 1990)

Activity	Affiliates	Nonaffiliates	Total
Agriculture	50.9	49.1	100.0
Mining	85.2	14.8	100.0
Industry	73.9	26.1	100.0
Construction	69.8	30.2	100.0
Business	56.7	43.3	100.0
Government S.S.	88.6	11.4	100.0
Oersibakes S.S.	49.0	51.0	100.0
Community S.S.	82.2	17.8	100.0
Transportation	72.5	27.5	100.0
Other	74.8	25.2	100.0

Source: Author's calculations, based on CASEN 1990.

Table 2.22. Distribution of Non-Affiliates by Decile
(Percentages in November 1990)

Decile	Percentage
1	10.86
2	11.48
3	10.87
4	11.68
5	10.83
6	10.68
7	9.03
8	9.20
9	7.98
10	7.40
Total	100.00

Source: Author's calculations, based on CASEN 1990.

uniformly among all sectors. The poorest 50 percent of households account for about 55 percent of all nonaffiliates.

Table 2.23 shows the distribution by decile of autonomous and monetary income for individuals who do not belong to any formal social security system. There are two interesting figures presented in this table. First, by comparing the distribution of the autonomous income of nonaffiliates with the distribution for the population as a whole, a major disparity is observed among nonaffiliates (Table 2.9), suggesting the state intensify efforts to assist this group. Nevertheless, by examining the distribution of monetary income of nonaffiliates (which includes monetary allowances), it is clear that, with the sole exception of the first decile, government monetary allowances have little effect on the share of nonaffiliates. These results are substantiated by Table 2.24. This table

Table 2.23. Distribution of Autonomous and Monetary Income of Nonaffiliates (Percentage by decile)

Decile	Autonomous income	Accumulated	Monetary income	Accumulated
1	0.47	0.47	0.52	0.52
2	2.15	2.62	2.18	2.70
3	3.03	5.65	3.05	5.75
4	3.37	9.02	3.40	9.15
5	5.98	15.00	6.00	15.15
6	6.59	21.59	6.61	21.76
7	7.02	28.61	7.04	28.80
8	8.62	37.23	8.62	37.42
9	14.48	51.71	14.46	51.88
10	48.29	100.00	48.12	100.00
Gini		0.5562		0.5537

Source: Author's calculations, based on CASEN 1990.

Table 2.24. Autonomous Income Adjusted for Monetary Allowances of Nonaffiliates and the Total Population

Decile	Autonomous income	Non-affiliates	Total population
1	100.00	10.95	11.26
2	100.00	1.97	6.72
3	100.00	1.55	4.99
4	100.00	0.81	3.43
5	100.00	0.89	3.02
6	100.00	0.68	1.82
7	100.00	0.81	1.44
8	100.00	0.39	0.84
9	100.00	0.24	0.49
10	100.00	0.05	0.67

Source: Author's calculations, based on CASEN 1990.

shows the percentage increase in the autonomous income of nonaffiliates and the total population due to monetary allowances granted by the state. The increase in autonomous income for nonaffiliates is consistently smaller than for the population as a whole.

Final Considerations

Examination of social security reform in Chile reveals that the amount of the recognition bond and its financing determines the nature of the transition period following the reform. The amount of the recognition bond determines the amount of the social security deficit the state must assume and, consequently, the weight of the restriction on formulation of fiscal and social policy.

Another insight is that the biggest challenge facing the decade-old social security system is expansion of its effective coverage. As pointed out in many studies,[3] the inclusion of low-income, self-employed individuals may prove to be too costly.

The fixed monthly commissions collected by the PFAs are regressive and responsible for the inadequate coverage of low-income, self-employed workers. Fixed commissions, based on fixed costs of the administration of individual accounts, are unavoidable and therefore must be included in fees charged by administrators. The regressive impact of these commissions can be neutralized through compensatory subsidies for low-income workers.

The basic problem is that the social security system is organized into "packages" which are expensive for low-income workers. A way of expanding coverage would be to offer self-employed workers the option of joining specific insurance programs offered by the system. Negative selection problems could be avoided by allowing affiliation in groups.

Finally, the evidence suggests that expanding coverage of the social security system would improve the effectiveness of social policies.

Higher Education and Equity

This section will evaluate the equity of government financing of higher education in Chile. A definition of the higher education system is provided in part one of this study, with special emphasis on financial aspects of the system. In part two, the equity of current government financing of higher education is analyzed with unpublished data from the recent CASEN survey. Data on the educational system and income distribution in Chile are presented, the beneficiaries of higher education are identified, and the profitability of post-secondary education is evaluated utilizing income equations and rates of return. Based on the above information, the distributive impact of government spending on higher education is evaluated.

Higher Education in Chile in the 1980s

Higher education has been provided by eight universities, two being state universities and the rest private. All, however, were financed by the state. The state's contribution, as a percentage of university revenues, fell from 80 percent in the 1960s to 66 percent by the end of the 1970s. Between 1965 and 1980 state spending on higher education varied between 1 and

---

[3]   A recent analysis of the subject is found in Arellano (1990).

2 percent of GDP, or about a third of total government expenditures on education.

In 1981 a reform of the higher education system began with the goal of increasing efficiency and equity. There were three major changes at the institutional level. First, higher education was diversified. Universities were required to offer programs of five years or more for academic degrees; establish professional institutes for intermediate programs (four to five years); and create technical training centers for short programs of two to three years. Second, the reform promoted private involvement in higher education by encouraging private enterprise to create universities, professional institutes, and technical training centers. Third, regional universities were created to eliminate the dependence of regional centers on traditional universities.

The principal financing reform was to divide state assistance into three components: a direct contribution to finance research and extension activities, an indirect contribution distributed among universities to attract the best students, and government loans to help students pay for their education.

The results of the reform were different from what had been planned. Not only was the state's actual contribution less than the budgeted amount but its composition continued to reflect the pre-reform situation with a preponderance of direct contributions.

There were three major reasons for this. First, the adjustment process following the external debt crisis restricted the state's resources. Second, the economic crisis caused government personnel changes, with individuals gaining power who were not supportive of new (private) universities joining the system. Third, the reforms met with strong opposition within the universities.

In 1986 the economy recovered and the more liberal sectors regained positions of influence in the government. Some of the government's resources were allocated for the establishment of a scientific and technological research fund, Fondecyt, which awards grants to applicants through a national research competition. The responsibility for administering and collecting student loans, which was difficult to manage politically, was transferred from the government to the universities themselves. In 1988 restrictions on access to Fondecyt for new universities were lifted and in 1990 any university or professional institute became eligible for indirect state assistance. Nevertheless, the state's contribution continued falling, indicating that higher education was no longer a public priority. In 1990, state aid to the system was almost half of what it had been in 1980 (Table 2.25).

Higher education enrollment (Table 2.26) grew slowly throughout the decade (1 percent per annum). However, the reforms failed to motivate traditional universities to expand their enrollment. This was the objective of indirect state aid and was caused by the universities' failure to provide faculty incentives. However, enrollment in professional institutes and technical training centers grew significantly in the 1980s, accounting for almost half of total enrollment in higher education in 1990.

Table 2.25. Government Spending on Higher Education
(1980 = 100)

	1980	1982	1984	1986	1988	1990
Real expenditures	100.00	105.30	87.20	66.60	65.30	51.30
% of GDP	1.05	1.28	1.03	0.78	0.60	0.44
% of government spending on education	28.90	25.00	23.10	21.10	21.00	16.90

Sources: Lehmann (1990) and Treasury of the Republic (1991).

Table 2.26. Enrollment in the Higher Education System
(Thousands)

	1980	1982	1984	1986	1988	1990
Universities	118.9	119.2	129.1	132.9	127.3	132.5
Traditional	118.9	73.8	77.6	77.1	75.9	
Regional	—	42.7	48.6	49.5	42.2	
Private	—	2.7	2.9	6.3	9.2	19.5
Professional institutes	—	25.2(a)	30.0	29.0	33.7	40.0
with state funding	—	17.7(a)	19.0	10.3	9.9	
without state funding	—	7.5(a)	11.0	18.7	23.8	
Technical training centers	—	33.2	45.4	57.8	73.8	77.5

Sources: Lehmann (1990), González (1990) and Higher Education Research Commission (1991).
Note: (a) Figures for 1983.

Higher Education, Government Financing and Equity

Education and Income Distribution

A phenomenon observed in other countries as well as in Chile illustrates the relationship between education and earning power. Table 2.27 shows the close relationship between the educational level of heads of family and the level of family income.

This pattern tends to be cyclical, since children and young people from affluent households receive more and better education than those from households with limited means.

Although the coverage of elementary education is relatively uniform for all income levels (Table 2.28), the coverage of secondary education is clearly differentiated according to family income level. In the poorest quintile, 46.3 percent of young people between the ages of 14 and 17 attend high school; in the top quintile this figure is almost 80 percent.

Table 2.27. Family Income and Education of the Head of Household
(Percentages)

Education of	Quintile					
Head of household	I	II	III	IV	V	VI
Elementary not completed	51.3	44.1	37.9	28.2	14.2	34.7
Elementary completed	15.6	13.9	11.2	9.5	4.9	10.9
Secondary not completed	18.0	20.7	21.0	16.5	8.5	16.9
Secondary completed	12.1	17.6	22.4	29.0	25.7	21.6
Higher - 4 years or less	2.2	2.6	5.1	11.2	19.9	8.3
Higher - 5 or more years	0.8	1.1	2.4	5.6	26.8	7.6
Total	100.0	100.0	100.0	100.0	100.0	100.0

Source: Author's calculations, based on CASEN 1990.

Table 2.28. Educational Coverage
(Percentages)

	Quintile					
	I	II	III	IV	V	Total
Elementary	89.5	90.0	90.6	91.1	91.4	90.2
Secondary	46.3	56.6	60.9	72.3	79.2	59.5
Higher	4.1	6.6	9.3	15.6	32.2	11.9

Source: Author's calculations, based on CASEN 1990.

Table 2.29. Socioeconomic Distribution of Students, by Institution

Quintile	I	II	III	IV	V	Total
Traditional universities	7.4	10.3	18.8	23.9	39.6	100.0
Regional universities	11.7	16.5	16.9	28.0	26.9	100.0
Private universities	0.8	3.4	9.3	14.4	72.1	100.0
Professional institutes	4.9	10.4	17.0	31.4	36.3	100.0
Technical training centers	9.3	13.6	25.4	28.9	22.8	100.0
Total	7.0	11.0	18.4	26.4	37.2	100.0

Source: Author's calculations, based on CASEN 1990.

The most significant change, however, occurs in the transition from secondary education to higher education. Most students who attend a postsecondary institution are from high-middle and high-income families. The percentage of young people who pursue higher education is eight times greater in the highest quintile than in the lowest.

Available information indicates inequality in elementary and secondary education, depending on whether a student attends a private school or a tuition-free, state-financed institution. This is illustrated by the results of national aptitude tests administered at the fourth and eighth levels of elementary education. Scores earned by students on national university entrance examinations also illustrate this point.

In summary, available data indicate that education contributes significantly to income and, conversely, that family income determines the level and quality of education received. Thus, education is central to any public policy issue of equity and income distribution.

What is the current situation in public education? The traditional universities (Table 2.29) attract mostly high and high-middle-income students (39.6 percent are from quintile V and 63.5 percent are from quintiles IV and V). Still, a significant percentage (17.7 percent) are low-middle and low-income students (quintiles I and II). The enrollment at regional universities is more uniform, with 28.2 percent of students coming from the poorest 40 percent of households. Thus, the state's contribution goes to institutions where many students are from affluent families but a significant percentage are also from low-income families. It is important to keep this in mind when discussing the policy of financing higher education. Private universities basically attract upper-class students (72.1 percent are from quintile V, Table 2.29). Students in these institutions are likely those whose scores were too low to grant entrance to traditional universities[4] but who can nevertheless afford the tuition at private universities. The enrollment at these schools is generally no larger than at traditional institutions; the difference is that private universities cannot provide government-financed loans for their students, making it difficult for students from modest households to attend these universities.

In the nonuniversity higher education system, students in professional institutes are socioeconomically distributed much as they are in traditional universities, while those who attend technical training centers more closely resemble students in regional universities.

The Personal Rate of Return of Higher Education

How much income can a university graduate expect? How profitable is it to pursue a higher education? These questions are central to the formulation of higher education financing policies and they are the primary focus of this section. Since the professional institutes and technical centers are all new and have graduated only a small number of students, the following analysis focuses on university education.

Figures 2.1 and 2.2 profile lifetime earnings according to the type of education received. The information is cross-sectional and comes from the 1990 CASEN survey.

The figures show the close relationship between education and income. It is clear that for both men and women a higher education substantially increases personal income.

---

[4] At least in the most prestigious traditional universities, Universidad de Chile and Universidad Católica.

Figure 2.1 Income of Men by Educational Level

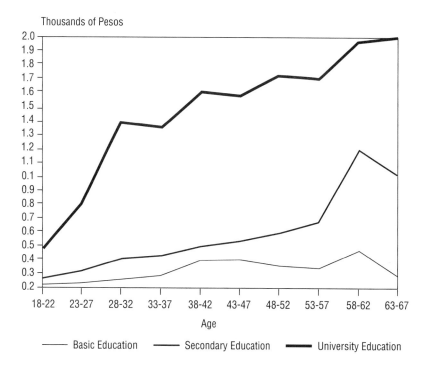

The information summarized in Figures 2.1 and 2.2 was used to formally estimate the relationship between education and earned income. The results of the estimate were used to calculate the private rates of return of higher education. These, in turn, correspond to the discount rate that brings to zero the present value of the flow of net benefits of pursuing a higher education. The benefit is calculated as the difference over a lifetime between the estimated income of a university graduate and the estimated income of a high school graduate, all other known variables being held constant (sex, age, etc.). The costs of a higher education are of two types. First, the alternative cost of pursuing a higher education is the income received by high school graduates who are employed. Second, the direct cost of a higher education consists of tuition and the terms of available credit.

The rates of return were estimated for two types of university professions. Type A comprises 12 professions that the 1981 reform assigned to universities, generally the professions with the most prestige and highest potential incomes. Type B professions cover all other nontechnical university programs. Estimates were also made for technical programs,

Figure 2.2 Income of Women by Educational Level

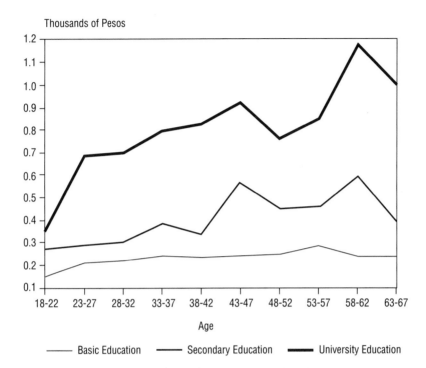

Thousands of Pesos

with results similar to those for type B professions. Technical program estimates are not presented in the text.

Table 2.30 shows results of three typical cases. The first is the rate of return from taking university courses while paying tuition without a student loan. The second is that of a student who uses a student loan to finance tuition. The loan is paid back, according to the terms in effect, within ten years of the second year after graduation at a real interest rate of 1 percent. The last case is that of a student who obtains a student loan but does not pay it back. This is extremely probable: the current delinquency rate for student loans is 70 percent. The results are presented for an auto-selection bias adjustment factor of 0.8 and 0.6, respectively.[5]

The main conclusions presented in Table 2.30 are first, that university studies are highly profitable. The profitability of preparing for a type A profession is 22.7 percent for a student who pays tuition without ob-

---

[5] Individuals who enter a university generally have more skills than those who do not. Since it is impossible to control the skills variable in terms of the income function, the correction was based on the estimated values for other countries.

Table 2.30. Personal Rates of Return of Higher Education

	Type A professions		Type B professions	
	0.8	0.6	0.8	0.6
Private tuition payment	22.7	19.3	16.0	13.3
Payment with student loan	31.5	26.6	20.2	16.6
Payment with unpaid student loan	32.8	28.2	22.0	18.4

Source: Author's calculations

taining a student loan. For type B professions, profitability is 16 percent. These percentages drop to 19.3 percent and 13.3 percent, respectively, if the 0.6 factor is applied to correct the auto-selection bias. Second, student loans substantially raise the personal rate of return of higher education. In the case of type A professions, the return is 31.5 percent and for type B 20.2 percent (26.6 percent and 16.6 percent with a factor of 0.6). Finally, comparing the rates of return for the two cases in which a loan is obtained indicates the latter is not affected by the decision to pay back the loan. This is a direct result of subsidizing the real interest rates applicable to student loans.

Distributive Impact of State Spending on Higher Education

This subsection presents an estimate of the distributive impact of state spending on higher education. The objective is to determine who receives government subsidies for higher education. Two types of subsidies are used in calculating the distributive impact: those contained in student loans and the subsidy implicit in state aid to universities.

Table 2.31 shows the distribution of student loans according to the beneficiary's family income level. The first row shows the percentage of students who obtain loans. As indicated in the table, 36.1 percent of all students who receive credit belong to the low-middle-income levels (quintiles I and II), while 46.1 percent belong to the high-middle levels (quintiles IV and V). The second row shows the distribution of student loans according to amounts received. Students in the two lowest quintiles of income receive 43.6 percent of the total credit, while those in the two highest quintiles receive 36.2 percent.

Two types of subsidies are received through student loans. First, credit is granted at subsidized real interest rates (1 percent per annum). Second, there is a high percentage of delinquency in servicing the loans. In this case, the subsidy is the difference between the opportunity cost of the government funds and the present expected value of recovering the loans. The distributive impact of the subsidy provided through state aid to universities is estimated based on the socioeconomic composition of the student body of traditional and regional universities.

Table 2.32 shows the results of the estimate, indicating a clearly regressive pattern in state aid to higher education. Approximately 77 percent of government spending on university education goes to young people from middle- and high-income households (quintiles III, IV and V). The results underestimate the degree of regressivity since the calculations do not reflect the fact that students who are now poor will later become affluent professionals, making the analysis one of static rather than dynamic impact.

An Evaluation of State Aid to Higher Education

In this section the equity of state aid to higher education is evaluated with a focus on government spending to subsidize a university education. The results discussed suggest that there are at least two reasons for questioning the rationale of this subsidy. First, those who attend higher education institutions come primarily from middle and high-income levels. Second, the personal rate of return of pursuing a university education is high.

What part of government spending on higher education goes to research and extension and what part to education? This question is relevant since there are economic reasons justifying state aid to research and extension, which is also related to the externalities these activities generate.

A complete answer to the above question requires information not available in Chile, such as estimates of the production and cost functions of higher education. The only (public) indicator available that illustrates relative weight given higher education is the amount of time academics spend on these functions, which is provided by Arriagada (1989).

Table 2.31. Who Receives Government-funded Student Loans?
(Percentages)

Quintile	I	II	III	IV	V	Total
Students	17.6	18.5	17.8	22.9	23.2	100.0
Amount	25.4	18.2	20.2	18.4	17.8	100.0

Source: Author's calculations, based on CASEN 1990.

Table 2.32. Distributive Impact of Government Spending on Universities

Quintile	I	II	III	IV	V	Total
% of govt. spending	10.5	12.7	18.6	24.1	34.1	100.0

Source: Author's calculations, based on CASEN 1990.

If, as an exercise, the use of time by academic professionals is linked to the cost of university research and extension, it can be concluded that about half of undergraduate education is financed with state subsidies. Another basis for the estimate would be tuition, since about 23 percent of the university budget is financed with tuition payments. Undergraduate teaching requires a substantial percentage of the resources of higher education (60 percent of the time of academics), so there is clearly a significant gap that ought to be financed by the state.

In these circumstances, some thought should be given to increasing tuition, so the cost of higher education is paid by those who receive it. However, given that the current level of tuition represents a significant percentage of the income of most Chilean families (see Table 2.33), any policy concerning tuition must be accompanied by a student loan policy. Otherwise, regressivity of the system will be accentuated because of market failures (difficulty of obtaining private credit), making access to a university education impossible for students from low-income families.

The next step is to examine the impact—on the personal rate of return of an education—of university financing policies that do not include subsidies and which make higher education possible for all applicants with the requisite abilities. This exercise is conducted for two scenarios: (1) tuition is kept at its current level and a nonsubsidized

Table 2.33. Percentage of Family Income Required to Pay Tuition

Quintile	Type A professions	Type B professions
I	91.0	64.8
II	48.0	34.4
III	34.0	24.0
IV	23.6	16.9
V	8.1	5.8

Source: CASEN 1990 and newspaper articles.

Table 2.34 Impact of Policy Alternatives on Profitability and Income

Adjustment factor	Rate of return		Debt service as a percentage of income
	0.8	0.6	
Type A Profession			
Interest: 6 percent	30.5	25.4	13.0
+ 50 percent tuition increase	29.2	23.9	19.5
Type B Profession			
Interest: 6 percent	19.2	15.4	14.4
+ 50 percent tuition increase	17.7	14.0	21.7

Source: Author's calculations.

interest rate is paid for credit (real 6 percent); (2) tuition is increased 50 percent and 6 percent interest is paid.

The results of this exercise are presented in Table 2.34. The personal rate of return is still good in both situations. Getting an education is still profitable, even when the interest rate on student loans is not subsidized and tuition is raised. The high cost of servicing the debt with earned income (about 15 percent if tuition is not raised and 20 percent if it is) could be reduced by extending the repayment period.

Final Considerations

Available evidence indicates the current financing system subsidizes university education. The rationale of this subsidy is questionable because of both the socioeconomic distribution of those who enter the higher education system and the high profitability of a higher education.

The evidence examined shows that the higher the level of education, the more skewed the socioeconomic distribution of students toward the middle and high-income levels. The change is particularly noteworthy in the transition from secondary to higher education. A factor that reinforces this argument and points out the need to reorient social spending on education is the return of investment in higher education. The results show that university studies are a profitable investment, even when a student pays tuition without a government-funded loan.

Summary and Conclusions

This study examined important aspects of income distribution in recent years and the relationship of distribution to social policy in Chile.

The second section examined the relationships between economic reforms, stabilization policies, social policies, and income distribution. The increase in social spending is due to two factors: first, the growth of pensions caused by the change in the social security system and second, the implementation of social assistance programs designed to compensate for the impact of the economic environment on income. Spending on education, housing, and health care declined during the period, reflecting the impact of the reforms on the composition of social spending. Some progress was made in targeting social spending, in particular the creation of specific programs aimed to offset the effects of recessionary cycles on employment and wages. The progress achieved in the redirection of social spending, however, was not enough to make up for the deterioration of income distribution.

The third section evaluated the impact of social security reform on the level of pensions, the coverage of the system, and the social security deficit. The general conclusion is that a determining factor of the transition period is the size of the social security deficit and how it is financed. The impact of reform on the public sector budget and savings depends essentially on the size of intergenerational transfers involved in the method of financing and the estimation of the recognition bond. One challenge facing the current social security system is the inclusion of self-employed workers in the system. An obstacle to the wholesale entry of these workers into the system is related to the way social services are offered. At present, services are offered in the form of "packages" that include a full array of benefits that cannot be obtained separately. The alternative of offering workers independent and separate access to benefits of the current social security system is a step closer to expanded coverage and consequently merits consideration in future studies.

Finally, the fourth section evaluated the redistributive impact of the current system of financing higher education. The conclusion is that higher education subsidies are extremely regressive and that higher education is very profitable. The combination of these two findings suggests that the rationale for the current system of financing higher education is an issue for public debate.

Bibliography

Arellano, J. P. 1989. La seguridad social en Chile en los años 90. *Estudios CIEPLAN* (no. 27, September).

——————. 1990. *El desafío de la seguridad social: el caso Chileno.* Documentos de Trabajo No. 340, PREALC.

Arriagada, P. 1989. *Financiamiento de la educación superior en Chile: 1960-1988.* Santiago: FLACSO.

Behrman, J. 1990. *The action of human resources and poverty on one another. What we have yet to learn.* Living Standards Measurement Study 74, the World Bank. *Boletín Mensual del Banco Central de Chile.* n.d. Santiago: Banco Central de Chile.

Ffrench-Davis, R., and D. Raczynski. 1990. The impact of global recession and national policies on living standards: Chile 1973-89. *Notas Técnicas CIEPLAN* (no. 97, November).

González, L. 1990. La formación de técnicos superiores en los centros de formación técnica. In *La educación superior en Chile: un sistema en transición*, ed. M.J.Lemaitre. Santiago: Corporación de Promoción Universitaria.

Haindl, E., I. Irarrázaval, and E. Budinich. 1989. *Gasto social efectivo: Un instrumento que asegura la superación definitiva de la pobreza crítica.* Santiago: ODEPLAN-Universidad de Chile.

Iglesias, A., and R. Acuña. 1991. *Chile: Experiencia con un régimen de capitalización 1981-1991.*

Indicadores económicos y sociales 1960-1988. 1989. Santiago: Banco Central de Chile.

Indicadores económicos y sociales regionales 1980-1989. 1991. Santiago: Banco Central de Chile.

Instituto Nacional de Estadísticas. n.d. *Encuesta de presupuestos familiares.*

Lehmann, C. 1990. Antecedentes y tendencias en el financiamiento del sistema de educacion superior Chileno. In *Financiamiento de la educación superior: antecedentes y desafíos*, ed. Carla Lehmann. Santiago: Centro de Estudios Públicos.

MIDEPLAN. n.d. *Informe Social.*

Tesorería General de la República. n.d. *Informe financiero del tesoro público.*

Una política para el desarrollo de la educación superior en la década de los 90. 1991. Comisión de Estudios de la Educación Superior.

CHAPTER THREE

THE DISTRIBUTIVE IMPACT
OF FISCAL POLICY IN THE
DOMINICAN REPUBLIC

Isidoro Santana[1]
Magdalena Rathe

Introduction

Due to favorable external conditions, the Dominican Republic promoted in the 1970s a program of import substitution industrialization
with substantial tax, credit, and exchange incentives. This led to an
unusual level of foreign exchange availability and sustained growth of
per capita GDP until 1977. The social aspects of development were
ignored and little attention was paid to basic services. The development model caused a structural shift in the balance of payments and in
the public sector budget which destabilized the entire economy.

In the early 1980s the economy was seriously affected by deterioration of trade and the external debt crisis. This, together with distortions caused by years of misdirected macroeconomic policy, forced
the adoption of an adjustment program with restrictive fiscal, monetary and exchange policies that continued until 1986. Given the state's
lack of interest in social expenditures, the public services situation,
already precarious, became even worse.

---

[1] This chapter was prepared with the invaluable assistance of the entire ECOCARIBE
staff, particularly Juan E. Cabral and Tammy Pou.

By 1986 the economy had been adjusted and economic growth was renewed. There was also substantial price stability. The new 1986 government stimulated the economy through an ambitious program of public investments. To do this, the government continued reducing the level of real current expenditures on public services, increasing budgetary savings. This led to a contraction of the real wages of government workers, a reduction in the state's management capability, and institutional debilitation.

To make this investment program viable, the Central Bank released the government from many of its obligations, and assumed responsibility for servicing the external debt and providing subsidies to state enterprises, thereby giving rise to an extraordinary increase in the money supply. This resulted in both the further deterioration of the balance of payments position as well as unprecedented levels of inflation. By the second half of 1990 the economy needed a strict, new economic adjustment program and a stand-by agreement was concluded with the IMF in 1991.

In recent decades, the economic literature has paid considerable attention to income distribution and welfare in developing countries, as well as to the economic policy tools available to address social imbalances. In the area of fiscal policy, the idea that government revenue and spending must be progressive has long prevailed. It has also emphasized that the state's financial activities influence income distribution in the following ways:

- Through taxes, which alter the relative position of the most affluent by reducing their disposable income.
- Through transfers, which improve the situation of the poorest sectors of the population.
- Through the provision of basic services, the assumption being that if they are delivered in sufficient quantity and quality, the most pressing needs of the lowest income groups will be satisfied.
- Through the creation of public property, which, in theory, is accessible to all, including the poorest.

In terms of fiscal policy, the prevailing idea is that public revenues and expenditures must be progressive and that the tax systems are based on personal income, profits, property, capital gains, and certain consumer goods and services. Nevertheless, the distributive effects of taxation are rarely satisfactory due to the low tax burden in underdeveloped countries, especially in Latin America, and there is strong political and institutional resistance to the administration of heavy, progressive taxes.

Consequently, the best distributive mechanisms are spending-related, which means that the focus of tax policy must be to maintain a reasonable tax burden so that sufficient funds will be available to implement an effective social spending policy.

The provision of basic services is an essential budget item. In some cases, however, more selective tools must be utilized, such as the granting of monetary allowances or in-kind contributions to the poor. This is necessary because public services policy sometimes fails to differentiate between income levels, resulting in services being utilized entirely by middle and high-income groups to the exclusion of the low-income groups.

The use of selective mechanisms is a more appropriate method of providing assistance, but it loses effectiveness in societies where poverty is widespread. In such cases, and without underestimating the value of direct assistance to specific population groups, it is better to utilize indirect methods that benefit broader segments of the population, such as the provision of public services.

This chapter is a summary of the research conducted by ECOCARIBE concerning the effects of government revenue and spending policy on income distribution in the Dominican Republic. An attempt is made to analyze the distributive impact of taxes and to quantify the degree of social progressivity of the country's public expenditures. The goal is to draw clear conclusions about which social groups bear the cost of government spending and which receive the benefits.

The first section is a study of income distribution in the Dominican Republic and the social aspects of its economic history. The second section contains a comprehensive study of the impact of taxes, while the third attempts to determine which social groups receive the benefits of government spending. The allocation of government resources in the 1980s is analyzed, followed by a close look at the distributive impact of government spending on health care and housing, identifying the social groups they benefit.

A final section offers general recommendations for amending fiscal policy to achieve greater distributive efficiency.

Income Distribution and Social Conditions

Income Distribution

Income distribution is extremely unequal in the Dominican Republic. Between 1976 and 1984, when the National Family Income and Expenditures Surveys (ENIGF) were conducted, some improvement in income distribution was registered, but the distribution pattern worsened considerably in the latter half of the 1980s. The Gini coefficient fell two percentage points between 1976 and 1984, reflecting some alleviation of social disparity, presumably because of the greater attention given in the early 80s to rural areas, where the lowest income sectors of the population are concentrated.

However, between 1984 and 1989 a disturbing concentration of income occurred, resulting in an economic crisis, inflation and misdirected government spending. The Gini coefficient rose from 0.43 to 0.51, revealing an unusual concentration through this five-year period.

In 1989, the poorest 34.3 percent of families received only 8.8 percent of the national income, while the richest 11.9 percent received 44.2 percent.

Table 3.1. Distribution of Income by Decile Groups of Households (1984 and 1989)

	1984			1989		
		Cumulative percent			Cumulative percent	
Decile	Percent income received	Households	Income	Percent income received	Households	Income
1	2.1	10.0	2.1	0.8	8.1	0.8
2	3.3	20.1	5.4	1.9	16.5	2.7
3	4.2	30.1	9.6	2.5	25.0	5.2
4	5.2	40.1	14.8	3.6	34.3	8.8
5	7.0	50.1	21.8	4.5	43.5	13.3
6	7.0	60.1	28.8	5.9	53.4	19.2
7	9.5	70.1	38.3	9.0	65.0	28.2
8	13.9	80.1	52.2	11.2	76.5	39.0
9	14.6	90.2	66.8	16.4	88.1	55.8
10	33.2	100.0	100.0	44.2	100.0	100.0

Source: Prepared by ECOCARIBE, based on Central Bank data.
Note: The 1989 grouping does not coincide exactly with the decile groups of households because the grouping was originally done by deciles of individuals.

The deterioration of income distribution was due to excessive and recurrent public sector deficits (financed by the issuance of paper money and the decapitalization of major public enterprises, creating a lengthy process of inflation), shortages of basic goods and services, and a decline in real wages. In addition, there was an emphasis on public construction projects to the detriment of current expenditures on public services.

Between December 1985 and December 1990, the real minimum wage of public employees declined 56.6 percent and that of private sector employees 25.2 percent. Likewise, there was a substantial concentration of material wealth in the country. In 1984 the average income level of the top decile was more than 15.8 times that of the poorest; in 1989 it was 20.3 times that of the poorest. The top decile includes all households with a family income in excess of US$500 per month, referred to as the middle and upper classes.

The change in income distribution can be better perceived in the Lorenz Curve shown in Figure 3.1.

To accurately assess the distributive efficiency of fiscal policy, it is important to know the geographic location of the population's poorest levels. The results of the 1984 ENIGF show that there are no significant differences between the internal stratification of rural areas and that of the cities (intrazone). There are, however, profound imbalances in interzonal income levels.

Figure 3.1 Lorenz Curves on Income Distribution in the Dominican Republic 1984 and 1989

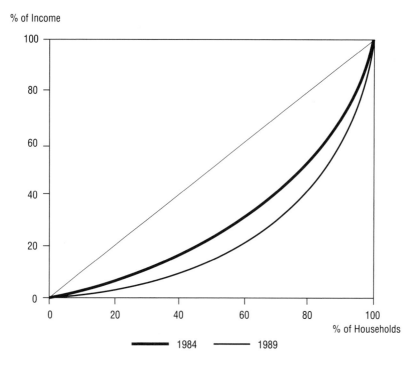

Source: Prepared by ECOCARIBE, based on Central Bank data, 1984 ENIGF, and 1989 Social Expenditure Survey.

Figure 3.2 shows the differences in family incomes in urban and rural areas. The vertical axis is a logarithmic scale, the purpose of which is to smooth out the curve. It is shown that for both high and low groups, income is much greater in urban areas than in rural areas, with the median 69 percent higher in urban areas.

Poverty Level

The trend of the economy and income distribution leads to the conclusion that poverty is widespread in the Dominican Republic. Many people live in a state of deprivation with no possibility of adequately satisfying basic human needs. Where there is poverty, there is also malnutrition, inadequate housing, low educational levels, poor sanitary conditions, and erratic participation in productive activities.

Figure 3.2 Levels of Monthly Family Income by Area, 1984

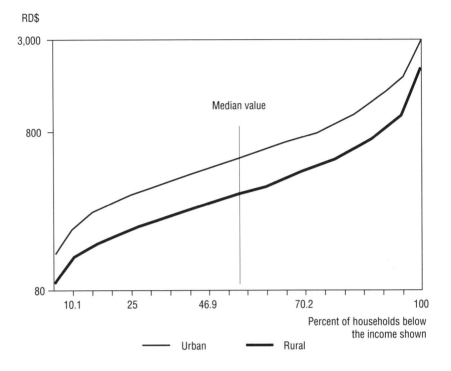

RD$

Median value

Percent of households below
the income shown

——— Urban   ▬▬▬ Rural

Source: Prepared by ECOCARIBE based on Central Bank data and 1984 ENIGF.

Many efforts have been made to establish criteria for measuring the extent of poverty. One is to define poverty on the basis of percentage of income spent on food. In the Dominican Republic, the poverty line has been defined as the income level where 60.5 percent of income is used to buy food, and where the basic food basket necessary to satisfy nutritional requirements is barely provided. The indigency line is defined as that level where the entire income is spent on food, but the basic nutritional needs are not adequately satisfied.

According to these definitions, 47 percent of all Dominican households in 1984 could be described as poor, with 23 percent of these same households also falling into the indigent category. Looking at the 1989 data, the picture becomes considerably worse: 56 percent of the Dominican population was below the poverty line, and within this group, 35 percent was indigent. This situation was exacerbated by a decline in real GDP of around 13 percent between 1989 and 1991. We estimate that, at present, some 4.2 million Dominicans (more than half of the population) are poor and approximately 2.5 million are indigent.

Figure 3.3. Level of Monthly Family Income by Decile Groups of Households, 1984 and 1989

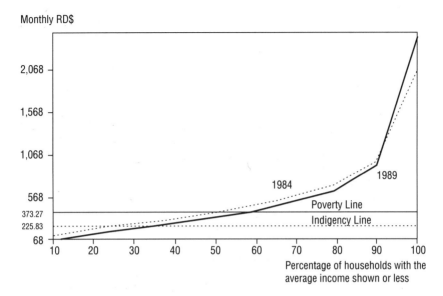

Source: Prepared by ECOCARIBE, based on Central Bank data, 1984 ENIGF, and 1989 Social Expenditure Survey.

The level of poverty reflected in the data examined thus far is well above the Latin American average.

Social Conditions

The low income levels, skewed distribution of monetary income, precarious nature of services provided by the government, and lack of access to other elements of material well-being give a picture of the inadequate living conditions of a large part of the population. Based on the national family budget survey of 1976-77, it has been estimated that 90 percent of the Dominican population is to some extent undernourished. This situation has recently worsened. In every food category, the richest 5 percent of the population consumes twice as much as the poorest group; in the case of meat and milk, four times as much.

Another survey conducted in 1986 by the National Population and Family Council revealed that 31 percent of children under three years of age in urban areas and 46 percent of those living in rural areas suffer from severe malnutrition, as evidenced by their weight being too low for their age. The most critical levels of malnutrition are found in the country's southwest region.

In the housing sector, there is a substantial qualitative deficit; some 33 percent of existing housing is estimated to be worthless and only 24 percent is considered adequate. It is estimated that more than 80 percent of the country's existing housing was built by the informal sector.

The health care situation, which currently covers barely 36 percent of outpatient consultations and 50 percent of hospitalizations, is deficient and has deteriorated in recent years due to cuts in government spending. A growing proportion of the population, including those in low income levels, rely on expensive private health care services.

A good indicator of the viability of health care is infant mortality, which, although it has declined, is still high at about 80 per thousand live births. Similarly, life expectancy at birth is 65 years, which is low for Latin America.

Social security is practically nonexistent in the Dominican Republic, where the government spends less than 1 percent of GDP on this sector, one of the lowest levels in the world. The four official agencies responsible for social security provide only partial protection to 9.5 percent of the total population. This means that the vast majority of the population has no protection against unemployment, old age, disability, sickness, and other contingencies.

Although some long-term improvement has been observed in the education indicators, serious problems persist and the government has neglected this sector as well. More than a million people are illiterate and functional illiteracy is a problem for the majority of adults.

Only about 86 percent of children aged 7-14 are enrolled in elementary school, and only 43 percent of those between 15 and 18 years of age are in secondary school. But these data overstate the coverage of the educational system because they include many overage students, resulting in available places being occupied by older students who are behind in their education. Added to this are students who repeat grades and those who drop out. In the public elementary schools, the percentage repeating grades rose from 17 percent in 1984 to 19 percent three years later. The situation is most serious in the first grade, where the rate of repetition is 38 percent because there is almost no pre-school education.

Approximately 10 percent of the children who enroll do not complete the school year, and nearly 18 percent of those who pass do not return the following year, resulting in a 23 percent dropout rate between years. It is estimated that only 19 percent of those who begin elementary school complete it within the officially allotted time. This percentage rises to 40 percent in secondary school.

The situation is also dramatic in the case of drinking water. In 1984 only 30 percent of all households in the country had indoor water. The situation is worse in rural areas, where only 4 percent of households had indoor connection. But even among those who do have a connection, service is problematic and intermittent in many areas.

Only a fourth of the households are connected to the official sewerage system, while 7.5 percent of families have no means of disposing of waste. Similarly, it was estimated in 1987 that only 40 percent of the country's urban areas have frequent garbage collection.

Electrical service is deficient and has deteriorated markedly since 1987. It is estimated that the electric company currently supplies less than half the normal energy requirements. At the level of individual households, it is estimated that a fourth of the population has no access to power lines, especially in rural areas.

The most notable characteristics of the labor market are high rates of unemployment and underemployment, large numbers of children and old people in the work force, and the growing presence of women in the labor market. A large-scale migration exists from the country to the city and, to a lesser extent, from the Dominican Republic to other countries (primarily the United States), as well as from Haiti to the Dominican Republic. Similarly, with the decline in real wages, there is a trend toward moonlighting and the informalization of labor.

The Distributive Impact of Tax Payments

This section will provide a comprehensive view of the current Dominican tax system and its recent growth, as well as determine the impact of the payment of taxes.

The Dominican Tax System

For the purposes of this analysis, detailed data were collected on government revenues in the 1980s and calculations made for each type of tax. To accomplish this, all tax receipts collected were categorized according to type of tax.

There are two reasons why this was necessary: first, in most statistics on public finances, some taxes are always categorized incorrectly, depending on the offices that collect them. Second, the statistics do not reflect the actual tax burden since they include only some of the taxes. Specifically, taxes established not by law but by Executive Order, resolutions of the monetary authorities, special agreements, and other sources are usually omitted.

The first task was to collect and process the data on government revenues so they could be organized for this research, given that the country's system for preparing and publishing statistics is extremely deficient.

One characteristic of the Dominican tax system is that the coefficient of taxation is relatively low in comparison with that of other countries. Furthermore, it declined in recent decades and only re-

Table 3.2. Structure and Trend of Government Revenues (1979-1990)
(Millions of RD$)

Year	Gov't. revenues	Tax receipts				Non-tax revenue	Special revenue
		Total	Taxes	Rates	Other taxes		
1979	913.8	621.6	605.3	16.3	—	50.9	241.3
1980	1,063.8	713.7	696.2	17.5	—	155.2	194.9
1981	1,080.9	749.2	734.8	14.4	—	159.1	172.6
1982	1,024.4	676.3	661.3	14.9	—	68.8	279.3
1983	1,172.6	798.1	782.5	15.6	—	107.5	267.0
1984	1,316.5	1,067.5	1,049.1	18.3	—	81.4	167.5
1985	2,458.2	2,095.8	2,075.6	20.2	—	80.1	282.3
1986	2,644.4	2,163.0	2,139.7	20.2	3.1	99.3	382.1
1987	3,156.5	2,632.9	2,529.5	32.3	71.2	288.9	234.7
1988	5,575.1	4,884.7	4,689.0	50.3	145.4	302.1	388.3
1989	7,043.1	6,447.6	6,285.4	69.4	92.8	248.4	347.2
1990	8,470.7	7,766.4	7,177.4	151.6	437.5	247.4	456.9

Source: Prepared by ECOCARIBE, based on National Treasury data. The heading "other taxes" includes both taxes and rates, but the available information does not permit separating them.

cently stabilized at about 12-13 percent of GDP. This downward trend in the central government's ability to generate revenue persists despite numerous changes in tax legislation, which has caused enormous variations in receipts during the last decade. Many of these changes were made without approval of the National Congress and have prevented an even greater deterioration of the coefficient of taxation, as shown in Figure 3.4.

All efforts to change the tax system to expand the country's tax base are met with organized resistance from various social groups. One of the arguments most commonly used by low and high-income groups against the imposition of new or higher taxes is their regressivity; i.e., the responsibility for paying them falls primarily on the poor.

Another reason for popular resistance to higher taxes is the public perception that there is little connection between taxes paid and benefits received through public services. This view is explained by the often irrational allocation of government funds to low-priority activities, inefficiency in the provision of services, and administrative corruption.

The reason cited most often for resistance is regressivity of the tax system. The basis for this assertion is that one of the chief characteristics of the tax system is its heavy reliance on consumption taxes, which are considered transferable.

Table 3.2 shows the trend of the Dominican tax structure and reveals that direct taxes, in this case revenue taxes and taxes on net worth, represent approximately 25 percent of the total tax receipts, resulting in the government being financed primarily with indirect taxes.

Figure 3.4 Trend of the Tax Burden as Percentage of GDP

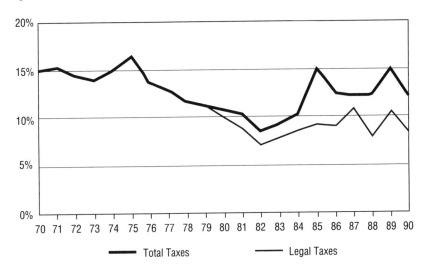

Source: Prepared by ECOCARIBE, based on National Treasury data.

As can be seen, taxes on net worth represent the smallest percentage of the total, though they are paid by the most affluent sectors of the population. With respect to revenue taxes, nearly all government receipts in this category are income taxes, which represented 96 percent in 1989. This method of taxation, which accounts for a fifth of the government's current income, is below the average for Latin America as a whole.

Revenue and property taxes represent a small proportion of total receipts, mostly because tax administration is inefficient; consequently, indirect taxes are preferred because they are easier to collect.

One major characteristic of the Dominican tax structure, mentioned as a disadvantage in the last 20 years, is its reliance on receipts from taxation of foreign trade. This accounts for about 45 percent of the total tax receipts, the largest proportion consisting of taxes on imports. The variability of export taxes is from their having been imposed on a cyclical basis, to taxing extraordinary income when prices were high. Tax variability also exists because the taxes were established as temporary surcharges on exports.

Domestic consumption taxes exhibited regular, sustained growth in the last decade, and their importance as a source of government income is on the rise. The tax on sales of manufactured goods and services (ITBIS) is the most dynamic, representing the fourth largest source of receipts in 1990.

Other important taxes are the selective consumption taxes, especially those on alcoholic beverages, foreign travel, fuels, long-distance telephone calls, and processed tobacco (cigarettes).

The System Effects of Income Groups

The purpose of this section is to determine the impact of the Dominican tax system, i.e., to identify groups that actually pay the taxes.

It is hoped that the impact of the tax system will be progressive, i.e., that the higher income groups will be taxed more heavily since their ability to pay is greater. This is called the justice or fairness of the tax system. It is not easy to incorporate these ideals while achieving growth and increasing the government's ability to generate revenues needed to finance public expenditures.

The word "impact" is understood to mean the burden borne by the taxpayer who actually pays the tax. This is not necessarily the person legally responsible to pay the tax because of the process of transferral— where attempts are made to avoid the tax and to pass it on to other social groups. The impact, therefore, is the result of the transferral.

Nevertheless, the problem of identifying which social groups should bear the tax burden is not a simple one. This difficulty has been recognized since the dawn of economic thinking, and the theory of public finances has attempted to approach it from many angles.

A great deal of empirical research is still needed to validate the impact theory, especially regarding Third World countries. Most of the work in this field has been done in industrialized countries, and even so, there is no general consensus on how these transferral processes function and how they affect various productive entities.

This has implications on the type of taxes that are appropriate, which is more a problem for developing countries than industrialized nations, given the greater social imbalances in the former. Studies of this type can provide governments with a solid basis for decision-making.

For the purpose of this study, a tax is considered progressive when the percentage of income needed to pay it increases with family income. There are cases where a tax is initially progressive and then becomes regressive at the higher levels, in which case the burden falls more heavily on the middle class. Taxes were divided into two categories, based on the old classification of direct and indirect taxes, to determine the progressivity or regressivity of each of these two major groups.

Conventional wisdom holds that indirect taxes, i.e., those that are transferred, are regressive because they are normally levied on consumption while the percentage of income devoted to consumption increases as the level of income decreases. Nevertheless, this regressivity would be assured only if the application of consumption taxes were general and the tax rates proportional to income. If this were the case, the mere act of consuming would necessitate payment of the tax, regardless of the thing consumed.

Consequently, a tax system based on direct taxes is usually considered progressive, while a system based on indirect taxes is thought to be regressive. But, in fact, this is not true. No tax is considered general, strictly speaking, since the consumption of certain goods and services is normally exempt. Even if there were a general tax, different rates would probably be applied, depending on the type of consumption. In addition to the general tax, selective taxes are usually applied to widely consumed goods and services.

In the Dominican Republic there is a selective general consumption tax, the ITBIS, which exempts a wide range of goods and services that absorb a large part of the budget of poor families.

Another consumption tax is that on imports, given the imported component of almost all consumption. Nevertheless, even in this case, highly differentiated rates are applied, depending on the type of goods imported. The imported component is substantially larger in the consumption pattern of higher income levels than in the lower levels.

Finally, there are selective consumption taxes which are intended to place more of the burden on high-income groups.

Indirect tax policy in the Dominican Republic attempts to mitigate or eliminate the natural tendency of this type of tax toward tacit regressivity. This is relatively easy to accomplish in a society where poverty is widespread and pronounced, and in which the poor must devote a significant portion of their budget to satisfying basic needs.

To determine the impact of tax payment according to social group, the method used by the Central Bank to classify the population by income level was adopted, wherein the poorest 40 percent of households are considered the low-income group, the next 35 percent the low-middle-income group, the following 20 percent the high-middle-income group, and the top 5 percent the high-income group. The base year for the study was 1989, so the results refer to the tax structure in effect that year.

There are many opinions about the transferral of taxes. They are explained in detail in the final report of this study, but are not included in this summary. The methodological explanations of how the taxes were apportioned to the various social sectors are also not included. Only the findings are presented here.

Direct taxes, those that are levied on net worth, are progressive and affect only the richest 25 percent of Dominican households. The overall burden, however, is of little significance.

Revenue taxes, which constitute the bulk of direct taxes, also affect households progressively, even assuming that corporate income taxes are partially indirect since a portion of these taxes is passed on to consumers. Table 3.3 shows the distribution of revenue taxes.

Since the Dominican Republic has a low average level of income, much of the population in the poverty level is not involved in productive activities affected by the tax system and, consequently, undergoes no di-

Table 3.3. Distribution of the Tax Burden by Family Income Group Revenue Taxes,1989
(Millions of RD$)

| Item | Income Groups | | | | |
	Low	Low middle	High middle	High	Total
Individual income taxes				32.0	32.0
Payroll taxes				336.8	481.1
• Distribution (percent)			144.3	70.0	100.0
			30.0		
Tax on games of chance	0.8	1.9	2.2	1.8	6.7
• Distribution according to consumer					
spending on recreation	12.0	28.1	33.2	26.7	100.0
Transferable corporate taxes					297.7
• Forward transfer	34.6	71.7	76.4	40.6	223.3
Percent total consumption expenditures	15.5	32.1	34.2	18.2	100.0
• Backward transfer			22.3	52.1	74.4
Distribution according to wages (percent)			30.0	70.0	100.0
Transferable taxes on					
export companies	0.1	0.2	0.3	0.2	0.8
• Distribution according to rural					
sector income (percent, 1984)	16.0	28.8	33.8	21.4	100.0
Total revenue taxes	35.5	73.8	245.5	463.4	818.3
Number of households, 1989	532,720.0	465,806.0	266,328.0	66,697.0	1,331,551.0
Monthly tax per household	5.6	13.2	76.8	579.0	51.2
Average income per household, 1989	590.5	1,573.0	3,424.7	10,730.2	2,053.2
Percent average income paid in revenue taxes	0.94	0.84	2.24	5.40	2.49

Source: Prepared by ECOCARIBE, based on Annex 3.1 of the "Documento de trabajo 107," Inter-American Development Bank, Washington, D.C., March 1992, and the 1984 ENIGF.

rect taxation. Table 3.4 shows the distribution of direct taxes among the social strata.

To apportion indirect taxes by family income group, the kinds of goods and services usually included in the family budget of each social group were examined in detail as well as the extent to which they were affected by each type of tax. Table 3.5 shows the impact of indirect taxes.

Table 3.4. Total Direct Taxes Paid by Family Income Group, 1989
(Monthly tax per household, in RD$)

| | | Income Groups | | | |
Item	Low	Low middle	High middle	High	Total
Revenue tax	5.6	13.2	76.8	579.0	51.2
Taxes on net worth	0.0	0.0	4.0	35.2	2.6
Total direct taxes	5.6	13.2	80.9	614.2	53.8
Average income per household, 1989	590.5	1,573.0	3,424.7	10,730.2	2,053.2
Percent average income paid in direct taxes	0.94	0.84	2.36	5.72	2.62

Source: Prepared by ECOCARIBE, based on Annex 3.1 of the "Documento de trabajo 107," Inter-American Development ment Bank, Washington, D.C., March 1992, and the 1984 ENIGF.

Table 3.5. Distribution of the Tax Burden by Family Income Group: Indirect Taxes, 1989
(Millions of RD$)

| | | Income Groups | | | |
Item	Low	Low middle	High middle	High	Total
Selective consumption taxes	37.1	148.7	287.1	188.7	661.6
Tobacco	21.7	40.0	30.1	10.0	101.8
Alcoholic beverages	5.9	74.7	101.2	48.1	229.9
Nonalcoholic beverages	0.4	0.7	0.6	0.2	1.9
Fuels	3.2	12.8	19.1	16.9	52.0
Foreign travel	0.0	0.1	87.4	43.9	131.4
Shows and entertainment	0.6	1.6	1.6	1.5	5.2
Communications	5.3	18.8	47.1	68.1	139.3
Taxes on sales of manufactured goods	61.2	181.1	242.1	178.7	663.0
Import taxes	222.9	585.7	737.4	481.5	2,027.4
Total Indirect Taxes	321.1	915.5	1,266.6	848.8	3,352.0
Number of households, 1989	532,720.0	465,806.0	266,328.0	66,697.0	1,331,551.0
Monthly tax per household (RD$)	50.2	163.8	396.3	1,060.6	209.8
Average income per household, 1989 (RD$)	590.5	1,573.0	3,424.7	10,730.2	2,053.2
Percent average income paid in indirect taxes	8.5	10.4	11.6	9.9	10.2
Including:					
Other taxes	373.4	1,023.7	1,381.9	910.2	3,689.2
Percent of average income	9.9	11.6	12.6	10.6	11.2
Export taxes	393.5	1,059.9	1,451.2	999.5	3,904.1
Percent of average income	10.4	12.1	13.3	11.3	11.9

Source: Prepared by ECOCARIBE, based on Annex 3.1 of the "Documento de trabajo 107," Inter-American Development Bank, Washington, D.C., March 1992, and the 1984 ENIGF.

Since the burden of direct taxes on the lower income sectors is virtually nil, the tax system's impact on them can only come from consumption taxes. Nevertheless, the shopping basket of 75 percent of lower income families contains mostly food. Many of these are agricultural products or are considered essential; therefore, the level of taxation is very low.

The table shows that, depending on the structure of the family budget by social group, even indirect taxes are progressive. Once all selective consumption taxes, the general consumption tax (ITBIS) and import taxes are computed and apportioned, it was determined that the average paid indirectly by low-income families in 1989 was RD$50 per month. Low-middle-income families paid RD$164, high-middle-income families paid RD$396, and high-income families paid approximately RD$1,060 each month.

For the first three groups, this amount represented 8.5 percent, 10.4 percent and 11.6 percent of their respective incomes. However, for the high-income group, it represented only 9.9 percent of the average family income, showing that these taxes affect the middle class more than they do the rich. Although consumption among the middle groups is more diversified than among the poor, consumption expenditures are still a significant item in their budget.

Combining both direct and indirect taxes, the system exhibits a degree of progressivity, as shown in Table 3.6. The main conclusion, therefore, is that the Dominican tax system is not regressive, as is commonly believed. If the impact is measured in terms of average consumption instead of income, the level of progressivity increases.

Despite the relative progressivity of the Dominican Republic's tax system, the poorest groups still bear a substantial burden, primarily as a result of import taxes, because the poor consume products that are either imported or contain an imported component.

A sensitivity analysis was conducted, assuming, in one case, a total transfer of the income tax paid by corporations and, in the other, no such transfer. This experiment reveals that modifying the transfer assumptions, even in extreme cases, has no significant effect on the results.

Table 3.7 shows the impact of the tax system for each type of tax and the total, as a percentage of average monthly family income. The taxes with the greatest progressivity in the Dominican Republic's tax system are:

- Revenue taxes.
- Taxes on net worth.
- Fuel taxes.
- Taxes on communications.

Export taxes are regressive in the first two income levels but are progressive from that point on.

The taxes that are progressive for 95 percent of households, but which are regressive in the top level are:

Table 3.6. Overall Impact of the Dominican Tax System, 1989
(Monthly tax per household, in RD$)

Item	Low	Low middle	High middle	High	National average
			Income Groups		
Revenue taxes	5.56	13.20	76.82	579.04	51.21
Tax on net worth	0.00	0.00	4.04	35.20	2.57
Export taxes	3.15	6.48	21.67	111.56	13.45
Import taxes	34.86	104.78	230.74	601.54	126.88
Taxes on sales of manufactured goods	9.57	32.40	75.74	223.31	41.50
Tobacco taxes	3.39	7.16	9.42	12.48	6.37
Alcoholic beverage taxes	0.92	13.37	31.66	60.09	14.39
Nonalcoholic beverage taxes	0.07	0.12	0.19	0.24	0.12
Fuel differentials	0.50	2.29	5.99	21.11	3.26
Taxes on foreign travel	0.00	0.02	27.34	54.89	8.23
Taxes on shows and entertainment	0.09	0.28	0.50	1.82	0.32
Taxes on communications	0.84	3.36	14.74	85.09	8.72
Other taxes	8.18	19.36	36.08	76.68	21.10
Total Tax System	67.70	203.90	535.70	1,848.00	298.10
Average income per household, 1989	590.5	1,573.0	3,424.7	10,730.2	2,053.2
Percent average income paid to the tax system overall	11.5	13.0	15.6	17.2	14.5
Percent variation	—	13.1	20.7	10.1	—
Avg. consumption per household, 1989	665.3	1,497.6	2,790.7	8,301.3	1,913.1
Percent average consumption for all taxes	10.2	13.6	19.2	22.3	15.6
Percent variation	—	33.9	41.0	16.0	—

Sources: Prepared by ECOCARIBE, based on Annex 3.1 of the "Documento de trabajo 107," Inter-American Development Bank, Washington, D.C., March 1992, and the 1984 ENIGF.

- Import taxes.
- Taxes on sales of manufactured goods and services.
- Taxes on foreign travel.
- Taxes on alcoholic beverages.

   The clearly regressive taxes are:
- Taxes on tobacco.
- Taxes on nonalcoholic beverages.
- Other taxes (not specified).

   The last category, "other taxes," contains a large number of small taxes. These taxes are apportioned on the basis of overall family consumption. In addition, entertainment taxes affect families unevenly.

Table 3.7. Impact of the Tax System by Type of Tax, 1989
(As percentages of average income received)

Item	Low	Low middle	High middle	High	National average
			Income Groups		
Revenue taxes	0.941	0.839	2.243	5.396	2.494
Taxes on net worth	0.000	0.000	0.118	0.328	0.125
Export taxes	0.533	0.412	0.633	1.040	0.655
Import taxes	5.904	6.661	6.737	5.606	6.180
Taxes on sales of manuf'd goods	1.712	2.128	2.231	1.947	2.021
Tobacco taxes	0.577	0.456	0.275	0.116	0.311
Alcoholic beverage taxes	0.156	0.850	0.925	0.560	0.701
Non-alcoholic beverage taxes	0.011	0.008	0.005	0.002	0.006
Fuel differentials	0.085	0.145	0.175	0.197	0.159
Taxes on foreign travel	0.000	0.001	0.802	0.506	0.401
Taxes on shows and entertainment	0.015	0.018	0.015	0.017	0.016
Taxes on communications	0.141	0.214	0.430	0.793	0.425
Other taxes	1.385	1.231	1.054	0.715	1.028
Total Taxes	11.367	12.894	15.620	17.364	14.522

Sources: Prepared by ECOCARIBE, based on Annex 3.1 of the "Documento de trabajo 107," Inter-American Development Bank, Washington, D.C., March 1992, and the 1984 ENIGF.

The above results reflect the impact of taxes on social groups, but determine nothing about the degree to which the poorest groups are affected in absolute terms. Taxes on net worth and foreign travel do not affect these sectors at all. Taxes on communications, revenue, and alcoholic beverages have little effect on the poor.

The price differentials or fuel consumption taxes, taxes on entertainment, and tax on sales of manufactured goods and services, have an average impact on the poor.

Finally, the tax burden on the poor is heavy with respect to import taxes, other unspecified taxes and, above all, tobacco taxes. This can be seen in Table 3.8.

The Distributive Effects of Government Programs

The goal of this section is to analyze the trend and structure of Dominican Republic government spending and to determine to what extent budget expenditures benefit various income levels.

The Trend of Government Spending

The basic problem with government spending is that official statistics are outdated, inaccurate, incomplete, and omit disbursements made through accounts managed personally by the President.

Table 3.8. Taxes Arranged in Relation to the Percentage Paid by the High-Income
Group
(Cumulative percentages - high income group = 100 percent)

Item	Low 40%	Low middle 75%	High middle 95%	Total
	Income Groups			
Tax on net worth	0.00	0.00	31.39	100.0
Tax on foreign travel	0.00	0.08	66.95	100.0
Alcoholic beverage taxes	2.06	5.69	36.18	100.0
Taxes on communications	3.81	17.30	51.11	100.0
Revenue taxes	4.34	13.36	43.36	100.0
Fuel differentials	6.15	30.77	67.50	100.0
Export taxes	9.35	26.20	58.45	100.0
Taxes on shows and entertainment	9.62	40.39	71.15	100.0
Taxes on sales of manuf'd goods	9.74	37.96	74.78	100.0
Import taxes	10.99	39.88	76.25	100.0
Other taxes	15.51	47.60	81.79	100.0
Nonalcoholic beverage taxes	21.05	57.90	89.47	100.0
Tobacco tax	21.37	60.69	90.20	100.0

Source: Prepared by ECOCARIBE.

To obtain government statistics, which are not usually published in the Dominican Republic, one must consolidate the accounts of the central government with those of local governments, social security institutions, and decentralized government agencies (except state enterprises.)

The quantitative differences between these results and the central government data were not particularly significant, because local governments are of little economic and political importance in the country. In addition, expenses of other government agencies, although they entail considerable sums of money, are made with funds transferred from the central government, so they are already included in its financial statistics.

Compared to other countries, the level of government spending in the Dominican Republic is relatively low: consistently below 20 percent of GDP, which is far below the averages of all major regions of the world (Table 3.9).

The government's top priority in recent years has been construction of the country's physical infrastructure; while the provision of public services has been ignored. Between 1985 and 1988, the investment in construction multiplied seven times in real terms. The government's capital expenditures represented 57 percent of the budget, an uncommonly large outlay. Figure 3.5 illustrates this situation compared with other regions.

The share of capital expenditures in total government disbursements in the Dominican Republic is one of the largest in the world.

Table 3.9 Total Government Spending, by Country
(As percentage of GDP)

Region/Country	Year	Percent GDP
World	1986	40.65
Industrialized countries	1988	41.43
United States	1988	36.44
Canada	1988	44.47
France	1988	48.78
Germany	1988	47.77
England	1988	40.45
Africa	1987	35.18
Asia	1987	26.24
Middle East	1986	32.60
Latin America	1984	29.37
Argentina	1988	27.90
Barbados	1988	35.69
Bolivia	1989	18.64
Chile	1988	30.60
Costa Rica	1989	27.47
Dominican Republic	1989	18.20
Panama	1988	31.07
Paraguay	1988	9.04
Uruguay	1984	26.01

Source: IMF, Government Finance Statistics Yearbook, 1990.

According to the Government Finance Statistics Yearbook published by the IMF, in 1989 only Guinea-Bissau had a slightly larger share of 58 percent. Four countries had percentages above 40 percent, and the simple average for Latin America was 14.6 percent.

In government spending by sector, education expenditures were cut in the last decade from 2.2 percent of GDP in 1980 to 1.4 percent in 1989, an excessively low percentage in an international context. Real per capita expenditures fell from RD$25.4 to RD$15.1 in 1980 pesos in the same period (Table 3.10).

Health care expenditures as a percentage of GDP remained stable during the decade (less than 2 percent), but the level was also far below world averages. In real terms, these expenditures were 6.4 percent lower in 1989 than they were 10 years earlier.

Spending on housing took a giant leap in 1987, climbing to eight times the 1986 figures and doubling in each of the following years.

The drinking water and sewerage sector was another high priority in recent years, primarily as a result of disbursements made to begin construction of an aqueduct for the city of Santo Domingo.

Figure 3.5 Structure of Central Government Expenditures
(Simple averages for country groupings)

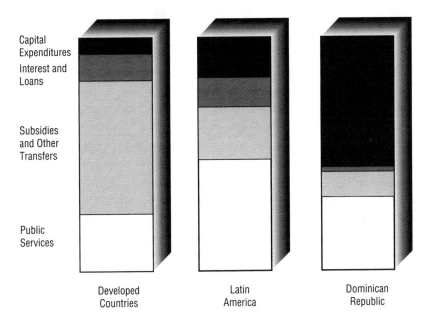

Capital
Expenditures

Interest and
Loans

Subsidies
and Other
Transfers

Public
Services

Developed   Latin   Dominican
Countries   America   Republic

Source: IMF, Government Finance Statistics Yearbook.

Distributive Effects of Government Spending on Health Care and Housing

The objective of this section is to select several government spending programs and identify the social groups they benefit. This is a complicated task, not only because of limited information but also because of the risk involved in asserting that specific individuals were the beneficiaries of a given expenditure.

Individuals or groups can receive different types of benefits. There are three ways of determining the effect of a government disbursement on an individual or a segment of the population:[2]

---

[2] See Federico Herschel, "El Gasto Público y su Efecto en la Economía," document presented in the VII Inter-American Budget Seminar, Buenos Aires, August 1978.

Table 3.10. Total Government Spending by Sector, 1980-1989
(Percentages of GDP)

Sector	1980	1981	1982	1983	1984	1985	1986	1987	1988	1989
General services	3.6	3.3	3.1	3.3	2.7	2.7	2.6	1.9	2.5	1.9
Education	2.2	2.3	2.2	2.2	2.0	1.8	1.7	1.5	1.6	1.4
Health	1.6	1.6	1.5	1.5	1.4	1.3	1.1	1.4	1.7	1.7
Social security	1.2	1.3	1.2	1.3	1.2	1.1	1.1	0.8	0.6	0.7
Sports, municipal & community services	0.9	0.8	0.7	0.9	1.2	1.0	1.0	0.8	0.8	0.6
Housing	0.3	0.3	0.3	0.5	0.2	0.3	0.2	1.2	1.4	1.9
Sewerage & drinking water	0.4	0.2	0.1	0.2	0.1	0.1	0.2	0.5	1.1	1.1
Agriculture and fishing	1.9	1.9	1.2	1.4	1.5	1.8	1.9	1.4	1.3	1.0
Irrigation	0.7	1.2	0.5	0.5	0.5	0.7	0.6	1.4	2.5	1.4
Transportation, communications and local roads	1.8	2.0	1.6	1.7	1.4	1.5	1.4	1.8	2.1	2.5
Urban development	0.2	0.3	0.3	0.2	0.1	0.1	0.2	0.9	0.9	0.9
Energy	1.6	0.5	0.2	0.3	0.5	1.1	0.7	1.2	0.9	0.6
Debt and financial services	1.0	1.0	1.3	1.6	0.8	0.7	0.3	1.7	1.6	1.7
Other sectors	0.6	0.4	0.3	0.3	0.4	1.3	1.6	0.7	0.8	0.8
Total	17.9	17.1	14.5	15.8	14.1	15.4	14.4	17.4	19.8	18.2

Sources: 1) National Budget Office; Budget Performance Report and official publications of the period. 2) Central Bank; monthly newsletters of the period.

- The first criterion is the monetary flows approach, where an attempt is made to identify recipients of a government disbursement. For example, in the implementation of a vaccination program, money is paid to the personnel who administer the vaccines and their suppliers. This method of analysis is useful for determining the government multiplier effect on the economy.

    This approach is not useful in measuring the distributive effect, although it can be helpful in the case of transfer expenditures, where the recipient of the money is also the beneficiary of the program. It would be helpful to study the effects of public spending programs on employment.

    This approach can also be helpful if, for ethnic or social reasons, social or racial discrimination blocks access of certain groups. This element is usually present in Latin American societies, but is not a determining factor.

- The second is the benefit criterion, which determines who receives the good or service provided by the state. In the vaccination program, the beneficiary is the person who receives the vaccine. This method is the most practical and widely used.

- The third method considers the overall expenditure impact on the economic system and how this system affects individuals and groups. In the vaccination program, not only does the benefit go to the supplier or the person receiving the vaccine, but to other members of society who will live in a healthier environment as well as those who benefit from an increase in labor productivity.

This section will analyze the effects of public spending from a broader perspective. Many spending programs such as education, health care, agriculture, highways, electricity, etc., have significant effects other than those on the direct beneficiary. Although there is an increasing interest in the distributive effect of government spending, distribution is not the sole aim of public policy. Attention must also be given to growth as well as to the social and legal system that govern life in society.

Concern for growth justifies the large sums of government resources allocated to higher education, for example, despite the fact that such programs do not have the same distributive effect as elementary education.

Following are more detailed studies designed to determine the social strata of the beneficiaries of government health care and housing programs.

Health Care

The health care system in the Dominican Republic is directed by the Secretary of State for Public Health and Social Assistance (SESPAS). Other important institutions are the Dominican Social Security Institute (IDSS) and the Armed Forces and National Guard Social Security Institute (ISSFAPOL). There are, in addition, other public sector institutions of lesser importance, as well as private non-profit agencies and private sector institutions.

Health services are provided by SESPAS and social security agencies through a system of specialized national hospitals, regional, area, and local hospitals, and health centers, subcenters and rural clinics, depending on the region. Almost all specialized hospitals are in the city of Santo Domingo. There are also mobile health units that provide certain minor services such as vaccinations and family planning.

The government subsidy of services is complete, meaning that office visits, hospitalization, surgery, etc. are free of charge, as are food and medicine during hospitalization.

To determine the income level of the beneficiaries, a survey was conducted among SESPAS hospital users. In this summary of the research, the methodology of the survey has been omitted. One of the findings is that despite the existence of a large private sector health care system, even families with a relatively high level of income use public hospitals.

The highest average user incomes were found in hospitals in the Cibao Central (Santiago, Moca and La Vega), which is the most eco-

Table 3.11. Grouping by Monthly Family Income Level of the Beneficiaries of Government Health Spending, 1989

Decile	Family income RD$/month	No. of beneficiaries in the sample	Percent of the total	Cumulative percent
1	0.00 - 1,067	37	7.4	7.4
2	1,067 - 1,517	91	18.2	25.6
3	1,517 - 1,870	47	9.4	35.0
4	1,870 - 2,079	36	7.2	42.2
5	2,079 - 2,774	87	17.4	59.6
6	2,774 - 3,369	49	9.8	69.4
7	3,369 - 3,582	13	2.6	72.0
8	3,582 - 4,543	46	9.2	81.2
9	4,543 - 7,527	70	14.0	95.2
10	7,527 and over	24	4.8	100.0
Total		500	100.0	-

Source: Prepared by ECOCARIBE, based on a hospital survey.

nomically advanced region of the country outside Santo Domingo. In the capital, user incomes were smaller, presumably because private medical services are more widely utilized, leaving the capacity of the public sector open for lower income groups. Family income levels of beneficiaries in the southwestern region of the country (Barahona and San Juan) and in the southeast (Baní and Villa Altagracia) are considerably lower.

To determine the social groups to which users of public health services belong, the national population was divided into decile groups of monthly family income. The distribution of beneficiaries, by family income level, is shown in Table 3.11.

Although families of all income levels receive a subsidy in one form or another, the largest percentage goes to the poorer households. For example, families in the first two deciles (comprising the poorest 16.5 percent of the households in the country, who receive scarcely 2.7 percent of the national income) receive 25.6 percent of the benefits of government health expenditures.[3]

The first five deciles (43.5 percent of the households) received 59.6 percent of the benefits. In the primary distribution of income, these families receive only 13.3 percent. These results confirm the belief that government spending on health care is an efficient mechanism for distributing national income.

---

[3] Not all decile groups of the 1989 family survey correspond exactly to 10 percent groupings since the original grouping was of individuals, making it necessary to rearrange them into deciles of households.

Table 3.12. Distribution of the Benefits of Government Health Care Spending, by Decile of Family Income, 1989
(Thousands of RD$)

Decile	Percent received	Amount received
1	7.4	52,162.6
2	18.2	128,291.8
3	9.4	66,260.6
4	7.2	50,752.8
5	17.4	122,652.6
6	9.8	69,080.2
7	2.6	18,327.4
8	9.2	64,850.8
9	14.0	98,686.0
10	4.8	33,835.2
Total	100.0	704,900.0

Source: Prepared by ECOCARIBE, based on ONAPRES data and hospital survey.

Households in the highest income level make less use of public services and, therefore, receive fewer benefits through the official health care system. The highest quintile (which includes 23.5 percent of families with the highest income and comprises all the middle and upper classes), received only 18.8 percent of the benefit despite the fact that its share of the national income is 61 percent.

Figure 3.6 shows the Lorenz Curves for distribution of national income and distribution of benefits of government health care spending. The latter curve is above the diagonal, meaning that the benefit is better distributed than national income (i.e., the poor receive relatively more than the rich) and also that the poor benefit more in absolute terms.

Table 3.12 shows the distribution of the total subsidy granted by the government in 1989 through public health care spending. Of the RD$704.9 million used for this purpose, approximately RD$420.1 million was received by households in the lower income levels (the poorest 43.5 percent).

Table 3.12 also shows that high-income sectors also received benefits. If the government's intention in providing health care was exclusively to benefit the poor, it would make no sense to subsidize high-income groups. Perhaps a way could be found to require the high-income sectors to cover the cost of the service.

Housing

Although there are many government institutions that provide housing services, the most important is the National Housing Institute. However, most recent spending in this sector has been controlled by the office of the President of the Republic.

Figure 3.6 Lorenz Curves with National Income Distribution and the Distribution of the Benefits from Government Expenditures on Health Care

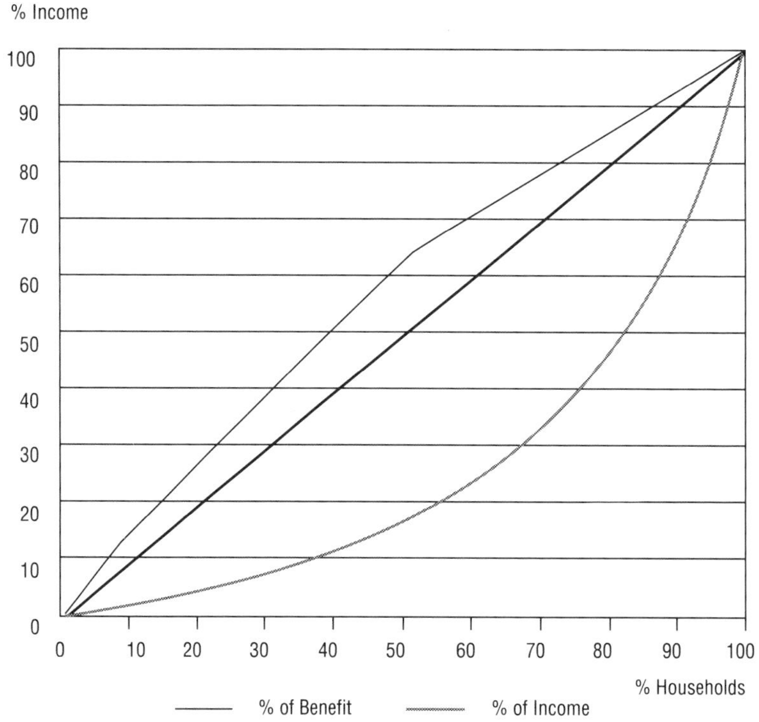

% Income

% of Benefit   % of Income

Source: Prepared by ECOCARIBE, based on a hospital survey.

The government's extraordinary effort in this sector has resulted in the construction of approximately 5,000 dwellings a year between 1986 and 1991, which, although considerable, does little to solve the country's housing shortage, as 30,000 new households are formed each year and the number of existing, run-down dwellings is about 460,000.

The concentration of taxpayer resources in this sector makes little sense from the social perspective since benefits are received by a small segment of the population.

The housing sector subsidy comprises almost all spending in this field, since the initial payments collected and the monthly rents charged to beneficiaries represent a negligible percentage of the original investment.

To determine the social groups benefiting from government housing projects, as well as the amount of monthly income received, a survey was conducted among the residents of the new housing projects. The methodological aspects of the survey are omitted from this summary.

Table 3.13. Grouping, by Monthly Family Income Level, of the Beneficiaries of Government-Built Housing, 1989

Decile	Family income RD$/month	No. of beneficiaries in the sample (valid)	Percent of the total
1	0,00 - 1,067	14	3.8
2	1,067 - 1,517	17	4.6
3	1,517 - 1,870	15	4.1
4	1,870 - 2,079	13	3.5
5	2,079 - 2,774	45	12.2
6	2,774 - 3,369	31	8.4
7	3,369 - 3,582	11	3.0
8	3,582 - 4,543	58	15.7
9	4,543 - 7.527	89	24.1
10	7.527 and over	76	20.6
Total		369	100.0

Source: Prepared by ECOCARIBE based on government spending on housing survey.

Research findings indicate that government spending on housing has not succeeded in its objective of helping the poor. Most of the benefit is received by families who are not poor, although not the wealthiest on the social scale.

The above table shows the social status of beneficiaries of government spending on housing, according to levels of family income identified in the survey.

No direct relationship is found between tenant income and the value of housing. In housing complexes with the highest market value, the beneficiaries are not in the highest income groups. The apparent reason is that these complexes were previously inhabited and the tenants organized to prevent the appropriation of their residences by groups with more economic, social and political power. The highest incomes are found in peripheral urban complexes that were not previously inhabited and therefore not the subject of controversy. Higher income groups with greater influence were able to obtain housing in these complexes.

The group with the lowest incomes, comprising the first four deciles, i.e., the poorest 40 percent of the households, receive 16 percent of the benefits of public spending on housing. It is also true that 10 percent of the poorest households receive 3.8 percent of the government subsidy through the construction of housing. Contributing substantially to this finding is the investment in rural housing in the southeast section of the country and several large, low-income housing projects in urban areas, such as the Guachupita district.

The top decile received 20.6 percent of the resources allocated by the government for this purpose. The last three deciles, which include the middle and high-income groups, received 60.4 percent of the total.

Excluding the first four deciles, 84 percent of the benefit was received by families who are not poor. Several residential complexes built specifically for high-income sectors, such as those on Calle Pedro Henríquez Ureña, Calle César Nicolás Penson and Av. José Contreras, were not included in the sample, partly because they are not finished and also because of the difficulty in obtaining reliable information. If projects of this type were included, the average income level of the beneficiaries of government housing expenditures would be even higher.

But even if all spending benefited poor families, considering the investment made, the distributive impact of building 5,000 units a year in a country where there are an estimated 720,000 poor households would be of little consequence. Therefore, government spending on the construction of housing is not an appropriate tool for achieving a more equitable distribution of income.

Table 3.14 shows the total amount spent on housing by the government in 1989, by decile groups of family income. Although the survey only included central government projects, the findings were extended to all public spending in this field. In any case, the central government contributed 90 percent of the total.

The most glaring detail in the table is that RD$169.5 million of the RD$822.8 million spent by the government on housing benefited families in the richest 10 percent of the Dominican population. Moreover, 60.4 percent was received by 30 percent of households in the middle-high and high-income categories. This means that 6.4 percent of the overall government budget was transferred to these families through expenditures on the construction of housing alone.

Although the high-income groups availed themselves to a larger percentage of government housing subsidy than the poor, the distribution of the subsidy is more equitable than the primary distribution of national income, as shown in Figure 3.7.

General Recommendations for Amending Fiscal Policy to Achieve Greater Distributive Efficiency

Research shows that fiscal policy is effective and can play an important role in achieving a less skewed distribution of income and improving the standard of living.

The poor receive a larger proportion of benefits of government spending than the percentage of taxes they pay. Since many goods and services produced by the state are public or semi-public, the share of poor households in the benefits of these programs is greater than their share of the primary distribution of income.

Unless the tax system is very regressive, requiring the poor to bear the costs to a greater extent than the rich, the net effect is usually that fiscal policy is beneficial to the poor. This means that a larger tax burden, provided it results in the government providing goods and

Table 3.14 Distribution of the Benefits of Government Spending on Housing, by Decile of Family Income, 1989
(Thousands of RD$)

Decile	Percent received	Amount received
1	3.8	31,266.4
2	4.6	37,848.8
3	4.1	33,734.8
4	3.5	28,798.0
5	12.2	100,381.6
6	8.4	69,115.2
7	3.0	24,684.0
8	15.7	129,179.6
9	24.1	198,294.8
10	20.6	169,496.8
Total	100.0	822,800.0

Source: Prepared by ECOCARIBE based on government spending on housing survey.

Figure 3.7 Lorenz Curves with National Income Distribution and the Distribution of the Benefits from Public Housing Expenditures

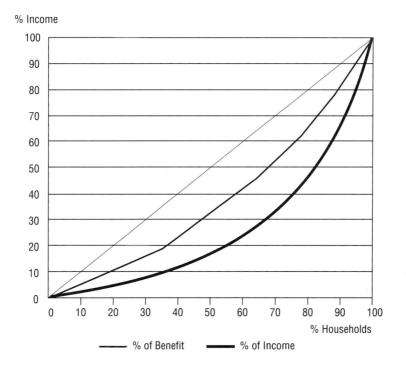

% Income

% Households

——— % of Benefit ■■■■■ % of Income

Source: Prepared by ECOCARIBE, based on Central Bank data, 1984 ENIGF, and 1989 Social Expenditure Survey.

services to the citizenry, tends to produce gains for the lower income sectors.

Since the tax burden in the Dominican Republic has been historically low, the system resists any real increase in the tax base. The budget for public services remains a small percentage of the country's total expenditures, which can create substantial distortions in the functioning of the economy.

Although taxes have little effect on the poor, it is recommended that priorities be established when increasing tax receipts to make the system more efficient in terms of distribution.

Taxes on net worth and revenue, considered direct taxes, remain the best means of increasing tax receipts. But in these categories, and especially with regard to revenue taxes, the greatest effort must be focused on improving administrative efficiency to curb tax evasion and eliminate avoidance mechanisms, given that the tax rates are already high.

Some domestic consumption taxes, such as taxes on foreign travel, communications, alcoholic beverages, and fuels might eventually be increased without significantly affecting low-income households. The distributive function is not the only one to be taken into account when making a decision about a given tax, since it may also have other economic effects.

A substantial raise in the price of goods or inputs for some sectors can affect the country's competitive position. It can also negatively affect revenues, depending on the price elasticity of the demand for that good.

Some of these taxes, although they have little effect on the poor, may constitute more of a burden on the middle class. This is true of taxes on alcoholic beverages and foreign travel.

Other taxes that could be increased and yet weigh less heavily on the poor than on middle-income groups are taxes on imports and the value added tax (ITBIS). Increasing the former, however, would conflict with efforts to avoid relative distortions in the protection of national production.

Consequently, of the indirect taxes, the most appropriate for increasing the tax burden, while having the least negative effect on the poorest groups, is the value added tax. But it would be advisable to retain the current tax base (i.e., retain the exemptions established in the existing legislation), and to raise only the rate of the tax.

If the tax were expanded and exemptions eliminated, despite making the tax regressive, it could still be justified, given the opportunity to neutralize regressivity through spending, with the poor being given access to services to improve their quality of life.

A decision to raise the rate before expanding the base requires the burden to fall on the middle class, which would necessitate finding other ways to compensate them. This could be achieved through the budget, i.e., the reorientation of government spending with a social objective.

The most important objective of spending policy is to allocate more resources to increase the coverage and quality of public services in general and social services in particular.

Since poverty is so widespread in the Dominican Republic, greater resources would be targeted to services that are more inclusive, i.e., those that reach broader segments of the population at a lower relative cost.

Our research focused on health care and housing expenditures. In health care, we found that the subsidy substantially benefits the poor because the per capita cost is low, enabling the government to provide a service for broad segments of the population at a reasonable cost.

There are other public services that have the same characteristics, such as education, sports, social assistance, environmental protection, community services, and agricultural development. Given that all of these services come under the heading of public or semi-public property, the poor's access to them is greater than their share of the national income suggests. From this perspective, their share of the benefits of these programs is greater than their share of the primary distribution of income. If these assertions are true, a concentrated effort on the part of the government in these areas would contribute to better income distribution.

One way the middle class would also be compensated for the increased tax burden would be to receive the benefits of these services as indirect income, inasmuch as they now have to allocate part of their family budget to pay private educational and health care costs of family members.

Unlike the activities mentioned above, the government must not allocate resources for activities which have such a high cost that they barely satisfy the needs of a few. This includes construction of housing, particularly when it has been demonstrated that the few beneficiaries are not always the poorest.

If resources are to be allocated for housing, it may be necessary to find ways of lowering the cost to the government. This includes sites with services, in which the state only supplies the site, the infrastructure, and the foundation, with the beneficiaries assuming responsibility for building the house.

To do this the first requirement will be to explain that the state's basic responsibility is not to save money for investment, but rather to satisfy the basic needs of its people. The effectiveness of fiscal policy cannot be judged by the size or number of public works it makes possible, but rather by its impact on the welfare of the population.

Any effort to implement an effective social policy must begin with the improvement of the government's ability to ensure increased efficiency and a thorough democratization of the decision-making policy on allocation of resources. This will provide for more efficient organization and for guarantees to taxpayers of greater transparency in the management of government receipts and expenditures.

Bibliography

Adler, J., E. Schlesinger, and E. Olson. 1952. *Las finanzas públicas y el desarrollo económico en Guatemala*. Mexico City: Fondo de Cultura Económica.

Alfonso, Abreu C.. 1982. Diagnóstico de la estructura tributaria dominicana. In *Seminario sobre reforma fiscal in la República Dominicana: Política y administración*. Santo Domingo: Publicaciones INCAT, Secretaría de Finanzas.

Andic, F., and S. Jones-Hendrickson. 1981. *Readings in Caribbean public sector economics*. Kingston, Jamaica: Institute of Social and Economic Research, Jamaica.

Anteproyecto de reforma del arancel de aduanas. 1980. Santo Domingo: Secretaría de Finanzas.

Auerbach, Alan. 1985. The theory of excess burden and optimal taxation. In *Handbook of public economics*, eds. A. Auerbach and M. Feldstein. New York: North-Holland.

Chapman, S.J. 1964. La utilidad del ingreso y la imposición progresiva. In *Ensayos sobre economía impositiva*, eds. R. Musgrave and C. Shoup. Mexico City: Fondo de Cultura Económica.

CIEPLAN. 1974. *Bienestar y Pobreza*. Santiago: Ediciones Nueva Universidad.

Corporación Dominicana de Electricidad. 1985. *Leyes, reglamentos y resoluciones*.

De Moya, F., M. Rathe, and I. Santana. 1984. *El gasto público y su efecto distributivo*. Santo Domingo: Editora Taller.

Del Rosario, G. n.d. Estructura del Consumo. Nutrición y pobreza en la República Dominicana, 1976-1984. Central Bank of the Dominican Republic. Mimeo.

Del Rosario, G., and T. Hidalgo. 1986. *Metodología para calcular el índice de salario nominal y su aplicación en la economía dominicana*. Santo Domingo: Banco Central de la República Dominicana.

Del Rosario, G., and S. Gómez. 1987. *Estructura impositiva y bienestar social en la República Dominicana, 1976-1984*. Santo Domingo: Fundación Friedrich Ebert.

Díaz S., Arismendi. 1990. Articulación de los seguros médicos privados en el desarrollo de la seguridad social en la República Dominicana. Dominican Republic. Mimeo.

Due, John F. La competencia monopólica y la incidencia de los impuestos especiales sobre las ventas. In *Ensayos sobre economía impositiva.* See Chapman, 1964.

ECOCARIBE. 1991. Los proyectos de reforma Tributaria: Observaciones preliminares. Mimeo.

Foxley, A. 1974. *Distribución del Ingreso.* Mexico City: Fondo de Cultura Económica.

Foxley, A., E. Aninat, and J.P. Arellano. 1977. *La distribución de la carga tributaria.* Notas Técnicas N°1, CIEPLAN, Chile.

Gómez Sabaíni, Juan Carlos. 1974. Análisis de la imposición sobre la renta de las personas naturales. Simposio Nacional sobre Política Tributaria como Instrumento para el Desarrollo, Secretaría de Finanzas, República Dominicana.

Guilliani, H. 1987. *El sistema tributario dominicano.* Santo Domingo: Fundación Friedrich Ebert.

Herschel, Federico. 1979. Reformas fiscales para América Latina. *Revista Tributación* 6 (no. 18, April-June).

Herschel, F., and J.C. Rossi. n.d. *Distribución de la carga tributaria en Argentina.* Buenos Aires: Cuadernos de Desarrollo.

Jarach, Dino. 1978. *Finanzas públicas: Esbozo de una teoría general.* Buenos Aires: Editorial Cangallo.

Kollikoff, L., and L. Summers. 1985. Tax incidence. In *Handbook of public economics.* See Auerbach, 1985.

La situación del empleo en Santo Domingo y Santiago en noviembre de 1979. 1981. Santo Domingo: Oficina Nacional de Planificación.

Los subsidios en la República Dominicana. 1990. Santo Domingo: Unidad de Estudios de Políticas Agrícolas (UEPA).

Mann, A.J. 1973. *La carga de las contribuciones y los beneficios de los gastos públicos, Puerto Rico, 1970.* Mayagüez: Universidad de Mayagüez.

McLure, C. 1979. El uso adecuado de la tributación indirecta en América Latina. *Revista Tributación* 5 (no. 19, July-September).

Musgrave, Richard A. 1968. *Teoría de la hacienda pública.* Mexico City: Aguilar.

_____. 1969. *Bases para una reforma tributaria en Colombia.* Bogotá: Biblioteca Popular.

_____. 1985. A brief history of fiscal doctrine. In *Handbook of public economics.* See Auerbach, 1985.

Organization of American States. 1973. La política tributaria como instrumento de desarrollo. In *Reforma tributaria para América Latina-IV.* Washington, DC: Organization of American States.

Pechman, Joseph. 1980. Tendencias internacionales en la distribución de la carga tributaria: Implicaciones para la política impositiva. *Revista Tributación* 6 (no. 21, January-March).

Petrei, A. Humberto. 1987. *El gasto público social y sus efectos distributivos: un examen comparativo de cinco países de América Latina.* Río de Janeiro: ECIEL.

Población y educación en la República Dominicana. 1989. Santo Domingo: Instituto de Estudios de Población y Desarrollo (IEPD).

Población y energía en la República Dominicana. 1985. Santo Domingo: Instituto de Estudios de Población y Desarrollo (IEPD).

Población y salud en la República Dominicana. 1987. Santo Domingo: Instituto de Estudios de Población y Desarrollo (IEPD).

Población y vivienda en la República Dominicana. 1984. Santo Domingo: Instituto de Estudios de Población y Desarrollo (IEPD).

Prats, I., et al. 1990. Evaluación de la extensión y eficiencia de los servicios educativos dominicanos. CIEA. Mimeo.

Ramírez, N., I. Santana, F. De Moya, P. Tactuk, and J. Canales. 1988. *Población y desarrollo en la República Dominicana.* San José, Costa Rica: IEPD-CELADE.

Rathe, Magdalena. 1982. La imposición al comercio exterior en la República Dominicana. In *Seminario sobre reforma fiscal en la República Dominicana: Política y administración.* See Abreu and Alfonso, 1982.

Rodríguez Grossi, J. 1985. *La distribución del ingreso y el gasto social en Chile-1983.* Santiago: ILADES.

Santana, Isidoro. 1982. El gasto público y su efecto en la economía. In *Seminario sobre reforma fiscal en la República Dominicana: Política y administración*. See Abreu and Alfonso, 1982.

_____. 1986. Participación de la población rural en la tributación y los beneficios del gasto público. *Revista Tributación* (no. 47/48, July-December).

_____. 1986. Política fiscal y estructura tributaria. In *Estrategias para la superación de la crisis económica nacional*. Santo Domingo: CODECO.

Santana, I., and M. Linares. 1990. Evaluación del sistema de seguridad social en la República Dominicana. CIEA. Mimeo.

Seligman, E.R.A. Introducción a la traslación e incidencia de los impuestos. In *Ensayos sobre economía impositiva*. See Chapman, 1964.

Thurow, Lester C. 1988. Corrientes peligrosas: El estado de la ciencia económica. Mexico City: Fondo de Cultura Económica.

Un aporte para enfrentar la crisis habitacional en la República Dominicana, Vols. 1 and 2. n.d. Santo Domingo: Oficina Coordinadora y Fiscalizadora de las Obras del Estado.

U.N. Development Programme. 1990. *Desarrollo Humano Informe 1990*. Bogotá: Tercer Mundo Editores.

The World Bank. 1990. Poverty. In *World Development Report 1990*. New York: Oxford University Press.

CHAPTER FOUR

PUBLIC ADMINISTRATION AND INCOME DISTRIBUTION IN PERU

Javier Escobal[1]
Arturo Briceño
Alberto Pascó Font
José Rodríguez

When the Alianza Popular Revolucionaria Americana (APRA) came to power in July 1985, it found that the principal macroeconomic adjustments needed to stabilize the Peruvian economy had been made by the previous government. Public finances were in balance, the balance of payments showed a surplus, there was $900 million in international reserves (approximately six months' worth of imports), and the exchange rate was slightly above its historic par value.

Still, inflation was climbing to alarming levels. The incoming government maintained that the cause of inflation was the constantly rising prices caused by public price adjustments adopted by the previous government. Consequently, a program was developed to combat inflation: production costs were controlled by freezing the exchange rate, imposing strict price controls, and lowering and fixing interest rates. In addition, there was an increase in aggregate demand through an expansive policy of public spending, wage increases, and reduction of indirect taxes.

---

[1] This chapter was coordinated by Javier Escobal, who also developed the section concerning the distributive impact of the policy governing agricultural prices and credit. The section on the fuel price policy and income distribution was prepared by Arturo Briceño and Alberto Pascó Font. José Rodríguez prepared the study on the distributive impact of public education expenditures.

All of the measures mentioned above were also part of a stated objective to improve the distribution of income. The goal of this chapter is to show how the results of a large part of this redistributive effort, carried out in the early years of the APRA government, were soon wiped out. To accomplish this, some of the most important tools that the government used in the 1985-1990 period to influence income distribution will be analyzed: public price policy, agricultural prices policy, subsidies, and education policy.

To provide a framework for evaluating the impact of programs carried out between 1985 and 1990, the first section describes the basic aspects of income distribution in Peru during that period. After describing the characteristics of poverty in Peru, this section summarizes the methods used in the 1985-1990 period to improve income distribution. The APRA government identified the need to redistribute income as a requirement for sustained growth. In accomplishing this, and although some specific spending programs with redistributive objectives were developed (such as the public education program and the Agricultural Revitalization and Food Security Fund, both of which are analyzed in this chapter), the general rule was to improve income distribution through massive intervention in commodities and factors markets, based on price controls.

Chief among the controls used were exchange control (the aim of which was to reduce the costs of producing and importing key goods consumed by the poorest sectors), the provision of credit at subsidized interest rates, and price control of public goods and services. Two of these instruments, the fuel price policy and the policy governing agricultural prices and credit, are analyzed in detail in the next two sections of this chapter. These instruments are not explicit spending programs; rather, they are implicit taxes or subsidies that affect the income of the producers or consumers of the goods involved in the programs.

The final section, which concerns the redistributive effects of public education expenditures, can be described as a traditional impact study. Obviously, education spending programs will have different effects in the short and the long terms; our goal is to analyze the first aspect, i.e., the immediate effect of transfers from the public treasury.

Income Distribution in Peru

Statistical evidence shows that income in Peru is highly concentrated. The Gini coefficient, the most conventional measure of the phenomenon of income concentration, has fluctuated between 0.55 and 0.58, according to the estimates made for years between the early 1960s and the mid-80s. The proportion of total income retained by the richest 20 percent of the population was between four and six times greater than that received by the poorest 50 percent. The gravity of the income distribution problem in Peru can be illustrated by comparing these figures with those of Brazil, perhaps the Latin American country most associated with the image of skewed income distribution: in 1970 Brazil had a Gini of 0.56, with an income ratio between the richest and poorest quintiles of 4 to 1.

Although it is not possible to accurately trace the medium-term trend of income distribution in Peru, some claim that the trend in the last 40 years has been toward deterioration.[2] Webb (1977) asserts that in the 60s income distribution was skewed toward the modern urban sector, which, including 70 percent of those in the richest quintile, received almost half of the nation's income. Included in this sector were not only the landowning class but also salaried workers and the state bureaucracy. Rural families (mostly highlanders) were on the opposite end of the distribution spectrum; the rural sector included 62 percent of the population in the poorest half and received barely 7 percent of the national income. Hence the overwhelming distinction between the rural poor and the modern urban sectors.

The characteristics of the distribution problem in Peru remained unchanged in subsequent years. The reforms in the productive structure introduced by the military government in the 1970s only caused a shuffling within the highest income quartile. Thus, neither the industrial nor the agrarian reform effected change in the overall structure of income distribution. The latter reform, for example, benefited only 38 percent of rural families (communities), who also received an average plot of land that was about one-tenth the size of the parcels allotted to other beneficiaries.

Figueroa (1975), who evaluated the redistributive effects of the institutional changes made—in particular, the change in the system of ownership of tangible assets between 1968 and 1972—asserts that the sectoral nature of the reforms limited their redistributive effects. In fact, the differences in productivity between sectors, which, according to Webb (1977) were significant and explained the biases of distribution of income, remained unchanged. Consequently, the reforms only benefited salaried workers in the modern sector, with a redistribution occurring within the top quartile. Meanwhile, the income of small agricultural producers, most of whom were included in the poorest groups, did not improve at all.

According to the National Food Consumption Survey (ENCA) conducted between 1971 and 1972, poverty was at that time still concentrated primarily in rural areas. Metropolitan Lima, with 20 percent of all Peruvian families, received 43.6 percent of the income; rural areas, where 54.4 percent of all families lived, received only 26.7 percent of the income. The severity of this situation is better perceived by noting that the average rural income was only 22.4 percent of the average income in Lima and 37.9 percent of the average income in other urban areas.

Figueroa (1982) suggests that around 1975 the structure of income distribution began to change because of the cyclical crises and the en-

---

[2] See Figueroa (1975), Webb (1977), and Amat y León (1981), among others.

Table 4.1. Distribution of Expenditures in Peru: 1985-1986

Deciles	Average monthly expenditures	Percent of expenditures
Decile 1	111.8	2.01
Decile 2	188.9	3.39
Decile 3	248.2	4.46
Decile 4	307.2	5.52
Decile 5	365.4	6.57
Decile 6	431.3	7.75
Decile 7	524.4	9.42
Decile 8	656.8	11.80
Decile 9	874.3	15.71
Decile 10	1,858.0	33.38
Total	556.6	100.00

Source: Glewwe (1987).

suing stabilization programs, which had a greater impact on the urban labor sectors. He asserts that the agricultural sector, although it was not a priority, began to improve its relative position in the urban/labor sector, which slowly fell on the income scale. Consequently, toward the end of the 1980s, poverty was not a uniquely rural/farm problem, but also involved the urban sectors.

Toward the middle of the 1980s, the inequality in the distribution of income continued to grow. The income levels of large urban sectors fell, substantially increasing the number of people below the poverty line.[3] A study by Glewwe (1987) reveals that the rural population, engaged primarily in agricultural work, lost less purchasing power than these urban sectors.

Between 1985 and 1986, a survey was taken to collect information about the welfare of the urban and rural populations of Peru. The National Living Standards Survey (ENNIV 1985) provides the clearest picture of the recent status of income distribution in Peru.[4] According to the survey, in 1985 the population decile with the highest income accounted for 33 percent of the total spending, while the lowest income decile accounted for only 2 percent. This disparity is reflected in the differences between the average expenditures of the various popula-

---

[3] The poverty line is defined as the minimum level of consumption that enables a person to satisfy basic needs.

[4] The status of income distribution in Peru in 1985 is described in two studies by Paul Glewwe (1987 and 1989). This section is based largely on those studies, although in some cases the information is presented differently, based on the original ENNIV data. To measure the standard of living, the total spending of the families is used as an indicator, so that in this sense the results are comparable to those obtained from the ENCA.

tion groups (Table 4.1): the average spending of the poorest 10 percent is about one-fifth of the average spending of the population as a whole, while the average spending of the top decile is almost four times higher than the national average. Only from the eighth decile upward does average spending per decile exceed the national average, illustrating the high concentration of income in the upper deciles.

ENNIV data for 1985 show that 28 percent of the poorest quintile lives in urban areas. This confirms a change in the composition of the poorest population group, which is no longer located exclusively in rural areas. Nevertheless, the preponderance of the rural population in the poorest group still stands. The large majority of this population is basically self-employed in agricultural work: 64.7 and 47.3 percent of those in the two poorest population quintiles. The structure of spending relative to the productive sector and population quintile shows that the agricultural sector accounts for 28 percent of the spending, despite comprising 40 percent of the population (Table 4.2).

Another characteristic of income distribution in Peru is the significant relationship between the educational level of the head of the family and the level of family spending. Ninety percent of the poorest quintile consists of families headed by an individual who has had no education or who had only basic education, while only 33 percent of families in the most affluent quintile were headed by someone with this educational background. Conversely, 66 percent of families in the highest income quintile were headed by someone with a university education (Table 4.2). According to Glewwe (1987), the educational level of the head of the family explains about 25 percent of the disparity in the spending levels in Peru.

Factors that were once significant causes of this imbalance have become irrelevant, according to the findings of the ENNIV. Such is the case with land ownership. Despite the considerable inequity in the distribution of this production factor, the poorest quintile has significant access to it, owning 13 percent of all cultivable land.

Another factor that once explained income distribution in Peru and that has now lost its significance is the place of residence. Glewwe (1987) clearly shows that regional differences and the urban/rural category explain no more than 15 percent of the disparity in the spending levels. This finding confirms the change observed in the composition of the distribution structure in Peru, the imbalances of which can no longer be explained solely by the differences between geographic regions. The differences are to be found within the regions.

The distribution of spending in Metropolitan Lima for the 1985-1986 period did not differ significantly from the country as a whole. It is also true that the poorest quintiles were largely comprised of families headed by someone with only an elementary education or no education at all, while more than 60 percent of families headed by someone with a college education were in the most affluent quintile (Table 4.3). The average income of individuals with an elementary education was 45 percent lower than the average for the population as a whole, and that of individuals with a college education 45 percent higher than the overall average.

Table 4.2. Household Characteristics by Quintile of Expenditure in Peru

Characteristics	Quintile 1	Quintile 2	Quintile 3	Quintile 4	Quintile 5	Total	Avg. per capita exp.	Percent of expenditures
Percentage of expenditure	5.4	10.0	14.3	21.2	49.1	100.0	556.6	100.0
Residence								
Lima	6.0	18.2	28.8	35.4	45.5	26.8	770.9	37.1
Urban coast	11.1	14.7	17.6	15.4	17.2	15.2	569.8	15.6
Rural coast	8.8	9.8	7.2	6.8	3.5	7.2	421.3	5.5
Urban sierra	9.0	9.6	10.2	11.5	14.8	11.0	649.9	12.9
Rural sierra	52.8	38.5	28.1	22.9	10.4	30.5	366.8	20.1
Urban selva	2.1	2.8	2.3	3.0	4.7	3.0	792.0	4.2
Rural selva	10.3	6.5	5.8	5.1	3.9	6.3	413.5	4.7
Employer								
None	5.1	5.8	6.0	6.4	6.6	6.0	582.4	6.3
Government	2.7	5.4	7.5	11.8	17.8	9.0	801.8	13.0
Semi-public	0.4	0.6	1.9	3.0	7.2	2.6	960.7	4.5
Private sector	15.0	21.0	23.0	21.0	23.0	20.6	599.2	22.2
Domestic	2.7	3.5	2.4	1.4	0.2	2.0	320.0	1.2
Self-employed	74.2	63.6	59.3	56.5	45.2	59.8	492.3	52.9
Employment sector								
None	5.1	5.7	6.0	6.1	6.6	5.9	583.7	6.2
Agriculture	64.7	47.3	38.5	31.8	17.5	40.0	389.4	28.0
Business & services	10.5	21.3	24.8	25.7	29.0	22.3	655.6	26.2
Industry & crafts	17.5	21.8	22.1	22.2	16.6	20.0	510.4	18.4
Professional	2.2	3.9	8.5	14.2	30.2	11.8	1,000.6	21.2
Other	0.0	0.0	0.1	0.0	0.0	0.0	375.4	0.0
Educational level								
None	28.1	17.2	12.4	7.4	3.8	13.8	329.0	8.1
Elementary Incomplete	62.1	63.5	57.4	50.0	29.0	52.4	436.8	41.1
Secondary Completed	5.9	9.7	13.1	14.2	12.6	11.1	576.0	11.5
Secondary	2.9	7.0	11.2	16.8	22.9	12.2	760.6	16.6
Post-Secondary	0.5	1.2	2.4	3.6	5.9	2.7	841.4	4.1
University	0.5	1.4	3.5	8.0	25.5	7.8	1,298.8	18.1
Other	0.0	0.0	0.0	0.1	0.3	0.1	2,935.6	0.4

Source: Glewwe (1987).

Table 4.3. Household Characteristics by Quintile of Expenditure in Lima: 1985-1986

Characteristics	Quintile 1	Quintile 2	Quintile 3	Quintile 4	Quintile 5	Total	Avg. per capita expenditure
Employer							
Government	9.8	12.6	18.3	24.9	29.8	19.1	9,474.3
Private sector	41.6	35.3	34.2	32.3	32.5	35.2	7,604.0
Domestic	3.7	1.2	0.8	0.5	0.0	1.2	3,931.5
Self-employed	10.0	43.5	36.7	32.4	29.0	30.3	7,126.7
Employment sector							
None	2.1	3.2	3.0	2.8	3.6	2.9	8,098.5
Agriculture	2.3	4.7	5.9	3.7	1.8	3.7	6,430.0
Business and services	34.6	27.3	24.2	23.4	29.2	27.7	7,532.4
Industry and crafts	47.6	49.9	38.6	35.3	15.1	37.3	5,858.5
Professional	10.6	10.6	21.2	27.3	45.1	23.0	11,307.8
Retired	2.5	4.3	6.2	7.2	4.6	5.0	7,495.9
Educational level							
None	5.4	5.0	2.0	1.2	0.5	2.8	4,288.5
Primary	58.3	43.9	40.6	27.5	15.3	37.1	5,677.6
General secondary	28.0	38.0	38.9	41.1	30.9	35.4	7,145.7
Technical secondary	1.8	6.2	4.5	9.7	4.1	5.3	7,087.5
University	3.4	4.1	10.1	15.5	44.5	15.5	15,112.2
Others	6.5	2.8	3.9	5.1	4.7	4.6	7,632.3

Source: Glewwe (1987).
Notes: 1) The columns do not total 100 percent due to the loss of 1.6 percent of the data. 2) The figures represent percentages of each quintile, where the head of the family indicates the characteristics mentioned.

As Table 4.3 shows, the population employed in the public sector was concentrated in the highest quintiles of income, as was true of professionals. An important difference at the national level is that many families in the poorest quintile were headed by someone employed in the private sector, not self-employed. Another difference is the small proportion of people employed in the agricultural sector; this is explained by the fact that in Metropolitan Lima there is little agricultural activity and the farmers on the outskirts of Lima, unlike those in the rest of the country, are located in the middle spending levels.

In summary, in the mid 1980s, income distribution in Peru was still highly concentrated, as compared with international levels. One of the most remarkable aspects of this is the significant correlation between the standard of living and education, which accentuates the importance of educational policy in a redistribution strategy. Another key point is that the urban population is considerably better off than the rural population, which is largely poor. Nevertheless, not all the poor live in the country, nor are all rural residents poor. A key aspect of income distribution in 1985 was that the regional differences were not sufficient to explain most inequities in the living standards of the Peruvian people.

How did this scenario change under the government of Alan García? The following section summarizes and analyzes the policies implemented by the APRA government between 1985 and 1990 from the perspective of their impact on income distribution. This analysis will provide a framework for the three studies that are the central part of this document and which concern the effects of three of the many measures that the government utilized to improve distribution: public prices and rates policy (with a specific analysis of fuels), agricultural prices and subsidies policies, and education policy.

The APRA Government and Income Distribution

In July 1985, when Alan García, the leader of the APRA, assumed power, the annualized rate of inflation was 200 percent and the country was unable to service its external debt. Nonetheless, and despite the seriousness of the imbalances, the APRA government inherited a somewhat stable macroeconomic situation with an orderly system of relative prices.

In late 1983 the previous government had initiated a process of economic adjustment aimed at balancing government finances and the foreign sector. To achieve this, a gradual adjustment of relative prices was undertaken, which consisted of a mini-devaluation policy and a gradual increase of the public rates, especially fuel prices. Towards the end of 1985, fiscal revenues were 13.5 percent of GDP, the highest of the decade. Thirty percent of the tax receipts came from fuel sales taxes, the main source of government revenue. Excluding payment of the central government's external debt (amortization plus interest), which in 1985 was equivalent to 8.8 percent of GDP, the central government had a surplus. Thus, the main source for financing the public sector deficit was external (primarily the arrears in servicing the debt), whereas internal borrowing was negative.

Similarly, in 1985, the trade balance was a positive $1.172 billion, which permitted an increase of $280 million in international reserves that year. In late 1985 the country had nearly $1.5 billion in reserves. This was the result of the mini-devaluation policy, which prevented the real exchange rate from falling in 1984 and 1985.

In summary, Peru underwent a severe process of internal adjustment aimed at generating the resources needed to service the external debt. This strategy caused serious problems and much discontent among the people, since the constant rise of public rates and the exchange rate caused an inflationary spiral. Near the end of the Belaúnde administration, the main problem was the government's inability to control the inflation caused by its own economic policy. The inflationary process had an impact on real wages, which, after a slight recovery in the early 80s, were at levels below those of the previous decade. Although the higher exchange rate benefited certain export sectors, some industrial sectors had serious problems due to the increase in the cost of imported inputs. The mini-devaluation system caused a strong dollarization of deposits and bank investments, creating difficulties for many businesses because of the continuing rise of financing costs.

Taking a populist approach, the APRA party capitalized on the discontent caused by the previous government's economic policy and made a campaign promise to look after the welfare of the poorest segments of the population. After an overwhelming victory, the APRA was in a position to make a radical change in past economic policy. Citing anti-imperialist arguments, Alan García announced that payment of the foreign debt would be limited to an amount equivalent to 10 percent of the value of exports.

The APRA economic plan was based on the old development strategies of import substitution industrialization. The main objective was to increase internal demand to reactivate the industrial sectors, in the hope that profits would be reinvested placing the country on the road to sustained growth. The government used the funds saved by not paying the external debt and the international reserves accumulated by the previous government to finance imports of the inputs needed to increase use of industry's installed capacity.

The APRA government believed that inflation was the result of constant cost increases with contraction of the domestic market, factors which forced merchants to raise prices to protect profits. The government agreed to control main production costs (exchange rate, interest rate, energy prices, etc.) and to revive the domestic market (by increasing tariff protection and the income of the population), so that merchants would agree to accept a smaller margin of profit per unit sold. This would be offset by higher sales volumes. To break the inflationary spiral and de-dollarize the economy, after a small exchange and public price adjustment, the government froze the exchange rate and public rates and launched a strict program of private price controls.[5]

The populist bent of the economic policy was manifested in the increase of nominal wages and in programs designed to provide temporary employment to the population in basically unproductive tasks. In addition, the government developed or supported specific programs aimed at improving income distribution: two of the most notable were the municipal school milk program and the zero-interest credit program for rural Sierra (called the "Trapecio Andino"). Nevertheless, and despite the compelling political argument, the programs that provided direct subsidies to specific sectors of the population were far less effective than those aimed at controlling the system of relative prices.

In the government's first year, the results were favorable: the GDP grew almost 10 percent and the rate of inflation was only 63 percent in 1986. However, near the end of that year, the arbitrary manipulation

---

[5] Although the increase in wages (a principal production cost) with the concurrent freezing of sales prices caused some discontent among merchants, increased sales soon alleviated tensions between the industrial unions and the government.

of relative prices was already causing serious imbalances. First, the freezing of public prices reduced the revenue of public enterprises and the central government. In 1986 the tax burden had been reduced to 13 percent and the value of the sale of public enterprises, which represented 30 percent of GDP in 1985, had fallen to only 20 percent of said value. Consequently, in 1986 the public sector had a deficit equivalent to 5.2 percent of GDP. These results were unaffected by the fact that external debt servicing had been cut by almost 40 percent.

Second, fixing the nominal exchange rate caused an appreciation of the currency, which affected exports and also coincided with a sharp increase in imports of industrial products. In 1986, exports fell by $400 million from 1985, while imports increased $700 million. As a result, in 1986, the current account balance was a negative $1.018 billion, with a loss of $520 million in international reserves. Similarly, setting interest rates below inflation initiated a process of financial disintermediation that intensified in subsequent years.

Instead of correcting the distortions of the relative price system, the government printed more money to finance expenditures. In 1987 and 1988, financing of the deficit by issuing new money exceeded 5 percent of GDP. The imbalances caused by these distortions exploded in mid-1987. The government's unwillingness to increase tax revenues and to correct the exchange lag, ostensibly for distributive reasons, plunged the country into its second worst hyperinflation in recent history. To avoid the "high social cost of adjustment," the economy was caught up in a hyperinflationary process that apparently had significant regressive effects (Glewwe and Hall 1991).

Although there are no exact figures on the trend of income distribution at the national level between 1985 and 1990,[6] authors such as Paredes and Sachs (1991) believe that income distribution worsened. Based on a living standards survey of Metropolitan Lima conducted in 1990, with a sample similar enough to permit direct comparison with the corresponding segment of the 1985 ENNIV, it can be shown that the economic policy of the APRA government had different effects in each sector of the population of Lima. The strongest impact was felt by the group which had the lowest income, the least education, and was either unemployed or self-employed.

Viewing the drop in the average real expenditures of families from the perspective of educational level (Table 4.4), the greatest loss of purchasing power occurred among those with no education or only an elementary education. Glewwe and Hall (1991) point out that in 1990, the average income of those with an elementary education dropped from 45 to 62 percent less than the city average.[7]

---

[6] In 1991 the World Bank undertook a national survey similar to the 1985 ENNIV. However, the results have not yet been processed.

[7] This supports the theory that lower educational levels make the population more vulnerable to changes in economic policy.

Table 4.4. Household Characteristics by Quintile of Expenditure in Lima (1990)

Characteristics	Quintile 1	Quintile 2	Quintile 3	Quintile 4	Quintile 5	Total	Avg. per capita real exp. in June 1990 INTIS	Decrease between 1986-88 & 1990
Employer								
Government	9.4	11.5	13.7	18.9	22.4	15.2	4,155.0	-56.1
Private sector	35.3	28.3	34.6	35.6	29.6	32.7	3,321.2	-56.3
Domestic	1.6	0.9	1.2	0.1	0.0	0.8	1,782.4	-54.7
Self-employed	39.4	40.7	35.5	33.5	33.4	36.5	3,466.2	-51.4
Employment sector								
None	7.8	7.8	4.9	2.6	3.1	5.2	2,763.5	-65.9
Agriculture	2.2	2.8	0.2	1.5	2.8	1.9	3,189.4	-50.4
Business and services	36.2	26.4	1.5	29.1	26.5	23.9	3,259.3	-56.7
Industry and crafts	44.2	36.5	35.0	32.2	17.1	33.0	2,793.3	-52.3
White collar	4.3	16.5	17.7	26.0	39.6	20.8	5,195.3	-54.1
Other	4.9	9.6	7.7	7.8	8.9	7.8	3,733.3	-50.7
Educational level								
None	7.9	4.8	2.8	0.7	0.9	3.4	1,770.7	-58.7
Primary	55.9	39.8	31.2	24.8	12.2	32.8	2,324.4	-59.1
General secondary	32.5	41.2	51.4	49.9	38.8	42.8	3,209.8	-55.1
Technical secondary	2.1	2.0	3.1	2.2	2.5	2.4	6,252.4	-11.8
University	1.1	7.7	8.8	14.1	37.1	13.8	6,945.7	-54.0
Other	0.5	4.5	2.7	8.4	8.5	4.9	4,665.0	-38.9

Source: Glewwe & Hall (1991).
Note: The columns do not total 100 percent because of the loss of 1.8 percent of the data.

Undoubtedly, the group hardest hit by the crisis was the unemployed, whose purchasing power fell 65.9 percent in real terms. This group, which had been distributed uniformly throughout different levels of expenditure, became concentrated in the lowest quintile of income: it went from having 14.3 percent of its members in this group to having 29.8 percent. Similarly, their income as compared to the mean fell substantially (from 23 percent to 41 percent below the mean).

Families headed by a self-employed individual also suffered losses in their relative position in the distribution structure according to spending levels. Although real expenditures of this group fell less than average, the percentage included in the poorest quintile went from 6.5 percent between 1985 and 1986 to nearly 22 percent in 1990. The percentage of self-employed individuals in the poorest quintile therefore rose from 10 percent to 39.4 percent in 1990.

Finally, indicators used to quantify poverty levels (such as the basket of basic goods and minimum wage) reveal that the percentage of Lima residents below the poverty line increased from a scarce 0.5 percent to almost 17.3 percent in 1990. Other indicators of the quality of life, such as access to drinking water, sewerage, and electricity show

Figure 4.1 Real Price of Fuels
(1979 intis)

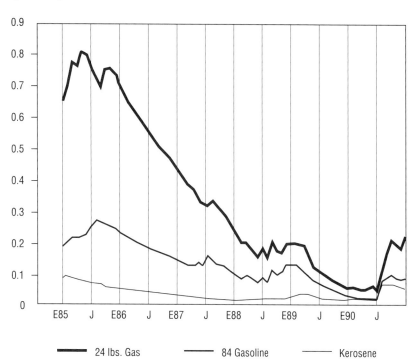

that the decline was substantial and unevenly distributed: only 52.8 percent of those in the lowest quintile of income had access to drinking water in 1990, as opposed to some 68.9 percent in the preceding five-year period; with regard to sanitation services (sewerage), the coverage fell from 90 percent to 57 percent. This is additional evidence that although some deterioration occurred in all quintiles of expenditure, the poorest sectors were the hardest hit.

Fuel Price Policy and Income Distribution

The public price policy was one of the most important tools used by the APRA government (1985-1990) to redistribute income more favorably to the poorest groups. This chapter evaluates the impact of this policy on income distribution, specifically with respect to fuel prices and taxes.

Alan García's ascent to power in July 1985 was accompanied by a drastic change in the management of fuel prices, given the new government's intention to reduce inflation by freezing and controlling prices. Following a price adjustment in early August, which included a

33 percent hike in the price of gasoline, García froze public prices and exchange rates for an indefinite period and implemented a strategy to control prices. In this way an attack was made on what was thought to be the main cause of inflation: rising costs.

The argument the government used to justify freezing the price of fuels, especially gasoline, was that constantly rising prices had regressive effects on income distribution. The rise in fuel prices, the government claimed, caused increases in the prices of food and transportation, two very important elements in the household budget of lower income families.

According to the APRA government, constant increases in the price of gasoline and other fuels during the previous administration had caused a decline in the real income of lower income families. It was for this reason that the new government, when it decided to increase the price of fuels, left the price of household kerosene and liquid gas unchanged. Furthermore, in 1985, the price of household kerosene was reduced by 15 percent.

This policy led to a real decline in the price of fuels, which increased the fiscal deficit. In December 1987 the prices of gasoline and household kerosene were 40 percent and 25 percent of July 1985 prices (Figure 4.1). Despite the exchange lag, gasoline was being sold at $0.29 per gallon in late 1987, and there was a time in 1988 when it cost only $0.22. Household kerosene fell to $0.05 per gallon.

This price cut lowered the central government's fuel tax receipts, which went from 33 percent of total tax receipts to 20 percent in 1987 and only 11 percent in 1988, years when the general tax burden also shrank considerably.[8] Despite this, the government continued with the "blocked" prices until early 1988.

In 1988, abrupt but relatively well-spaced adjustments were made to avoid further deterioration in fuel prices. These occurred on four occasions, usually at the end of each quarter; at no time did the price of gasoline increase less than 50 percent (in the so-called "black September price explosion" the increase was 296 percent). Unfortunately, the increases were either not sufficient or not accompanied by the fiscal discipline necessary to halt the issuance of paper money to finance the fiscal deficit. Consequently, the government only achieved a partial recovery in the real price of fuels. If these prices were converted to dollars, they would still have been below international standards: one gallon of 84 octane gasoline cost less than $0.60 and a gallon of kerosene was scarcely more than $0.10.

The political reasoning behind these price adjustments revealed a drastic change in the government's perspective. Now the government claimed that the increase in the price of gasoline was not regressive

---

[8] Worse still, Petroperú, the state enterprise responsible for producing and marketing oil and its by-products, experienced a reduction not only in the real price of its products but also in its share of total receipts from sales. In the case of gasoline, its share dropped from 33 percent in 1985 to 26 percent in the first quarter of 1988. Obviously, the result of this was the sudden decapitalization of Petroperú.

Figure 4.2 Relative Price of Fuels
(January 1980-December 1990)

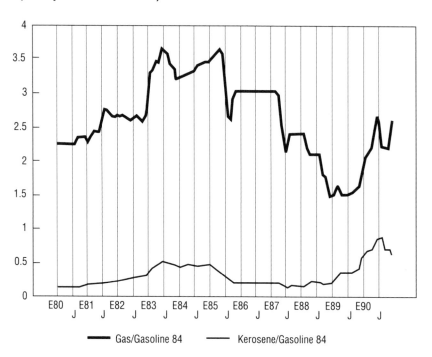

but rather progressive, since only higher income families had motor vehicles that used gasoline. Apparently, the government no longer considered that the effect of the price of gasoline on the price of other goods was important. Worse still, the trend observed in the relative price of various fuels throughout this period contradicts the political reasoning: the relative price of kerosene as compared to that of 84 octane gasoline increased under the APRA government (Figure 4.2).

In 1989, the strategy of abrupt but staggered fuel price increases was discarded and replaced by a policy of monthly adjustments, which were well below inflation. Moreover, because the government's efforts to revive the economy were tempered by its awareness of the upcoming elections, no increases in fuel prices were implemented in the final quarter of 1989; this only contributed to the further decline of real prices. In July 1990, before the change of government, the real price of gasoline had fallen 93 percent by July 1985, which was the lowest price in 12 years.[9]

---

[9] Toward the end of the APRA administration, Petroperu's share of the price of gasoline was raised to almost 90 percent. However, this increase was not enough to overcome the severe crisis the company was experiencing, especially since a gallon of gasoline cost only $0.23 in June 1990.

Fuel Tax Policy

Until July 1984, the only tax on fuels was the general sales tax. However, because receipts of this tax were low, the government increased revenues by replacing the general sales tax on fuels with higher consumption taxes. This also provided greater latitude for regularly changing the taxes on fuels without affecting the overall rate of the general sales tax.

Usually, goods and services subject to the consumption tax were considered luxury items;[10] consequently, progressivity was one of the motives for instituting the tax.[11] Nevertheless, as explained below, some fuels such as kerosene cannot be included in this category; the only explanation for it being subject to the consumption tax is its discretionary advantage.

One characteristic of the trend of fuel taxes in the APRA period is that numerous rate changes were made in a short time. In addition, the consumption tax on household kerosene was lower than for any other fuel; for several months the rate was even zero. On the other hand, the consumption tax on gasoline remained high. This fact reveals the existence of an active policy of gasoline taxes with clear redistributive objectives.

The Redistributive Impact of Fuel Price and Tax Policies

To analyze the redistributive impact of fuel price and tax policy it is first necessary to identify fuel consumption by income level. Then the total subsidy received by families must be determined, separating the subsidy created by manipulating prices from the one granted through tax policy. In addition, a distinction must be made between the direct subsidy received through the direct consumption of fuels and the indirect subsidy received through transportation expenses.

Based on information from the Multi-Purpose Surveys (ENAPROM) conducted in 1986, 1988 and 1989, it is possible to distinguish fuel consumption by income level. This survey groups households into five income levels. Level I (the poorest) comprises 60 percent of the population, Level II, 23 percent, Level III, 11 percent, Level IV, 4 percent and Level V, (the most affluent) 2 percent of the population.

It is easy to link the use of certain fuels to specific income levels: families with higher incomes consume more gasoline and related products (2.5 percent of their income) than do families with lower incomes (0.6 percent). Conversely, lower income families consume more household kerosene (0.77 percent) than higher income families, who use

---

[10] In addition to fuels, the goods and services subject to the general sales tax included cigarettes, liquor, precious stones, and video rentals.
[11] The tax is progressive, since those who consume goods and services of this type have high incomes.

Figure 4.3 Subsidy on Domestic Consumed Fuels
(Millions of dollars)

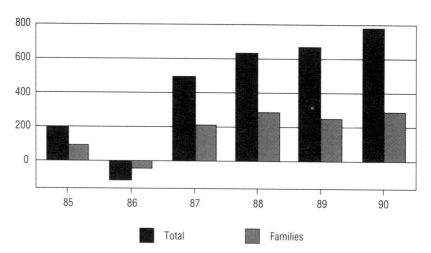

almost none (less than 0.15 percent). Finally, middle-income families use much more propane gas than lower income families.

Urban and inter-urban transportation expenses account for 6 to 8 percent of total family expenditures, depending on the income level. Unlike other fuels, the consumption of which varies considerably from one level to another, transportation expenses are much the same for all sectors.[12]

The fuel subsidy granted through manipulation of prices and taxes equals the difference between the sales price (if imported) and the price actually paid by the consumer.[13] The total subsidy granted for fuel consumption between 1985 and 1990 was $2.651 billion. In 1985 it was $195 million; in 1986, due to the fall of international prices, the amount of the subsidy was negative $104 million (i.e., domestic prices were greater than import price). In the following years, due to the gradual decline of prices, the total annual subsidy kept increasing until it reached a maximum of $775 million in 1990 (Figure 4.3).

---

[12] This is due to the fact that most Peruvian families —including the most affluent— own very few private vehicles, so that they are forced to use public transportation.

[13] The implicit assumption is made that the opportunity cost of a fuel is its international price. This is a sensible assumption since Peru is not a large producer of oil on the world market; on the contrary, it is nearly a net importer.

Figure 4.4 Fuel and Transportation Subsidy by Income Level
(As percentage of income level)

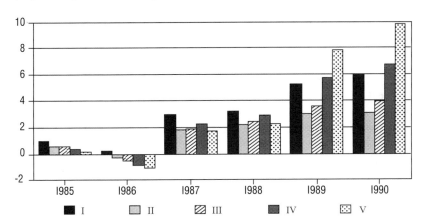

Of the total subsidy between 1985 and 1990, $1.1 billion went to families (41 percent of the total). The largest subsidy was for kerosene ($501 million), followed by gasoline ($310 million). In the latter instance, the trend was from a negative net transfer in the first two years to ever-increasing subsidies in subsequent years.

In per capita terms, the largest subsidy was granted for transportation (gasoline and diesel combined), far exceeding the subsidy for other fuels. Since the most affluent groups consume the most gasoline, the fuel price policy was regressive. In the case of transportation, there are clear signs of regressivity beginning in 1988, since the largest absolute subsidy went to the most affluent quintiles of the population (Figure 4.4). Something similar, although on a much smaller scale, occurred with propane gas. In the case of kerosene, the most popular fuel, the per capita subsidy received by the poorest quintiles was greater than that granted to the most affluent; nevertheless, the subsidy for kerosene was insignificant compared to the per capita subsidy for gasoline.

Regarding distribution of the total subsidy by income level, it is clear that the policy followed by the APRA government had regressive effects. Although in 1985 the poorest segment received 60 percent of the total subsidy and the most affluent sector only 1 percent, in 1990 the share of the poorest sector had fallen to 41 percent, while that of the most affluent sector had risen to 18 percent (despite the fact that it only included 2 percent of the population). This situation is explained by the acute regressivity of the gasoline subsidy, especially in 1989.

Per capita subsidy rates in relation to per capita income increased in 1987 as a result of lower tax rates and the fall in real prices of fuel. In 1989, rates for the most affluent sector were higher than those for the poorest sector. Thus, the fuel subsidy was regressive in the final years of the APRA period, both in absolute and relative terms. However, this total subsidy conceals differences based on the type of fuel.

In the case of gasoline, subsidy rates in the first two years were negative for all income levels due to the fall of international prices discussed above. In 1987, the rates of the subsidy became increasingly positive, especially for the most affluent sectors, revealing the regressivity of the subsidy. For propane gas, the same trend in the net rates is seen; negative at the beginning of the APRA period and positive afterwards. With respect to the subsidy rate by income level, those in the middle received the highest rate. In the case of kerosene, subsidy rates were positive for all levels throughout the period. Rates increased gradually, especially for the poorest sectors. Consequently, this subsidy and the indirect transportation subsidy are the only ones upon which the price policy had progressive effects.

One component of the total subsidy for fuel expenditures results from the manipulation of taxes, specifically the consumption tax. It is important to distinguish the distributive effects of this policy since, if a decision is made to base the price of fuels on global parity, it is necessary to determine the margin of maneuverability for a redistributive policy through manipulation of the tax structure.

A look at the effective rate of fuel taxes by income level (Figure 4.5) reveals two different periods: one from 1985 to 1989, in which the tax rate fell substantially from 1.1 percent in 1985 to 0.3 percent in 1989; and 1990, when the rate returned to its 1986 level. The year 1990 was also divided into two different periods, before and after the July inauguration of the Fujimori government, whose management of the economy was totally different from that of Alan García. The new government raised the real prices of fuels and standardized fuel taxes at 124 percent.

The decline in the first period is explained more by the fall in fuel prices than the change in tax rates. This decrease was not the same for all levels: the largest relative reductions benefited those with lower incomes (levels I, II and III). Nevertheless, an analysis of the tax imposed on these three levels reveals that the poorest level bore the heaviest burden. One characteristic of the aggregate fuel tax burden in the 1985-90 period is that in the three lowest income levels there was regressivity toward the poorest level, mainly as a result of the tax on kerosene.

Although the more affluent sectors paid more taxes, the level of taxation depended on the type of fuel under consideration. The gaso-

Figure 4.5 Effective Rate of Fuel Taxes by Income Level
(Percentages)

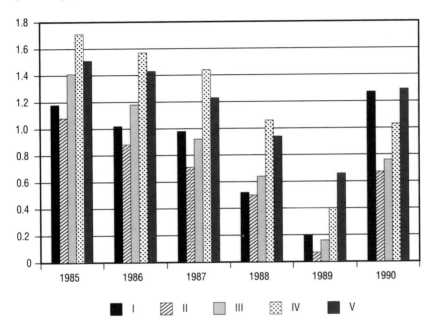

line tax was cut in half between 1985 and 1989, with the more affluent sectors paying the most, reflecting a certain progressivity in the tax. The tax on propane gas fell from 0.2 percent in 1985 to 0.01 percent in 1989, due to the reduction of the tax rate and the price. In this case the tax is regressive since these rates were higher for the lower income sectors (a situation that was reversed in 1990). The tax on kerosene also declined between 1985 and 1989, from 0.3 percent to almost zero, but it was regressive because the burden on the poorer sectors was greater. The level of regressivity increased systematically throughout the period, which means that the reduction of the real prices of fuels helped to reduce the absolute amount of the tax burden but not to eliminate the regressivity of the taxes on kerosene. This is true despite the fact that the consumption tax on kerosene was abolished for part of 1988 and 1989.

In conclusion, the taxes on gasoline had a progressive effect, while the taxes on kerosene were regressive. Consequently, during the period in question, tax policy tended to reduce the effective rates of fuel taxes while benefiting the lowest income sectors. These findings must be taken into account if the fuel tax policy is to be used as a means of improving income distribution.

Conclusions and Recommendations

The principal conclusion of this section is that the trend of the fuel subsidy was clearly regressive throughout the period in question. Although in 1985 the poorest sector received 60 percent of the total subsidy and the most affluent sector only 1 percent, by 1990 the poorest sector had a smaller 41 percent share while the most affluent sector increased its share to 18 percent, despite the fact that it included only 2 percent of the population. This is a result of the extreme regressivity of the gasoline subsidy, especially in 1989. In absolute terms, this means that although in 1985 the subsidy received by each member of the most affluent and poorest sectors was $2 and $5, respectively, in 1990 it was $125 and $9.

In addition to the negative impact of fuel price policy on income distribution under the APRA government, this strategy caused serious macroeconomic imbalances, the chief manifestation of which was the hyperinflation of 1988 and 1989. The erosion of government revenues caused by, among other things, the real deterioration of fuel prices, was alleviated by the issuance of paper money. This caused an acute inflationary process, which further deteriorated the fiscal position of the Peruvian government. In addition, this policy led to the decapitalization of Petroperú and the reduction of oil reserves.

The most important recommendations derived from these findings are, first, that Petroperú's net prices must be determined by the trend of international prices in order to avoid subsidies. Second, because of the different levels of gasoline consumption by various sectors, high taxes and prices should be imposed on the consumption of gasoline, since it is consumed mostly by the more affluent sectors. Lower taxes and prices should be charged for kerosene, since it is consumed primarily by the poorer sectors. Diesel prices and taxes should be set on an equitable basis since this fuel is widely used by mass transit vehicles. These measures would bring efficient progressivity to the current system of fuel prices and taxes. It is significant that in January 1992 the economic authorities decided to change the rates of the fuel consumption tax in accordance with the recommendations of this study, placing higher taxes on gasoline (123 percent higher for 84 octane and 136 percent higher for 95) and lower taxes on kerosene, propane gas and diesel fuel (66 percent lower).

Impact of the Agricultural Price and Credit Policy on Income Distribution in Peru: 1985-1990

In July 1985 the new government stressed the need to redistribute income as a requirement for sustained growth. To achieve this objective it decided to implement a state-directed spending program, among whose beneficiaries would be the country's poorest agricultural sectors. The Agricultural Revitalization and Food Security Program (PRESA), launched in 1986, constituted the basis of this strategy. This

Table 4.5. Regional Distribution of Poverty in Peru: 1985-86

Region	Poorest 10% of the population	Poorest 30% of the population	Most affluent 70% of the population	Total
Lima	2.4	7.8	34.9	26.8
Urban coast	5.0	10.8	17.1	15.2
Urban sierra	7.5	9.1	11.8	11.0
Urban selva	1.8	2.2	3.3	3.0
Rural coast	9.4	9.8	6.1	7.2
Rural sierra	62.7	50.2	22.2	30.6
Rural selva	11.2	10.1	4.7	6.3

Source: Glewwe (1989), Table 4, p. 17.

program, aimed primarily at guaranteeing farmers' growing demand at "income-producing" prices, was accompanied by a farm credit program to provide greater access to financial resources for the country's poorest agricultural sectors.

This section analyzes the effects of this policy on the real income levels of the agricultural sector and on their relative income (as compared with the income of other sectors). An attempt will be made to show how the lack of coordination between macroeconomic and sectoral policy prevented an effective redistribution of income. In fact, even assuming that there were no significant diversions of funds allocated, the bulk of subsidies provided by this program went to farmers in the two most affluent quintiles of the Peruvian population. Moreover, by comparing the producer and consumer prices of agricultural products under PRESA with the prices that would have prevailed had there been no distortions (shadow prices), it is clear that the program created an implicit tax, paid on practically every crop and by all farmers who were in any way involved in the market, regardless of their income level. As far as consumers are concerned, most of the subsidy generated by this system of prices went to the most affluent sectors of Peruvian society.

Spatial Distribution of Income

In analyzing the problem of income and its distribution in Peru from the geographic and productive viewpoints, we see that most of the poor live in rural areas and are engaged primarily in agricultural work. The most recent source of information on the Peruvian nation as a whole for evaluating income distribution and spending is the National Living Standards Survey (ENNIV) conducted from 1985 to 1986. By grouping the population according to the aggregate spending stated in this survey, one sees that most of the poor population is rural; 83.3 percent of the poorest 10 percent and 70.1 percent of the poorest 30 percent (Table 4.5). On the other hand, less than 18 percent of the rural population is in the highest income quintile. The residents of rural areas, who comprise 44 percent of the Peruvian population, receive an average income equivalent to 69 percent of the national average (76 percent, 65 percent, and 74 percent of said average income for residents of the rural coast, sierra, and selva regions, respectively).

The concentration of poverty in the Peruvian rural sector is especially striking in the sierra and selva regions. Among the provinces with the lowest average incomes are only three coastal provinces out of a total of 31, as compared to 20 out of 25 selva provinces and 86 out of 97 sierra provinces. A study by the Peruvian Central Reserve Bank (1981) confirms that the Peruvians with the lowest incomes live in rural areas, in particular in the Trapecio Andino.[14] In this region, the majority of the population lives in extreme poverty.

Agriculture is the main activity in the rural sector and most of the rural population is engaged in it on a self-employed basis. ENNIV data show that almost two-thirds of families who make up the poorest 20 percent of the Peruvian population depend on agricultural activities, while only a fourth have no family member employed in this activity.

According to the same survey, a farmer in Peru receives an average income equal to 70 percent of the national average and 21 percent of the average income of the most affluent decile of the population. Comparing agricultural income with other occupational categories, an industrial worker receives an average income that is 1.3 times greater than the average agricultural income, and the wages of an office worker are 2.6 times greater.

Despite the obvious imbalance in income distribution both between urban and rural sectors and between agriculture and other activities, inequalities within each sector can be even greater. Glewwe (1987), using an aggregate spending indicator,[15] presents a geographic and occupational breakdown of the inequality in seven regions (four urban and three rural). His study shows that the differences in average expenditures between the seven regions explain a mere 13 percent to 15 percent of spending imbalances in the country; this means that most of the imbalance is explained by the differences in spending within each region. Similarly, the breakdown of income by occupational level suggests that no more than 15 percent of the overall variation in income can be explained by the difference between average agricultural and nonagricultural income.

These findings are significant since the existence of pronounced productive differences between rural regions causes an extremely

---

[14] The Trapecio Andino comprises 42 of the 153 provinces into which Peru is politically divided. It covers most of the southern sierra (32 of the 38 provinces located in this region) and part of the central sierra (10 of the 50 provinces in this region). More than two-thirds of this area is rural.

[15] Glewwe uses spending as a criterion to avoid undervaluing the income stated in many surveys.

skewed income distribution within the sector. (It should be noted that the degree of imbalance in the rural coastal region is less than the degree of imbalance in the rural sierra and selva regions). Consequently, although the majority of the poor live in the country and engage in agricultural activities, not all farmers are poor. It is therefore necessary to distinguish poor farmers from those who are not. In doing so, it is useful to describe productive arrangements and growing methods used by farmers.

Table 4.6 shows that coastal crops such as rice and cotton are not grown by the poorest farmers. Their most important crops are highland crops such as sweet corn, wheat, barley, and coffee. Crops such as potatoes and hard yellow corn seem to be more uniformly distributed across all income levels.

Consumption figures reveal that some crops planted by the poorest sectors are not necessarily grown for sale; such is the case with coca, wheat, and quinoa. Undoubtedly, this relativizes the advantage of policies aimed exclusively at increasing the prices of crops grown by the poorest sectors, a large part of the production of which may be intended for self-consumption.

The technological model used for these crops shows that the poorer farmers use almost no mechanical energy or formal credit. According to INP-UNDP (1990), only 1.1 percent and 2.6 percent of the poorer farmers use these two "modern" inputs. Likewise, ENNIV data show that farmers in the two poorest quintiles use only 16 percent of all the fertilizer consumed, whereas more than 65 percent is used by the two most affluent quintiles. A modern vs. traditional duality is thus established in agriculture, which, as will be seen below, is a determining factor in the configuration of income distribution within the Peruvian agricultural sector.

To measure the distribution of welfare (or of poverty) and distribution's response to changes in the structure of relative prices, the levels and patterns of consumption must also be taken into account. The composition of consumer spending is extremely varied, both between the urban and rural sectors as well as within the rural sector. Table 4.7 presents a breakdown of family spending, emphasizing food purchases. The agricultural population is primarily located in the two lowest quintiles of income, and the most widely consumed products for these groups are, in descending order, wheat and wheat products, rice, and white corn. According to Glewwe (1988), the amount of wheat and white corn grown by farmers for their own consumption is greater among the poorest 10 percent of the population than in the poorest 30 percent; rice, however, is purchased by this group in the market.

Production for self-consumption provides 51.2 percent of all the food consumed by the population in the lowest decile, which is largely rural.[16] In the rural sector and especially in the sierra, farmers reserve

---

[16] This information will be used later to evaluate how the agricultural price policy of the APRA government affected consumption in each income level.

Table 4.6 Agricultural Production and Distribution of Expenditure in Peru: 1985-1986

Product[1]	Quintile 1	Quintile 2	Quintile 3	Quintile 4	Quintile 5	Total
Hard yellow corn						
Dist. of production	23.8%	23.0%	20.5%	16.2%	16.5%	100.0%
Dist. of sales	22.7%	24.8%	26.8%	13.3%	12.3%	100.0%
Kg. per capita	342.3	178.7	285.5	296.0	413.4	274.3
Sweet corn						
Dist. of production	40.1%	31.7%	14.7%	9.6%	3.9%	100.0%
Dist. of sales	4.2%	57.1%	20.7%	12.8%	5.2%	100.0%
Kg. per capita	79.1	112.0	67.8	78.2	111.1	85.9
Wheat						
Dist. of production	44.2%	21.5%	16.5%	11.4%	6.5%	100.0%
Dist. of sales	12.9%	12.4%	45.1%	19.0%	10.7%	100.0%
Kg. per capita	54.8	39.4	38.8	65.9	84.1	49.4
Rice						
Dist. of production	9.9%	19.1%	15.4%	18.0%	37.6%	100.0%
Dist. of sales	7.8%	19.2%	14.9%	17.1%	40.9%	100.0%
Kg. per capita	300.2	607.4	672.2	1,002.1	32,695.0	839.0
Barley						
Dist. of production	38.6%	19.5%	22.7%	10.8%	8.4%	100.0%
Dist. of sales	52.3%	17.3%	8.6%	6.8%	15.0%	100.0%
Kg. per capita	45.2	36.1	56.6	63.9	101.4	48.8
Potatoes						
Dist. of production	17.8%	21.9%	17.9%	13.0%	29.5%	100.0%
Dist. of sales	6.0%	15.4%	16.5%	11.0%	51.0%	100.0%
Kg. per capita	136.8	250.2	295.1	405.2	1,719.7	305.7

Continued on page 113
Continued on page 113

a large portion of their production for their own consumption, for seeds, or for barter. This means that the volatility of their income is not necessarily obtained by valuing total production at market prices: since not all of production is sold, the impact of macroeconomic and sectoral policy on farmers' real income depends on their products' degree of commercialization.

It is a fact that the poor in Peru live in rural areas and engage in agricultural activities. Nevertheless, not everyone in the rural agricultural sector belongs to the poorest segments of Peruvian society. Consequently, to evaluate the impact of the price and subsidy policies applied since July 1985 on the distribution of rural income and, therefore, on poverty, consideration must be given to the types of farmers, determining what they grow, what they consume, and their level of participation in the local, regional, and national markets.

Table 4.6 cont.

Product[1]	Quintile 1	Quintile 2	Quintile 3	Quintile 4	Quintile 5	Total
Coffee						
Dist. of production	11.9%	30.0%	16.0%	25.4%	16.7%	100.0%
Dist. of sales	11.9%	30.9%	16.7%	23.1%	17.3%	100.0%
Kg. per capita	31.2	92.1	116.2	135.8	350.2	92.7
Cotton						
Dist. of production	1.3%	3.7%	32.6%	42.3%	20.1%	100.0%
Dist. of sales	0.0%	3.4%	33.2%	43.0%	20.3%	100.0%
Kg. per capita	132.3	93.7	362.8	702.8	908.1	451.1
Sugar cane						
Dist. of production	46.1%	8.8%	29.8%	13.0%	2.3%	100.0%
Dist. of sales	86.6%	0.0%	2.5%	10.7%	0.1%	100.0%
Kg. per capita	182.7	267.1	324.4	313.5	28.2	199.9
Oca						
Dist. of production	54.3%	20.0%	13.6%	10.7%	1.4%	100.0%
Dist. of sales	6.1%	14.0%	17.8%	62.0%	0.1%	100.0%
Kg. per capita	93.8	58.4	59.9	85.6	41.5	76.5
Olluco						
Dist. of production	35.3%	22.3%	11.7%	25.9%	4.8%	100.0%
Dist. of sales	20.8%	12.5%	31.8%	7.6%	27.3%	100.0%
Kg. per capita	24.7	28.4	27.8	100.5	72.5	33.8
Quinoa						
Dist. of production	26.1%	22.3%	26.8%	14.1%	10.7%	100.0%
Dist. of sales	5.5%	28.6%	47.8%	18.0%	0.0	100.0%
Kg. per capita	4.9	7.5	11.3	8.9	13.8	7.7

Source: Prepared by the author, based on the National Living Standards Survey (ENNIV).
[1] The quintiles are shown in ascending order, from the lowest expenditures to the highest.

Characteristics of the Agricultural Revitalization and Food Security Program (PRESA)

As mentioned above, a stated goal of APRA was to redistribute income. According to National Planning Institute (INP) documents, the government sought to "improve the quality of life of the population, with special attention to the residents of the rural areas of the Trapecio Andino, to farmers in the sierra, and to the urban poor."[17]

The political reasoning of the government clearly stressed the priority due the agrarian sector. It established two central objectives for agrarian and food policy: (1) to make agriculture a more profitable activity due to better prices, lower costs and, eventually, better yields; and (2) to ensure the supply of staple foods at reasonable prices. An effort was made to simulta-

---

[17] INP (1987), pp. 105-107.

Table 4.7. Share of Food Consumption in the Budget: 1985-1986
(Percentage)

Product[1]	Quintile 1	Quintile 2	Quintile 3	Quintile 4	Quintile 5	Total
Meat						
Structure of demand	1.37	5.80	12.60	23.83	56.40	100.00
Percentage of the population	22.63	46.29	56.28	66.26	79.07	54.12
Pct. of expenditures	4.27	8.53	11.81	14.58	15.26	13.52
Corn and corn products[2]						
Structure of demand	5.17	8.08	12.43	18.30	56.02	100.00
Percentage of the population	15.92	22.99	30.12	36.93	42.67	29.73
Pct. of expenditures	2.07	1.53	1.50	1.45	1.96	1.74
Rice						
Structure of demand	8.55	14.05	15.43	25.97	35.99	100.00
Percentage of the population	22.63	46.29	56.28	66.26	79.07	54.12
Pct. of expenditures	17.56	13.65	9.56	10.50	6.44	8.93
Bread						
Structure of demand	21.77	20.07	17.50	19.93	20.72	100.00
Percentage of the population	75.07	74.46	74.49	76.15	79.06	75.85
Pct. of expenditures	25.75	11.23	6.24	4.64	2.13	5.14
Wheat and flour						
Structure of demand	5.94	10.65	14.62	25.02	43.77	100.00
Percentage of the population	18.69	27.11	31.03	39.73	44.42	32.20
Pct. of expenditures	1.78	1.51	1.32	1.48	1.14	1.30
Noodles						
Structure of demand	5.82	15.29	17.67	28.38	32.83	100.00
Percentage of the population	56.61	73.02	65.33	72.80	70.87	67.73
Pct. of expenditures	7.85	9.76	7.18	7.53	3.85	5.86
Potatoes and root vegetables						
Structure of demand	18.93	21.76	21.58	18.72	19.01	100.00
Percentage of the population	37.73	52.40	59.03	67.00	72.97	57.83
Pct. of expenditures	13.74	7.47	4.72	2.68	1.20	3.16
Sugar						
Structure of demand	8.52	13.94	17.75	24.80	34.99	100.00
Percentage of the population	78.20	73.16	67.54	68.86	71.16	71.78
Pct. of expenditures	7.43	5.75	4.67	4.26	2.66	3.79
Milk and dairy products						
Structure of demand	1.39	7.18	12.07	22.71	56.65	100.00
Percentage of the population	20.54	35.41	46.26	56.32	70.65	45.84
Pct. of expenditures	2.45	5.98	6.41	7.87	8.69	7.66
Percent of the budget						
spent in these categories	82.90	65.42	53.41	54.99	43.33	51.11

Source: Prepared by the author, based on the National Living Standards Survey (ENNIV).
[1] The quintiles are shown in ascending order, from the lowest to the highest expenditures.
[2] Refers mostly to white corn; hard yellow corn is basically an animal feed.

neously achieve these two objectives, which are not easily reconciled. The pivotal element of the policy was the Agricultural Revitalization and Food Security Program (PRESA).

The establishment of guaranteed prices and the creation of a fund to finance them comprised the nucleus of this program. The implementation of PRESA was based on the application of three key measures:

- The National Inputs Marketing Enterprise (ENCI) assumed exclusive responsibility for imports of major agricultural products (wheat, corn, sorghum, dairy products and oil seeds).
- In 1986 the Ministry of Agriculture imposed an additional 15 percent tariff on the CIF price of the above-mentioned products.
- The National Agricultural Revitalization and Food Security Fund (FRASA) was created to give farmers an adequate profit margin, regulate the supply of agricultural products, and stabilize prices of agricultural products and inputs.[18]

FRASA had four basic goals: to cover the difference between the cost of locally produced fertilizer and the cost of importing urea and other fertilizers; to make partial purchases of high-priority agricultural products (sweet corn, potatoes, wheat, barley, quinoa, broad beans and peas) to keep their prices from falling; to create reserve stocks of products with volatile prices (potatoes, sweet corn and other Andean crops); and to control consumer prices of hard yellow corn and milk through the ENCI, and of rice through the Food Marketing Enterprise (ECASA). The resources for this fund came from the profits earned by importing food at a preferential exchange rate and its subsequent sale at a higher price (resulting from the customs surtax), and from contributions from the Treasury.[19]

FRASA was designed to ensure that producer price increases were not passed on directly to consumers, thus protecting the diminished purchasing power of most of the population. In this way, PRESA—through FRASA—reconciled the objectives of the profitability of national agriculture and adequate food supply levels. This, in turn, improved income distribution.

The price system developed by the APRA government introduced new price categories, different from not only the existing free prices (subject to the free play of supply and demand) but also controlled prices (fixed by the government). The new types of prices were the guaranteed and shelter prices applicable to producers, and the supervised and regulated prices for consumers. Operation of the system was the responsibility of two public enterprises: ENCI and ECASA.

---

[18] In addition to FRASA, the government created other smaller funds to finance the purchase of imported and domestic sugar, powdered skim milk, powdered whole milk and alpaca wool. All these funds were consolidated in late 1988 into the Agrarian Fund.

[19] In 1988, most of the financing came from the National Bank, since the Treasury failed to meet its financial obligations to ENCI.

The purpose of support prices was not to change production patterns, but only to protect farmers' incomes. These prices were set during or after the harvest, generally when there was a surplus that caused a sudden fall in the price, exposing the producer to the risk of heavy losses. Few products had shelter prices in the 1986-1988 period and their impact on the production of these crops was small, since the share of total national production purchased by ENCI was minimal (less than 1 percent).

The purpose of guaranteed prices, on the other hand, was to guarantee the farmer a reasonable profit margin (between 20 and 40 percent) on the variable production costs of crops the government wanted to promote. The objectives of this mechanism were to redistribute income in favor of farmers and to restructure the supply of agricultural products by changing both their composition and the geographic location of the crops. The Ministry of Agriculture and ENCI were the organizations responsible for implementing the guaranteed price policy, the former setting the guaranteed prices and how frequently they were adjusted, and the latter determining the volume purchased in each region.

Crops to be assigned guaranteed prices were selected on the basis of the objectives of food security and revitalization of the agricultural sector. The demand for the crop in urban markets was a determining factor; also taken into consideration were both the share of the crop in national total acreage and the government's goal of developing specific geographic areas. Among the crops included in this program were vegetables, grains (rice, wheat, sorghum), Andean grains (quinoa, kiwicha, broad beans), agro-industrial products (basically hard corn and soybeans) and other perishable products (potatoes and onions).[20]

Direct Subsidies to Farmers

A look at the direct subsidies for basic agricultural products in the first three years of PRESA reveals that the total amount of the subsidy as a percentage of GDP was stable at 0.35 percent between 1986 and 1987, and climbed to 0.54 percent in 1988. In the early years of the APRA government, this subsidy for basic agricultural products and inputs was financed through FRASA, using the profits obtained by ENCI from importing food at a preferential exchange rate.[21]

---

[20] Although rice, hard yellow corn, sorghum and soybeans were not officially in the category of guaranteed prices, their prices were controlled and usually announced along with them.

[21] The values recorded in local currency were converted to dollars at the parity exchange rate, taking 1985 as the base year.

Table 4.8. Distribution of State Subsidies by Quintile of Expenditure
(Percentage and millions of dollars)

Year	I	II	Levels III	IV	V	Total
1986	6.8	14.3	11.7	12.1	27.6	72.5
1987	12.0	22.5	19.2	18.4	39.9	112.9
1988	17.0	28.7	25.6	22.9	48.9	143.1
1986-1988	11.1	20.0	17.2	16.3	35.4	328.5

Source: Prepared by the author, based on GRADE (1992) Tables 3.6 and 1.6.

Table 4.9. Distribution of Taxes on Agricultural Producers
(Percentage and millions of dollars)

Year	I	II	Levels III	IV	V	Total
1985	21.1	14.8	17.5	21.8	24.8	-406[a]
1986	34.9	12.5	16.0	28.8	7.8	-163
1987	-77.5	30.8	42.3	9.3	95.1	43
1988	18.5	16.7	16.4	20.7	27.7	-356
1989	13.0	13.5	22.0	28.7	22.7	-516
1990	15.2	15.5	18.6	23.4	27.2	-455
1985-1990	20.4	14.4	18.1	24.8	22.2	-1,853

Source: Prepared on the basis of ENCI, Ministry of Agriculture and ENNIV data.
[a] A negative number represents a tax.

Table 4.10. Distribution of Subsidies to Consumers of Agricultural Products
(Percentage and millions of dollars)

Year	I	II	Levels III	IV	V	Total
1985	9.4	14.9	16.9	24.6	34.2	194
1986	6.7	8.4	13.5	19.0	52.3	-75[a]
1987	8.5	11.2	14.3	21.2	44.8	-86
1988	8.6	14.5	16.1	26.5	34.3	96
1989	108.4	112.7	71.6	2.5	-195.2	-14
1990	-0.0	4.4	11.2	24.9	59.6	101
1985-1990	-0.3	7.3	12.6	30.0	50.1	216

Source: Prepared on the basis of ENCI, Ministry of Agriculture and ENNIV data.
[a] A negative number represents a tax.

Most of this subsidy was for rice. This probably polarized income distribution within the agricultural sector, since only 7 percent of farmers in the poorest decile grow rice. Most of the yield, especially in the coastal region, came from more modern farmers in the top quintile of rural sector income.

If the information on tax subsidies is compared with the distribution of sales for each quintile of the population, it is seen that 35.4 percent of the subsidy granted in the 1985-1988 period (approximately $328 million) went to farmers in the most affluent quintile, while only 11 percent went to farmers in the poorest quintile (Table 4.8).

Another way of evaluating the size of the subsidy is to compare the prices received by farmers with the prices that would have obtained in a stable macroeconomic environment with free trade. Using the "border prices" as shadow prices, it is possible to calculate the subsidy or tax the policy represented for producers and consumers. Generally, the subsidy to the producer for a given crop can be expressed as follows:

subsidy to the producer = $K * P_{producer} - (P_{CIF} + transportation)$ where $P_{producer}$ represents the price to the producer and P_{CIF} is the import CIF price;[22] k is a technical coefficient used to make two products with a different degree of processing comparable (e.g. raw cotton vs. cotton fiber, or paddy rice vs. milled rice). GAPA transportation costs (1986) were obtained by averaging the costs recorded in 1985, a year in which the structure of relative prices in the economy can be considered adequate and when there was no exchange lag.[23]

Consumer subsidies can be expressed as follows:

consumer subsidies = $(P_{CIF} + transportation) - K * P_{consumer}$

Based on the calculation of unit subsidies, sales levels of local producers, and demand for each product, it is possible to calculate the tax or subsidy granted for agricultural products in the period in question. This calculation was made for the following crops: rice, cotton, potatoes, sugar cane, hard corn, sweet corn, barley, wheat, and coffee, which together represent nearly 60 percent of the gross value of Peru's agricultural output in the years discussed. These data and the distribution of sales and purchases for each sector (according to ENNIV) show that there is a considerable tax on production and consumer subsidies for all of the products analyzed.

In fact, between 1985 and 1990, implicit taxes collected from producers totaled $1.9 billion. Only in 1987 did producers receive a small subsidy of $43 million (Table 4.9). The consumer subsidy for these products was $216 million in the same period, with a subperiod (between 1986 and 1987) in which taxes were recorded (Table 4.10). Add-

---

[22] The values recorded in local currency were converted to dollars at the parity exchange rate, taking 1985 as the base year.

[23] The CIF price is replaced by the FOB price in the case of exportable products.

ing the taxes on the producer and the subsidies to the consumer during the APRA government, the end result is a net tax of approximately $1.6 billion, which means a significant social loss as a result of the policy.

The distribution of these production taxes and consumer subsidies reveals that the program was regressive. While the distribution of taxes on the producer was relatively uniform, consumer subsidies were clearly regressive: barely 7 percent of the subsidy went to consumers in the two quintiles with the lowest spending levels; alternatively, more than 80 percent went to the two most affluent quintiles of Peruvian society.

Subsidies for Major Agricultural Inputs

Fertilizer Subsidy

Lowering the real costs of agricultural inputs and products was a key element of the agrarian revitalization model developed by the APRA government. This reduction in 1986 and 1987 was achieved by means of granting a heavy subsidy for imported fertilizers and pesticides. In 1986, the reduction of real unit costs varied between 25 and 34 percent; in 1987, it was smaller (between 4 and 18 percent), yet still significant.

In 1988 the trend of costs was different. At a time when real costs of water, machinery, chemical products, and pesticides were rising considerably, there was a substantial drop in the real cost of seeds, animal traction, fertilizers, and labor. Of particular note is that while the costs of some inputs and capital goods fell during that year, there was an increase in the real cost of most crops. This discrepancy is explained by the method of addition utilized and the substantial disparity between the real cost of each input for each crop. The distortion of relative prices in 1988 was of such magnitude that the average costs were not representative.

Nevertheless, despite the extreme fluctuation in relative prices, it can be said that after 1988 the costs of the poorest farmers' crops (sweet corn, barley, wheat, and potatoes) increased less than the costs of commercial crops (cotton, rice, and hard yellow corn) produced by more prosperous farmers. This is consistent with the assertion that the APRA price policy led in its expansive stage (1985-1987) to a concentration of income within the rural sector, followed by a dispersal process when the PRESA collapsed (in late 1987).

Another way of measuring the subsidy to consumers of fertilizers is to compare the prices during the period in question with those that would have been charged in a free trade system with a balanced macroeconomic environment. Calculations of the unit subsidy for the six leading fertilizers used in Peru (urea, triple calcium superphosphate, ammonium nitrate, ammonium sulfate, potassium chloride, and diammonium phosphate) show that after an implicit tax of approximately $16 million between 1985 and 1986, the lag in the price of fertilizers involved a subsidy of $81 million between 1988 and 1990. Nearly two-thirds of this subsidy went to farmers in the most affluent quintiles (Table 4.11).

Credit Subsidy

From the beginning, the credit policy of the APRA government was an active tool for the transfer of resources to agriculture. Between 1985 and 1987 agricultural credits grew rapidly, though not equally among crops: as more credit was granted for rice, hard yellow corn, sweet corn, potatoes, and wheat, less real credit was available for exportable crops such as cotton and, to a lesser extent, coffee. Similarly, despite efforts to decentralize credit, financing remained focused on coastal crops (cotton, rice, and potatoes) and on hard corn and coffee (Table 4.12).

In 1988, rising inflation prevented the continued growth of agriculture made possible by the expansion of aggregate demand. The depletion of international reserves meant that financing for the agricultural revitalization program had to come from Treasury and Central Reserve Bank contributions, which in turn exacerbated the inflationary process. This caused a drastic decline in real credit, which fell 48 percent between 1987 and 1988. In 1990 the credit capability of the Agrarian Bank collapsed: it loaned barely 7 percent of the total loaned in 1989.

The total Agrarian Bank credit to the agricultural sector between 1985 and 1990 was $2.95 billion. This figure, expressed in real terms, is 27.5 percent higher than that of the preceding five-year period; therefore, the credit policy of the APRA can be evaluated in terms of the costs and benefits of having channeled an additional $800 million to agriculture, of having transferred these resources at a reduced cost to farmers and, finally, of having attempted to change the regional structure of credit by means of an explicit policy of subsidies to the Trapecio Andino, the poorest sector of Peruvian agriculture.

The Agrarian Bank subsidy to agriculture during 1985-1990 (measured as the cost for the Agrarian Bank to loan at negative real interest rates) had two components. First was the preferential subsidy to the agricultural sector, resulting from the difference between the promotional interest rate charged and the rate that could have been charged if the resources had gone to sectors where the lending rates were higher. The second component was the general financial system subsidy to all sectors, resulting from charging negative interest rates in real terms, which did not reflect the real cost of money.

The preferential subsidy was small in comparison to the general subsidy, falling from 0.3 percent of GDP in 1985 to less than 0.2 percent in 1986 and to 0.1 percent in 1987, and then climbing to 1.1 percent in 1989 and finally falling to 0.5 percent in 1990 (Table 4.13). Conversely, the general subsidy granted to farmers by the Agrarian Bank went from 0.8 percent of GDP in 1985 to 4.8 percent in 1988, before falling to 1.6 percent in 1990.

Table 4.11. Distribution of the Fertilizer Subsidy by Quintile of Expenditure
(Millions of dollars)

Year	I	II	Levels III	IV	V	Total
1985	0.1	0.3	0.5	0.7	1.2	2.9
1986	-0.7	-1.7	-2.7	-3.7	-6.2	-15.0[a]
1987	-0.1	-0.2	-0.3	-0.4	-0.6	-1.5
1988	1.9	4.7	7.5	10.0	16.9	40.9
1989	1.0	2.5	4.0	5.4	9.1	22.0
1990	0.7	1.7	2.7	3.6	6.1	14.8
1985-1990	3.0	7.3	11.7	15.7	26.4	64.2
Percentage	4.6	11.4	18.3	24.5	41.2	100.0

Source: Prepared on the basis of ENCI and ENNIV data.
[a] A negative number represents a tax.

Table 4.12. Agrarian Bank Financing of Agriculture
(Millions of 1985 intis)

	1980	1981	1982	1983	1984	1985	1986	1987	1988	1989	1990
Total for agricultural purposes	3,223	3,268	2,932	2,662	3,204	3,633	5,467	5,316	2,755	2,314	160
Principal crops											
Cotton	1,092	779	649	490	764	1,316	799	683	598	456	28
Coffee	160	71	67	85	112	166	425	249	125	65	3
Sugar cane	65	194	132	108	191	57	64	39	25	16	0.4
Hard yellow corn	171	193	198	141	189	162	517	459	236	152	5
Sorghum	74	45	49	34	47	13	20	28	10	6	0.8
Rice	936	1,176	1,159	1,224	1,163	978	1,301	1,446	691	490	25
Beans	44	62	45	10	27	21	69	51	15	14	0.5
Sweet corn	12	13	10	11	14	40	88	82	48	38	4
Potatoes	368	458	292	313	455	489	1,259	1,213	521	688	68
Wheat	10	6	2	1	3	27	61	52	31	37	3
Other crops	286	266	324	241	235	375	860	1,008	449	348	19

Source: Agrarian Bank Loan Statistics.

Given the smallness of the preferential subsidy, the question arises of what percentage of the credit went to the poorer farmers. The debt balances of farmers in the Trapecio Andino represented a growing

Table 4.13. Agrarian Bank Credit Subsidy

Year	Total balances¹ US$	Trapecio Andino US$	Comm. interest US$ (%)	Agrarian interest rate (%)	Trapecio Andino interest rate (%)	Rate of inflation (%)	Total subsidy (% GDP)	Preferential subsidy (% GDP)	Trapecio Andino (% GDP)
1985	982.4	102.3	19.3	15.5	11.0	28.1	0.8	0.3	0.1
1986	1,519.8	200.0	8.9	6.6	1.0	12.6	0.5	0.2	0.1
1987	2,121.9	302.6	8.0	5.9	0.5	19.8	1.3	0.1	0.3
1988	1,379.1	219.6	31.2	23.9	10.9	96.7	4.8	0.3	0.8
1989	415.3	61.5	87.4	40.4	24.1	124.3	1.7	1.1	0.4
1990	308.0	46.6	87.6	38.6	48.1	203.6	1.6	0.5	0.2

Source: Prepared on the basis of raw data obtained from the Agrarian Bank.
¹ Average quarterly balances and quarterly rates.

Table 4.14. Credit Subsidy by Crop
(Millions of dollars)

	1985	1986	1987	1988	1989	1990
Cotton	47.2	10.4	36.5	192.4	73.4	63.7
Coastal rice	23.2	10.8	52.5	137.6	50.2	37.3
Coastal hard corn	4.9	7.3	14.5	26.4	12.1	7.6
Coastal sorghum	0.5	0.5	1.8	2.1	0.9	1.8
Coastal potatoes	2.0	3.6	9.2	9.6	15.0	11.0
Selva hard corn	1.5	6.2	17.3	53.1	12.8	5.5
Selva sorghum	0.0	0.0	0.1	1.4	0.2	0.0
Selva rice	15.8	14.9	33.7	88.7	33.2	22.6
Sierra potatoes	24.6	35.9	81.2	176.3	122.9	185.9
Other crops	28.0	19.4	77.0	220.9	105.2	56.0
Total subsidy	147.7	109.0	323.7	908.5	425.6	391.5
(Trapecio Andino)	20.6	30.2	72.4	164.2	72.3	59.6
(Other zones)	127.1	78.8	251.3	744.2	353.3	331.9

Source: Prepared on the basis of Agrarian Bank data.

proportion of the total debt balance, rising from 10.4 percent of the total in 1985 to 15.9 percent in 1988, and then declining slightly to 15 percent in 1990 (Table 4.13). However, the value of their debt balances was drastically reduced in 1987: from a total of $303 million in 1987 they fell to $47 million in 1990.

The distribution of the credit subsidy by crop type (Table 4.14) shows that almost half of it went to agro-industrial crops (rice, cotton, hard yellow corn, and sorghum) in the 1985-1990 period. It has been shown that most of the farmers who grow these products are not in the poorest groups of the rural sector. Another crop that received a considerable percentage of the subsidy was potatoes. Since this vegetable is grown in all regions and by all income levels, it is impossible to say whether that percentage of the subsidy had any redistributive impact.

Since the transfer of resources to the Trapecio Andino was one of the government's stated objectives, various operations in this geographical area, including those in support of the agricultural program, were financed at a zero interest rate. This caused the subsidy to increase in the first three years of the program, to a high of 0.8 percent of GDP in 1988. However, the precipitous fall of debt balances in late 1988 lowered the subsidy to 0.4 percent of GDP in 1989 and 0.2 percent in 1990.

In summary, it can be said that approximately $1.5 billion was transferred in the form of a credit subsidy between 1985 and 1988. Although a large portion of these funds (about $290 million) went to the Trapecio Andino, the more prosperous farmers received most of the subsidy. This, together with the redistributive effects of controlling prices in

Table 4.15. Distribution of Credit Subsidy by Quintile of Expenditure
(Millions of dollars)

Year	I	II	III	IV	V	Total
1985	4.8	17.6	15.1	37.7	72.5	147.7
1986	3.5	13.0	11.2	27.8	53.5	109.0
1987	10.5	38.6	33.2	82.5	158.9	323.7
1988	29.5	108.3	93.1	231.6	446.0	908.5
1989	13.8	50.6	43.5	108.4	208.6	425.0
1990	12.7	46.6	40.1	99.8	192.2	391.5
Total	75.0	274.7	236.2	587.8	1,131.7	2,305.4
Percentage	3.3	11.9	10.2	25.5	49.1	100.0

Source: Table 4.14 and ENNIV data.

the expansive period of the macroeconomic policy, resulted in a concentration of income. The subsequent breakdown in the management of the Peruvian economy reduced credit subsidies drastically; nevertheless, the subsidies remained focused on crops grown by relatively affluent farmers. Of the $817 million transferred through credit subsidies in the 1989-1990 period, only 16 percent went to the Trapecio Andino.

The regressivity of the credit program may be more clearly seen by observing the distribution of formal credit (primarily from the Agrarian Bank) by income level: three-fourths of the credit subsidy went to the two most affluent quintiles of Peruvian society (Table 4.15).

The subsidy granted by the Agrarian Bank was financed primarily with direct transfers from the Central Reserve Bank—in 1987 most of the funds loaned by the Agrarian Bank came from that source. The result of the APRA experiment, therefore, was that it left the Agrarian Bank in a deplorable situation. What had been a financial institution whose basic sources of financing were its own receipts and deposits became a mere conduit for the unlimited issue of paper money by the Central Reserve Bank, which was itself forced to devote a growing percentage of funds to agriculture at the cost of reducing domestic credit available to other sectors. In the second half of 1986 agricultural credit was the most dynamic component of growth in the money supply, more important even than the central government deficit. Thus, it became one of the main causes of the inflationary process in the Peruvian economy.

Conclusions and Recommendations

The agricultural price and subsidy policy applied in Peru between 1985 and 1990 involved a significant transfer of resources to and from the agricultural sector. At first, from July 1985 to late 1987, this was characterized by a growing state subsidy in the form of guaranteed and shelter prices for a large number of crops, a subsidy on the sale of fertilizers and pesticides, and a growing financial subsidy in the form of credit at promotional interest rates (lower than the rate of inflation and lower than the average rate for other productive activities).

Most of this subsidy went to the most affluent segments of the agricultural sector. Of particular note were the subsidized prices of rice and hard yellow corn, and the subsidized credit and inputs for these same products and cotton, crops rarely grown by poor farmers in Peru. Another crop that received a considerable subsidy was potatoes, a crop grown by farmers in all income levels, making it difficult to evaluate the redistributive impact associated with this transfer. Finally, a small percentage of the total subsidy (less than 20 percent) went to the Trapecio Andino, the geographic area where the poorest members of the agricultural sector live. Although the transfers to this zone seem to be larger than they were in the past, their size and that of other transfers to agriculture must be evaluated in light of the overall costs incurred in making them.

In 1988 the APRA government introduced an expansive spending policy, financed with the international reserves accumulated during the stabilization process carried out prior to 1985 and by the unilateral cessation of external debt payments. Thus, the subsidies program had to be financed by the unlimited issue of paper money, which, in late 1988, unleashed the inflationary process that reduced the real value of agricultural subsidies to a minimum.

By comparing producer and consumer prices with those predicted in a more balanced macroeconomic environment, it becomes obvious that the agricultural price policy resulted in a tax on all farmers associated with the markets involved. It has been estimated that this tax was more than $1.85 billion in the 1985-1990 period. This amount was only partially passed on to consumers in the form of lower prices (approximately $216 million). The difference (over $1.6 billion) can be characterized primarily as a social loss caused by the price policy adopted.

Considering the taxes and subsidies granted to producers through prices, credit, and the fertilizer subsidy, as well as subsidies to consumers, the distribution of taxes and subsidies which emerges is shown in Table 4.16, arranged according to spending level.

The distribution reveals that the price and subsidies policy actually caused a transfer of income from the poorest groups to the most affluent segment of Peruvian society. Nevertheless, the crisis brought about by the macroeconomic and social policy pursued in this period seems to have had several different effects within the agricultural sector. It is likely that the levels of income distribution within the rural sector fell, since farmers more closely associated with the market experienced a more rapid contraction of their income than farmers in the more traditional agricultural sectors. Because the kinds of crops and livestock they raised were diverse, poorer farmers were better able to protect themselves against the fall in relative prices. Similarly, the high levels of self-consumption acted as a buffer to slow the deterioration in their terms of trade.

Table 4.16. Net Total Subsidy by Quintile of Expenditure
(Millions of dollars)

Year	I	II	III	IV	V	Total
1985	-62.7	-13.6	-22.6	-2.3	39.2	-62.0
1986	-59.0	-15.5	-27.7	-37.1	-4.7	-144.0
1987	-30.4	42.1	38.9	67.9	160.8	279.3
1988	-26.2	67.4	57.4	193.3	396.9	688.8
1989	-67.2	-31.8	-76.0	-34.9	127.0	-82.9
1990	-55.7	-17.9	-30.6	22.1	134.8	52.8
1985-1990	-301.2	30.6	-60.6	209.1	854.1	732.0

Source: Tables 4.9, 4.10, 4.11 and 4.14.
Note: A positive sign indicates a subsidy, while a negative sign indicates a tax.

In this context, an appropriate price policy is a necessary but barely sufficient condition for improving income distribution. Obviously, what is needed are focused spending programs that will increase the productivity of Peru's most underdeveloped agricultural sectors and make their entry into the market both viable and desirable. Only in this way will producer prices more in tune with border prices lead to a better distribution of income in Peru. In any case, the objective of redistributing income must be attained with policies that are less costly in terms of economic efficiency. Recomendations include improved technological support, the provision of an adequate infrastructure, and directly redistributive tax policies.

Education and Income Distribution in Peru

In the last 50 years the Peruvian population has experienced significant improvement in educational achievement. In 1940, more than half of the population 15 years of age or older had no type of formal education; by 1985, 86 percent of the Peruvian population had reached some level of education. While in 1940, for every person with higher education there were 60 without any education at all, in 1985 this ratio was one to one.

The state has played a key role in this improvement. Nevertheless, little is known about the redistributive impact of resource transfers (because the public education system is tuition-free) or about changes in the educational composition of the population, particularly of the labor market.

The objective of this section is to evaluate the effects of transfers viewed as short-term measures from the state budget. These transfers are analyzed by reviewing public education expenditures by educational level and standard of living. The transfers will also be reviewed to determine their impact in terms of the distribution of family income (i.e., what percentage of family income consists of transfers through the free education system?). This analysis is based on official data from the education budget and the 1985-1986 National Living Standards Survey (ENNIV).

The Peruvian Educational System

Peru's current educational system is formally divided into four levels, each with its own subsystem. For children under six years of age there is the preschool option, which is the first level of the system. The second level (elementary education) is mandatory and tuition-free at state educational institutions. The minimum age is six years and there are six grades. The third level, or secondary education, also free at state educational institutions, includes five grades with five areas of specialization: i) agriculture, ii) arts and crafts, iii) human sciences, iv) commercial, and v) industrial. Higher education, which is the fourth level, requires the completion of secondary education. Generally speaking, there are two types of higher education: short-term (4-6 semesters of study), provided at Advanced Schools and Institutes, and longer-term (not less than 10 semesters), provided at universities. This option, greatly in demand among young people, leads to professional degrees, diplomas of specialization, masters degrees, and doctorates.[24]

Coverage of the Educational System

In 1940, more than half of the population 15 years of age and older had no formal education of any kind. Most of the population with a higher level of instruction (approximately 37 percent of the total population 15 years of age and older) had only attended elementary school, and less than 6 percent had gone on to secondary or higher education (Table 4.17).

The national population census in 1961 revealed a sizeable increase in the population's educational level. The percentage of individuals over 15 years of age with no education dropped to less than 40 percent, and the average years of education increased to more than three. On the other hand, the population of 6-14 year-olds who attended school grew at a faster rate than the total population in this age group. Consequently, their rate of enrollment was 58 percent (almost double the 1940 figure). The numbers for students 15-19 years of age are similar. This growth marked the beginning of an expansive trend in coverage of the educational system, as confirmed in subsequent censuses.

---

[24] In addition to these four levels, there are systems such as special education (for individuals with exceptional capabilities), occupational training, correspondence courses, and literacy programs.

Table 4.17. Distribution of the Population 15 Years of Age or Older, by Level of Education

	1940	1961	1972	1981	1985-1986
Total	100.0	100.0	100.0	100.0	100.0
No education	57.3	38.9	27.5	16.2	14.2
Primary	36.7	47.6	47.0	42.8	37.1
Secondary	4.7	11.5	21.0	31.0	36.3
Higher	0.9	1.8	4.5	10.1	11.7
Average years of education	1.9	3.1	4.4	6.0	n.a.

Source: Census of the Population and National Living Standards Survey.

In fact, the percentage of the population with no education shrank to less than 30 percent in 1972 and to approximately 14 percent in 1985-86. The average years of study increased to 4.4 in 1972 and 6 in 1981. The portion of the population attending educational institutions continued growing more rapidly than the overall population and, as a result, enrollment rates continued to climb. In 1981 enrollment rates were 90 percent among children 6-14, and 54 percent among young people 15-19 years old. Similarly, among those 20 years of age or older, especially the group 20-24 years old, attendance rates were high even by international standards (nearly 24 percent).

The "explosion" in the coverage of the Peruvian educational system is obvious. Although many developing countries have passed through this same stage in the last 10 years, in Peru it has been particularly accelerated; so much so that some authors have pointed out that the level of Peru's GNP is lower than its human resources (in terms of training) are capable of achieving.[25]

Nevertheless, remember that the indicators of expanded educational coverage are rough approximations for identifying improvement in the training of a country's human resources. Various authors have suggested that the growth of the system has occurred at the cost of— or at least ignoring—the quality of education.[26]

The State's Role

The Peruvian government, through the public education system, has played an important role in the provision of educational services. The statistics show that in the 1940s the state was educating nearly 90 per-

[25] Behrman (1987) and Tilak (1989) present evidence of the generalized expansion of educational levels in developing countries.

[26] Stelcner, Arriagada and Moock (1987) found that the public education dummy in a log-linear regression of wage rates was negative and statistically significant. This was attributed to the difference in quality between public and private education.

Table 4.18. Student Enrollment by State and Private Sector

Year	Students enrolled (%)	
	State	Private
1942	88.1	11.9
1948	87.2	12.8
1952	84.7	15.3
1958	83.0	17.0
1962	83.6	15.6
1968	85.3	14.5
1972	85.8	14.2
1978	85.0	15.0
1982	84.0	16.0
1988	84.4	15.6
1989	84.5	15.5
1990	84.7	15.3

Sources: From 1942 to 1958, Portocarrero and Oliart (1990); from 1962 on, Ministry of Education (various years).

Table 4.19. Share of the State Sector in Student Enrollment, by Level of Education

	1960	1970	1975	1980	1985	1990
Preschool	75.6	72.4	73.2	82.0	86.1	85.9
Primary	86.1	86.3	87.3	87.0	87.8	88.2
Secondary	69.9	83.9	85.5	86.1	86.4	86.8
Higher	89.1	79.6	68.9	72.1	65.9	67.1
Other	100.0	87.9	64.9	47.9	49.2	59.5

Source: Ministry of Education.

cent of all students enrolled; in the following decades the private educational sector grew at a slightly faster rate, so that the state's involvement had declined to about 85 percent by 1990 (Table 4.18). This involvement, however, is not uniform across the various levels and subsystems of the educational system.

Preschool education, having received significant state support, has grown steadily (in 1960, for every 100 students enrolled in elementary school there were two children in preschool—in 1990 the number of preschoolers was 25). From coverage that hovered around 75 percent of the total enrollment between the 60s and mid-70s, the state increased its involvement to a little more than 85 percent in the late 80s. Its participation in elementary education has remained the same for the past 30 years: between 86 percent and 88 percent. At the secondary level, however, the state's role has grown more rapidly than that of the private educational system. Most of this growth occurred in the 60s: while in 1961 the state educated 70 percent of the total number of students enrolled, in 1969 its involvement rose to nearly 85 percent, a level it maintained until 1990 (Table 4.19).

In higher education, the state's role has contracted due to the accelerated expansion of private higher education programs at universities and elsewhere. Until 1960 there were nine universities in Peru, only one of which was private. Between 1960 and 1965 seven private universities were founded, and nine others in the first half of the 80s. In 1990, of 51 universities, 23 were private.

Public Spending on Education

Portocarrero and Oliart (1988) have assembled data showing that from the early 1940s the state has made significant efforts to expand the coverage of the educational system. This is suggested by the increase in education funding both in gross terms and as a percentage of total government expenditures. This trend was pronounced in the early 1940s, when the annual rate of growth of real resources for education rose from 4.2 to 8.8 percent. Throughout the 1945-1968 period the growth of this sector was even greater, with growth rates varying from 9 to 16 percent.

In the late 1960s the real resources allocated to education began to fluctuate even more markedly than the overall GDP. Between 1967 and 1968 education expenditures contracted by over 40 percent; recovery from this fall did not begin until 1971, the year before the enactment of the Education Reform Law, and it continued until 1974-1975. Later on, the Peruvian economy entered the most widespread and serious economic crisis of its entire history, which has continued to the present day.

In the period since 1975, real spending on education experienced brief recoveries at the start of the Belaúnde and García governments. Nevertheless, in recent years it has declined to such an extent that in 1988 and 1989 real spending was at the same level as it was in 1970, and in 1990 it was almost 40 percent less (Figure 4.6). Education's share of total spending has fallen steadily since 1968, and exhibited unstable behavior in the second half of the 80s.

When the distributive impact of the growth of education is analyzed, the usual perspective is the medium and long term.[27] However, the fact that the public education system is tuition-free at all levels also implies a kind of short-term transfer of resources, whose redistributive impact on the welfare of individuals—and their families—warrants analysis.

---

[27] This is due to the fact that the redistributive mechanism of education functions completely in the long-term, through the system of opportunities and social and economic mobility associated with it.

Figure 4.6 Peru: Public Spending on Education, 1968-1990
(Billions of 1979 intis)

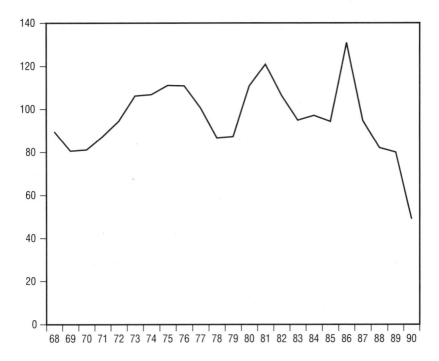

Sources: Central Reserve Bank and Ministry of Education

Table 4.20. Central Government Spending on Education as a Percentage of GNP

Countries	1970	1975	1976-1980	1981-1985	1986-1988
Low-middle-income	3.3	3.9	3.7	3.8	3.9
Bolivia	3.3	3.5	4.0	3.0	3.1
Brazil	2.9	3.0	3.5	3.8	4.5
Chile	5.1	4.1	3.9	5.0	3.6
Colombia	1.9	2.2	2.1	2.9	2.7
Mexico	2.4	3.8	4.2	3.6	3.2
Peru	3.4	3.8	2.9	3.0	2.4
High-middle-income	3.5	3.7	3.5	4.5	4.7
Argentina	2.7	2.7	3.0	3.3	3.4
Uruguay	3.6	—	2.1	2.5	3.1
Venezuela	4.7	5.3	5.3	6.7	—
Latin America	3.2	3.5	3.6	3.8	3.7

Source: Yang (1990).

The total education expenditure per student enrolled in the educational system[28] in 1968 averaged thirty-three 1979 intis (at the average official exchange rate then in effect, approximately $83). This transfer continued to decline until it was only 36 and 21 percent of the 1968 value in 1989 and 1990, respectively.

In 1970, on average, the equivalent of 3.2 percent of GDP was transferred through public education in the Latin American countries. In that year, a slightly higher percentage was transferred in Peru, exceeded only by those countries traditionally identified as heavy investors in education. In subsequent years this percentage increased in all countries of Latin America, varying from 3.7 percent to 3.8 percent between 1981 and 1988. In Peru, however, the transfers only increased until the mid-70s and then fell to 2.4 percent in the 1986-1988 period. It should be noted as well that Peru is the country with the worst performance in education spending among the low-middle-income countries (according to World Bank figures).[29]

The decline of education expenditures, also an indicator of costs per student enrolled in the public system, as well as the contraction of the transfer as a percentage of GDP, is consistent with the indirect evidence on the deterioration of the quality of public education in recent years. Much of this deterioration is associated with the substantial decline in teachers' wages.[30] If the ratio between salary expenses and the number of teachers is taken as an indicator of teacher wages, the steady decline becomes obvious. Compared to the 1968-1975 period, real wages fell 15 percent between 1976 and 1980; between 1981 and 1985 they fell another 22 percent; and between 1986 and 1990 they were only 40 percent of what they were between 1968 and 1975.

Distribution of Current Education Expenditures

In 1965 nearly 60 percent of the education budget[31] went to the elementary level, 23 percent to secondary education, 16 percent to universities and only 3 percent to nonuniversity higher education (Table 4.21). This structure has been changing gradually in favor of secondary and university education.

Between 1965 and 1987, the number of students enrolled in the four levels grew 2.5 times, reaching 5 million in 1987. But growth was

---

[28] Includes the total expenditures (current and capital) on education, and the total students enrolled at the elementary, secondary, and higher education levels.

[29] The contraction of the transfer in terms of GDP is not so dramatic as the spending on education per student, partly because of the 15 percent drop in per capita GDP between 1968 and 1990.

[30] In the 1968-1990 period, the expenditure on the educational infrastructure was a fraction of the total education budget (5 percent), and salaries accounted for 68 percent of the current expenses.

[31] The analysis includes only current expenditures and does not include the subsystems of relatively minor importance such as special education, special professional training, and preschool.

Table 4.21. Distribution of Current Spending on Education, by Educational Level

Year	Primary	Secondary	Nonuniv. higher	University
1965	59	23	3	16
1969	57	24	2	16
1973	54	28	3	15
1977	53	25	3	19
1981	47	31	3	20
1985	48	32	4	16
1987	43	30	3	24

Source: Based on Ministry of Education data.

Table 4.22. Relative Costs of the Different Levels of Education

Year	Primary	Secondary	Nonuniv. higher	University
1965	1.00	2.22	7.36	8.84
1969	1.00	1.79	4.25	7.94
1973	1.00	1.76	6.03	6.57
1977	1.00	1.25	5.59	6.92
1981	1.00	1.56	3.95	6.25
1985	1.00	1.51	4.35	4.59
1987	1.00	1.54	2.62	6.65

Source: Based on Ministry of Education data.

Table 4.23. Distribution of Families and Individuals by Quintile of Per Capita Family Income, 1985-1986

	Quintile 1 (%)	Quintile 2 (%)	Quintile 3 (%)	Quintile 4 (%)	Quintile 5 (%)	Total (%)	Total (thousands of individuals)
Families	20	20	20	20	20	100	3,234
Individuals	22	22	21	18	16	100	16,770

Source: ENNIV 1985-1986.

not uniform. While enrollment in elementary schools grew at an average rate of 3 percent, other levels expanded at rates above 7.5 percent per year. In 1965 elementary school enrollment was more than 80 percent of the total. Secondary and higher education were 14 and 3 percent respectively, but in 1987 secondary education moved up to 29 percent and higher education to 7 percent.

During this period, despite the fact that distribution of spending and enrollment by educational level moved in the same direction, the structure of relative spending changed. Gradually, the structure of relative spending tended to become less dispersed among the educational levels. According to the most recent information available (1987), in Peru, on average, it costs the same to educate one secondary student as it does to educate 1.5 elementary students; one nonuniversity higher education student, the same as 2.7 elementary students; and one university student the same as seven elementary students (Table 4.22).

Redistributive Effect of Public Education

Composition of the Demand for and Access to Education by Income Level

According to information obtained from the 1985-1986 National Living Standards Survey (ENNIV), 45 percent of the Peruvian population was between 6 and 25 years old, an age when people are usually in school. The rate of enrollment, defined as the percentage of the population between 6 and 25 years of age who have at some point had some education, totaled 95 percent at the national level and 99 percent in Lima. Nevertheless, the distribution of this population in the various educational levels is not the same for Lima and the other regions: while at the national level 62 percent of the population had only an elementary education, 53 percent of the population of Lima had at least attended secondary school. Forty-three percent of the national population between the ages of 6 and 25 who have a higher education lives in Lima, as does 55 percent of the total population with a higher education. Regarding rates of attendance, a little more than half (53 percent) of the population still attends educational institutions, with an even larger percentage in Lima (61 percent). Most of this education is provided by the state: 7 out of every 10 people are educated in public institutions.

To identify the major beneficiaries of the public education system, the families interviewed for the ENNIV were categorized and grouped according to per capita family income.[32] Table 4.23 shows the national population, grouped according to quintile of family income.[33]

Table 4.24 shows the distributions by quintile of (i) the total population in the 6 to 25 year age group (column 1), (ii) the population of this age group that attends some educational institution (column 2), and (iii) the population of this age group that attends a public education institution (column 3). The first distribution shows the composition by income level (in this case, the quintiles of per capita family income) of the potential demand for educational services. The second

---

[32] Income includes current monetary and nonmonetary remuneration for labor, profits from the ownership of tangible or financial assets, and transfers.

[33] Familes in the poorer quintiles are larger than families in the more affluent quintiles (IV and V); in the poorest quintile families have an average of 5.8 members, while in the most affluent quintile they average 4.2 members.

Table 4.24. Population of 6 to 25 Year-Olds, and Attendance at Some Educational Institution: Peru, 1985-1986
(Thousands of individuals)

		Who attend some educational institution				
	Total (1)	Total (2)	% (2/1)	Public (3)	% (3/2)	% (3/1)
Total	7,578	4,011	53	2,856	71	38
Percent	100	100		100		
Quintile 1	1,728	776	45	553	71	32
Percent	23	19		19		
Quintile 2	1,804	940	52	748	80	41
Percent	24	23		26		
Quintile 3	1,648	887	54	676	76	41
Percent	22	22		24		
Quintile 4	1,326	738	56	515	70	39
Percent	17	18		18		
Quintile 5	1,072	670	63	364	54	34
Percent	14	17		13		

Source: ENNIV 1985-1986.

distribution shows the composition of the users of the educational system, or effective demand. Finally, the third distribution shows the composition of effective demand met by the public education sector, i.e., the coverage of the public education system.

It should be noted that the two quintiles with the greatest potential demand (column 1) are the relatively poorest groups (quintiles 1 and 2). Comparing these distributions with the demand covered by the public system, it is seen that quintiles 2 and 3 tend to be slightly over-represented in the coverage of the public education system.[34]

Thus, at the national level, quintiles 2 and 3 are the ones best served by the public education system. These two groups together account for 50 percent of the total demand met by state educational institutions, while the poorest quintile accounts for only 19 percent of the enrollment in state institutions. The demand in the poorest quintile is not met to the same extent as it is in the next two quintiles (71 percent as opposed to 80 and 76 percent for quintiles 2 and 3, respectively), illustrating the state's inability to offer public education in many rural areas, where more than two-thirds of the target group in the poorest quintile live. Many rural communities finance their own schools because they are not covered by the state public education system.

A more accurate way of ascertaining who is best served by the public education system is to determine for each income quintile the

---

[34] This means that the percentage enrollment in state educational institutions (coverage of the public system) from quintiles 2 (26 percent) and 3 (24 percent) is greater in proportion to the potential demand (24 and 22 percent, respectively).

proportion of effective demand met by the public sector as compared to the total potential demand (the potential rate of coverage). The potential rate of coverage is simply the probability that all individuals between the ages of 6 and 25 have of attending a public educational institution, which can be broken down into (i)the probability of attending school and, if the individual attends school, (ii) the probability of attending a public school.

The potential rate of coverage, indicated in the last column of Table 4.24, shows that at the national level 38 percent of all persons of school age attend state educational institutions. This rate hovers around 32 percent for quintile 1 and 41 percent for quintiles 2 and 3, meaning that the middle levels benefit the most.

Although the probability of attending an educational institution increases in direct proportion to family purchasing power, the probability of attending a state educational institution increases as income decreases, except in the poorest quintile, where, surprisingly, the probability is lower than in the next highest quintile. This trend, instead of denoting an actively progressive role on the part of the state, is rather a result of the selection process, whereby more affluent families choose private schools. The very fact that individuals in the poorest quintile are less likely to be educated in a public school is proof of the state's limited ability to focalize public education expenditures. The data also suggest that low attendance rates—especially at the national level— explain the public education system's seeming inability to absorb more students from the lower income groups.

On the other hand, the rates of coverage for higher education also show that the middle-income groups receive relatively more benefits from the public system. The potential rate of coverage shows that a greater percentage of the demand in the most affluent quintile is satisfied, due to a higher level of enrollment in state universities (Table 4.25).

Redistributive Impact of Transfers Through the Free Public Education System

There are at least two ways of evaluating the redistributive effect of public education spending in the short term. The first consists of evaluating the distribution of spending (i.e., how much of the total public expenditure is received by each quintile?) The second consists of determining what proportion of each quintile's income is represented by public sector spending on education. The progressivity or regressivity of public education spending can be analyzed from both perspectives, with apparently contradictory results: it is true that the poorest quintile receives less than 20 percent of the total spending on education; however, this transfer can represent, in terms of its income, a larger proportion than the proportion received by the most affluent quintile. This is due in part to the great disparity in income distribution in Peru. Therefore, any discussion of effectiveness in terms of the equity of public policy must take these factors into account.

Table 4.25. Distribution of the Population of 6 to 25 Year-Olds Who Study at Public Education Institutions, 1985-1986
(Percentage)

	Quintile 1	Quintile 2	Quintile 3	Quintile 4	Quintile 5	Total
Public	19.4	26.2	23.7	18.0	12.7	100
Primary	23.5	28.4	22.1	16.3	9.7	100
Secondary	13.7	23.0	26.7	20.8	15.8	100
Nonuniv. higher	8.6	13.4	26.7	28.3	22.9	100
University	7.1	25.0	19.8	17.9	30.2	100

Sources: Based on data from the Ministry of Education and ENNIV 1985-1986.

Table 4.26. Distribution of Spending on Education, by Educational Level and Quintile
(Percentage)

	Quintile 1	Quintile 2	Quintile 3	Quintile 4	Quintile 5	Total
Total	17.1	25.5	23.4	18.5	15.5	100.0
Primary	11.3	13.6	10.6	7.8	4.7	48.0
Secondary	4.4	7.4	8.6	6.6	5.1	32.0
Nonuniv. higher	0.3	0.5	1.1	1.1	0.9	4.0
University	1.1	4.0	3.2	2.9	4.8	16.0

Sources: Based on data from the Ministry of Education and ENNIV 1985-1986.

If each quintile's share of total spending on the four levels of education is calculated (based on the structure by quintile of enrollment in each educational level and assuming that unit costs at each level are the same for the various income levels),[35] it is found that the share of total spending increases between the first and second poorest quintiles, and then gradually decreases between the second and most affluent quintiles. Therefore, the distribution of education spending is progressive only from the second poorest quintile up (Table 4.26). But spending on higher education becomes concentrated in the most affluent quintiles. Thus, public spending on the basic levels of education tends to benefit the poorest groups more, while funds allocated for higher education are concentrated in the most affluent quintiles.

Comparing the distribution of aggregate spending by quintile and the distribution of the school-age population (Table 4.24), the slight progressivity previously observed begins to disappear. In fact, there is

---

[35] In other words, working with an average cost for each additional level.

Table 4.27. Distribution of the Population of 6 to 25 Year-Olds in Public Educational Institutions
(By educational level)

	Quintile 1 (%)	Quintile 2 (%)	Quintile 3 (%)	Quintile 4 (%)	Quintile 5 (%)	Total (%)	Unit cost*
Total	100.00	100.00	100.00	100.00	100.00	100.00	924
Primary	74.10	66.00	57.10	55.20	46.50	61.00	678
Secondary	23.90	29.70	38.30	39.00	42.10	33.90	1,025
Nonuniv. higher	0.60	0.70	1.50	2.10	2.40	1.30	2,950
University	1.40	3.60	3.20	3.80	9.00	3.80	3,111
Students per family	0.85	1.16	1.05	0.80	0.56	0.88	

Sources: Based on ENNIV 1985-1986 and Ministry of Education data.
* 1985 intis.

a slight concentration in the middle-income groups, while the richest 20 percent and the poorest 20 percent of the population receive a smaller percentage of spending than the percentage of enrollment they represent. This lesser progressivity can even turn to regressivity if the comparison is made with respect to the distribution of enrollment in public schools. Comparing the first rows of Tables 4.25 and 4.26, one sees that the state spends proportionally less in the poorer quintiles than it would if distribution of spending were determined by public school enrollment in each income level.

To calculate the impact on income structure of the resource transfers represented by the tuition-free nature of public education, we determined the unit cost for each educational level in 1985, the composition by educational level of the student population within each quintile, and the average number of people who attend school in each quintile (Table 4.27). Taking into account the average spending per student and per educational level, the average number of individuals attending school in a family, and the educational structure of the population, one can calculate the average amount of the subsidy per family for each income quintile.

Thus, at the aggregate level, the average subsidy through public education spending for a Peruvian family is 2 percent of total family income or, put another way, 9 percent of per capita income (Table 4.28). This per-family subsidy was the equivalent of $73.50 in 1985. By comparing the size of the transfer by income level, differences appear that suggest the existence of a progressive structure: while the poorest quintile receives a transfer equivalent to 9.3 percent of family income, the most affluent quintile receives the equivalent of 0.6 percent of family income.

However, this apparently progressive transfer must be contrasted with the transfer that would result if all those who are old enough to go to school had equal access to public schools (maintaining both the structure and level of unit costs in effect in 1985). The potential transfer for the poorest quintile represents more than 33 percent of its in-

Table 4.28. Transfers from the Public Educational System and its Redistributive Impact on Income: Peru, 1985-1986
(1985 intis)

	Quintile 1	Quintile 2	Quintile 3	Quintile 4	Quintile 5	Total
Transfer	687	1,026	968	761	614	808
Per capita income	1,246	2,852	4,840	8,308	27,354	8,918
Family income	7,381	16,549	25,963	39,207	108,883	39,591
Real transfer						
Percentage family income	9.3	6.2	3.7	1.9	0.6	2.0
Potential transfer						
Percentage family income	33.2	15.6	9.1	4.8	1.4	5.5
Noncovered deficit						
Percentage family income	23.9	9.4	5.4	2.9	0.8	3.5

Sources: Based on ENNIV 1985-1986 and Ministry of Education data.

come, reducing the transfer necessary in more affluent quintiles. For the most affluent quintile, the transfer would represent only 1.4 percent of its income (Table 4.28). The difference between the transfer actually effected and the potential transfer reveals a rather large deficit for the lower income groups. It can therefore be concluded that the state, despite its somewhat progressive spending structure, does not provide the same educational opportunities to the poorest segment of the population as it does to the more affluent.

Summary and Policy Implications

Assuming distribution of public spending is progressive when poorer groups receive a percentage of the expenditure larger than the percentage they represent in the total population, it can be concluded that public education spending in Peru is progressive, except for the poorest quintile. Thus, the second poorest quintile receives 25 percent of the spending on education and the third poorest 23 percent, while the richest 20 percent of the population receives less than 16 percent. However, the poorest 20 percent receives scarcely 17 percent of education spending (Table 4.29).

Another criterion for evaluating the progressivity of education spending is the percentage of income transferred to each family in each quintile. Using this criterion, public spending on education is again progressive since the transfer per family—as a proportion of income—decreases between the first and last quintile.

However, the progressivity of education spending must also be evaluated in light of other considerations. In fact, the public education system is not so progressive if the differences in the average number of school-age individuals and the rates of attendance among the various socioeconomic levels are taken into account. We have seen that fami-

Table 4.29. Public Spending and Income Distribution
(Percentage)

	Quintile 1	Quintile 2	Quintile 3	Quintile 4	Quintile 5	Total
Distribution of expenditure	17.1	25.5	23.4	18.5	15.5	100.0
Distribution of population	20.0	20.0	20.0	20.0	20.0	100.0
Distribution of public school enrollment	19.4	26.2	23.7	18.0	12.7	100.0
Disribution of total enrollment	19.3	23.2	22.2	18.3	17.0	100.0
Distribution of school-age pop.	23.0	24.0	22.0	17.0	14.0	100.0

Source: Tables 4.24, 4.25, and 4.26.

lies in the poorest quintile have 2.7 members in the 6-25 year age group, and only 45 percent of them attend an educational institution; conversely, the most affluent families have 1.7 individuals in this age group, 63 percent of whom attend school.

Thus, since the demand for education is not the same at all levels, it is clear that public spending on education is less progressive than earlier figures suggest. While the top and bottom quintiles receive a percentage of spending that is less than their share of total enrollment, the middle quintiles receive proportionately more.

Concerning the potential demand for education, there is a deficiency in each of the income quintiles that increases as the income level decreases. While the most affluent quintile has to allocate only 0.8 percent of its income to cover the portion of demand for education not met by the state, the lower income quintiles are forced to spend 23.9 percent of their income. For the poorest families, sending all their school-age children to elementary school (even at the costs of the public education system, which are themselves fairly low in comparison with other Latin American countries) would cost them 24 percent of their total income. Worse still, if the composition of enrollment by educational level of this income level were similar to that of the most affluent quintile, this expenditure would represent 40 percent of the family income.

The differences between the subsidy granted to the poorest sector and the one granted to the next sector, combined with the fact that a considerable segment of the poorest quintile is forced to pursue a private education, proves that the state's coverage at this level is deficient and must be improved. Consequently, the state must continue expanding education coverage to low-income families. In addition, more appropriate arrangements must be made to attract members of these socioeconomic levels to school and keep them there. Increasing the school attendance rate among the poorest families must be one of the key objectives of the public education system since, as mentioned in the introduction to this study, educational level explains a considerable portion of the difference in income between individuals.

Finally, in comparing the distribution of spending with the distribution of public school enrollment by income level, a certain regressivity is clearly discernible. The richest 20 percent of the population receives 15.7 percent of the spending, though it accounts for only 12.7 percent of public school enrollment; conversely, the poorest 20 percent of the population receives 17.1 percent of the spending, though it accounts for 19.4 percent of public school enrollment. This is explained by the fact that a larger percentage of public spending on basic education is directed toward poorer sectors, while the public funds for higher education—which are more costly—are directed more toward affluent sectors. Thus, although real spending on education must be increased for all educational levels because of its currently depressed state, one must remember that the social return of additional money spent on elementary education will be greater than that spent on other levels of education.

Bibliography

Amat y León, C., and León, H. 1981. *La distribución del ingreso familiar en el Perú*. Lima: Research Center of the University of the Pacific.

Behrman, J.R. 1987. Schooling in developing countries: Which countries are the over- and underachievers and what is the schooling impact? *Economics of Education Review* 6 (no.2).

Figueroa, A. 1975. Redistribución del Ingreso y de la Propiedad en el Perú: 1968-1973. In *Distribución del Ingreso en el Perú*, eds. R. Webb and A. Figueroa. Perú Problema No. 14. IEP, Lima.

—————. 1982. *El problema distributivo en diferentes contextos sociopolíticos y económicos: 1950-1980.* Working Documents. CISEPA, Lima.

GAPA. 1986. Estudio de comercialización, producción y consumo de productos agrícolas. Area: transportes. Lima. Mimeo.

Glewwe, P. 1987. The distribution of welfare in Peru in 1985-86. Living Standards Measurement Study. Working Paper No. 42. The World Bank, Washington, D.C.

Glewwe, P., and D. de Tray. 1989. *The poor in Latin America during adjustment. A Case Study of Peru.* Living Standards Measurement Studies. Working Paper No. 56. The World Bank, Washington, D.C.

Glewwe, P., and G. Hall. 1991. The social costs of avoiding structural adjustment: Inequality and poverty in Lima, Peru, from 1985-86 to 1990. Mimeo.

GRADE. 1992. Gestión pública y distribución del ingreso: Tres estudios de caso para la economía Peruana. Lima, Mimeo.

INP-UNDP. 1990. *La pobreza en el Perú. Diagnóstico y propuestas de política* Proyecto Regional para la Superación de la Pobreza UNDP DE 125, UNDP-INP, Bogotá.

Paredes, C., and J. Sachs. 1990. *Estabilización y crecimiento en el Perú: Una propuesta independiente.* Lima: GRADE.

Plan de desarrollo de mediano plazo 1986-1990. 1987 Lima: Instituto Nacional de Planificación.

Portocarrero, G., and P. Oliart. 1989. *El Perú desde la escuela.* Lima: Instituto de Apoyo Agrario.

Stelcner, M., A.M. Arriagada, and P. Moock. 1987. Wage determinants and school attainment among men in Peru. Living Standards Measurement Study, Working Paper No. 38 (June). The World Bank, Washington, D.C.

Tilak, J. 1977. *Education and its relation to economic growth, poverty, and income distribution. Past evidence and further analysis.* Washington, DC: The World Bank.

Webb, R. 1977. *Government policy and the distribution of income in Peru. 1963-1973.* Cambridge, MA: Harvard University Press.

Yang, H. 1991. *Government expenditure on social sectors in Latin America and the Caribbean Statistical Trends.* A View from LATHR No. 13, Human Resources Division, Technical Department, Latin America and the Caribbean Region, the World Bank, Washington, D.C.

CHAPTER FIVE

FISCAL POLICY AND INCOME DISTRIBUTION IN VENEZUELA

Gustavo Márquez
Joyita Mukherjee
Juan Carlos Navarro
Rosa Amelia González
Roberto Palacios
Roberto Rigobón

To any careful observer of the situation in Venezuela in the last decade, it is obvious that fiscal policy had a predominant impact on income distribution. Both the size and scope of the state's field of action make it clear that state involvement fundamentally changes the basic parameters of income distribution.

But here the consensus ends. For some, the impact of state intervention prior to 1989 was extremely progressive, since it protected lower income groups through the imposition of public controls on the basic prices of the economy. For others, this involvement was extremely regressive, in part because of the negative effects of these same controls. This disagreement permeates the analysis of Venezuelan public policy at all levels. This is not an academic debate, nor is its scope limited to major macroeconomic policies. The basic disagreement of this debate affects decisions about vital government programs such as education, health care and a whole range of indirect subsidies.

Studies of the impact of spending have shown that under certain conditions, some expenditures can have a progressive impact. But in addition to all of the qualifications applicable to this sentence, the fact that these studies were carried out in a context of partial equilibrium —and the scarcity of adequate general equilibrium models—suggests that these results should be viewed with caution. Moreover, the state's impact is more profound than can be determined by analyzing government spending. The economic institutional framework created by the state, the effectiveness of its actions, and the efficiency of its management are aspects that can change a progressive program into one that is extremely regressive.

This study is based on that very premise. The Venezuelan government's action with regard to income distribution included the implementation of programs whose impact cannot be reduced to a simple analysis of spending and the effect of those programs on various groups. The impact of programs such as the social insurance system or education is communicated through an institutional structure whose effect is as important—or more important—than the level and distribution of spending. In fact, many times it is the institutional structure of a program that determines its beneficiaries.

Consequently, this study must be seen as a collective effort to analyze several programs. Our approach was not only to gain a comprehensive view of the public sector's impact on income distribution, but to also examine specific programs in an effort to identify the channels through which the state influences income distribution. The resulting view is not very encouraging: in the programs we studied, the impact of state intervention was generally not progressive. The reasons for this vary from program to program. In some cases it resulted from the process of benefit distribution; in others, it is the structure of the market in which the program operates.

The main objective of this study is to analyze the impact of public sector programs on income distribution in Venezuela in the 1980s. First, the trends of income distribution and poverty in Venezuela in the 1980s are analyzed, with particular attention focused on recent periods of macroeconomic adjustment. From there, the focus shifts to measuring the potential impact of social spending programs on income distribution by assigning an equivalent consumption value to several distribution alternatives at different levels of the population. This hypothetical exercise provides a general analytical framework for the impact studies of four selected programs: electricity and gasoline subsidies, education spending and social insurance. Based on the results obtained, policy recommendations are given to improve not only the focus of the subsidies but the distributive impact of the spending and subsidy programs.

The first section presents estimates of various indicators of poverty and income distribution for 1981, 1987, 1989 and 1990. All the data are based on the Central Office of Statistics and Data Processing (OCEI) household survey for the second half of each year. The principal findings of this analysis show that the percentage of the population below the poverty line has increased dramatically, from 24 percent in 1981 to 59.2 percent in 1990. Moreover, the severity of poverty, measured as the distance between the incomes of poor families and the poverty line, also increased from 36 percent in 1981 to 47 percent in 1990. Other poverty indexes (Sen, Foster-Green-Thorbecke) were estimated, indicating the same trend toward an increase in the extent and severity of poverty in Venezuela in the 1980s. The section also analyzes the geographic distribution of poverty. Poverty increased more rapidly in those states with the largest urban concentrations. This means that the consequences of the adjustment were worse for the urban poor than for the rural poor. In 1990, 40 percent of all the poor (measured by the percentage of families below the poverty line) lived in the federal district and the states of Miranda, Carabobo, and Zulia.

Income distribution is also analyzed in the first section. The trend of income distribution in Venezuela is characterized by increased asymmetry in the 1980s. In 1987, the richest 20 percent of households received 43.9 percent of the total income, while the poorest 20 percent received only 4.9 percent. The change in the Gini coefficient between 1981 and 1990 is the equivalent of what income distribution levels would have been had a transfer of 4 percent of the income occurred (at 1990 prices) from the poorest to the richest households.

All indicators calculated in this section are based on two alternative measures of family income: total income and per capita income. An interesting discovery is that despite the general, indiscriminate use of these two measures, the position of each household in the distribution ranking they create is different. Specifically, given that consumption surveys are generally based on measures of total household income, the results are difficult to interpret in terms of poverty (measured by the per capita income of the household). All of the indicators suggest that income distribution deteriorated considerably between 1981 and 1990. For example, the standard deviation of the income logarithm (income power) shows an annual increase of 0.2 percent (total income)/0.8 percent (per capita income) between 1981 and 1987. Between 1987 and 1989 the increase was 2.2/3.2 percent, suggesting that the burden of the adjustment policy fell disproportionately on the poorest families. Between 1989 and 1990 all indicators show a slight improvement in income distribution.

In the second section, the electricity subsidy is studied. In this case, as is true of gasoline, this is not an explicit public spending program, but rather a pricing policy with an implicit subsidy to electricity consumers. The subsidy per Kwh is calculated as the difference between the rates paid by consumers to electric companies and the marginal cost of the electricity—the cost of supplying an additional unit of energy—measured as the cost of a Kwh of electricity produced by new power generation, transmission, and distribution projects. The subsidy is determined for 1986 and 1990, in both nominal and real terms.

Consumers of electricity in the residential sector are subsidized in two different ways. First, when they pay less for the electricity than it costs, and second, when they simply "take" the electricity without paying anything for the service. The first subsidy is calculated as the difference between the marginal, long-term cost of the electricity and the rates charged by distributing companies, while the second is estimated as the amount of energy stolen at its marginal cost.

The distributive impacts of these two subsidies are completely different. The subsidy implicit in the rates is regressive, given that most benefits were received by the most affluent segment of the population. The subsidy implicit in the theft of energy is progressive since it is received primarily by the poorest segment. The net effect of the two subsidies is somewhat egalitarian treatment for all concerned, with a slight bias in favor of the lower income population.

The third section contains an analysis of the social insurance system in Venezuela, with particular attention on all of the services currently provided by the Venezuelan Social Insurance Institute (Instituto Venezolano de Seguros Sociales [IVSS]). It is incorrect to discuss this as a government spending program, since most of the services provided by the system are financed by contributions from IVSS affiliates. Moreover, and contrary to the usual method of analysis in this field, we restricted our study to the system of old-age, disability, and medical care coverage, meaning that the basic analytical parameters are those of a social insurance system and not those of a social security system.

The advantage of this approach in Venezuela is its adaptability to available information. Analysis of the social insurance system as a producer of medical services, for example, would require information about the income level of the users of the health care system, and this information is not available in Venezuela. If we analyze the system as an insurance system, we can obtain reasonably accurate information about the equivalent cost of coverage by other producers and, consequently, reliable estimates of the transfers involved.

From the analysis of the old-age insurance system (pensions) comes the view of a complex system of transfers from the social insurance system to the state, through pension fund investments in public instruments at below-market interest rates. This transfer has substantially eroded the financial viability of the system and, consequently, the effectiveness of the types of coverage. Curiously, the rules governing the granting of the system's benefits change it from a distribution system to a system of capitalization at very low interest rates. Even when inflation rates are reasonable, the rate of return on the contributions is negative in real terms.

The transfer effected through the medical insurance system is extremely progressive: the higher income groups finance access to health care for the lower income groups. Nevertheless, this transfer is achieved through the informal establishment of a rationing system characterized by long lines and a quality of care that drives away higher income users. Whether this is the best way to subsidize the lower income groups is debatable.

The results of the analysis suggest that the social insurance problems necessitate institutional reforms to reorder the transfer system, with a shift of focus to the lower income groups, and the establishment of rules of competitive behavior for IVSS. This will require organizational reforms, changes in the methods of financing, and redefinition of the various types of coverage. These recommendations are part of the conclusions of this section.

The fourth section analyzes the distributive impact of education spending in Venezuela in 1986. By taking the amounts allocated in the budget to each educational level, the beneficiaries are identified, and, based on information on the composition of users of public education, grouped according to socioeconomic and income levels.

We determined that the distribution of spending is not equitable since, in this study, equality is defined as the relative equal share of users at a given socioeconomic level in public spending and in the total population. The principal cause of this inequality is the preponderant weight of higher education spending in contrast to the expenditure on other educational levels. Nevertheless, lower income households receive a relatively larger share of public education spending than do those in higher income groups.

In section five the implicit gasoline subsidy is studied. Unlike traditional impact studies, the subject here is not a government spending program per se, but rather the price structure of subsidized goods which are produced and sold by a public enterprise. The basic question that this section attempts to answer is the advisability of using the gasoline pricing policy as a means of subsidization. A comparison is made between subsidization alternatives (public transportation and freight shipment subsidies). The implicit subsidy is calculated as the difference between the frontier price of gasoline and the average price paid by the public. This calculation is made for 1986, 1989, and 1990, in both nominal and real terms.

This section contains an in-depth discussion of the rationale of using the reference price to calculate the implicit subsidy. The amount of the subsidy is defined as the difference between the average sales price at the pump and the result of subtracting the refinery-to-port transportation costs from the reference price and then adding the refinery-to-pump transportation costs. The amount of the subsidy depends on the international price of gasoline, the exchange rate, the local sales price, and the amounts consumed and exported. Data from the consumption survey conducted by the Central Bank of Venezuela were used to distribute the amount of the subsidy according to income level. These calculations provide an accurate view of the distribution of the implicit subsidy by income level.

The conclusion is that the subsidy is regressive since the higher income levels receive a proportion of the total subsidy larger than the percentage of the population they represent. This allows us to examine the merits of various subsidization alternatives and pricing policies. An interesting aspect of the discussion is the analysis of the destabilizing effects of basing the domestic price of gasoline on the (fluctuating) international price, with some alternatives being suggested for solving this problem. This section ends with recommendations concerning the gasoline pricing policy and various alternatives.

Income Distribution and Poverty in Venezuela

The objective of this section is to analyze income distribution and the extent of poverty in Venezuela. We do not claim to advance a formal explanation for the changes observed. The complexity of these changes and the need to keep our analysis focused on income distribution led us to choose a straight forward presentation of data and findings.

In the last 10 years, the standard of living in Venezuela has declined considerably, partly as a result of the drop in international oil prices in 1982 and partly because of a series of policies aimed at delaying the corresponding macroeconomic adjustment. This accelerated inflation and caused a permanent downsizing of the labor market. Concurrently, the inevitable fiscal adjustment significantly affected the ability of the population to accumulate and preserve its human capital, with predictable distributive repercussions.

The "lost decade" had serious consequences for income distribution in Venezuela. Between 1981 and 1990 the Venezuelan population grew 24.7 percent in absolute terms, the number of people living in poverty doubled, and the number of people above the poverty line fell 32.9 percent in absolute terms. The changes that occurred in the 1980s are striking both in the distribution of families by income level as well as in the share that each of these groups represents in the total income. Following the usual practice employed in market studies of mass consumer goods, we created eight income categories for 1990, based on the income brackets for what are informally called the "lower class," the "low-middle class," the "high-middle class" and the "upper class."[1] These income categories are deflated for 1981 using the change in median family income.[2] Finally, using the income categories for both years, we present two distributions: (1) the percentage of families per income category, and (2) the percentage of total income per income category.

In 1981 the largest group in the distribution of families by income level was in the third and fourth categories, while in 1990 the weight of the distribution moved downward. This is clearly indicative of a regressive change in income distribution, which not only increases the number of families living in poverty, but also regressively changes the distributive structure. In other words, although the substantial decline in the 80s made the country poorer, there were also profoundly regressive changes in income distribution.

A clearer picture of this phenomenon is provided by the second distribution, which shows the share of total income by income category. Based on this distribution (and with the income categories arranged side-by-side), Figure 5.1 shows the changes in the share of total income of the families in each level. It is remarkable that the group that lost the largest share of income was not the poorest but rather the low-middle class, while the most affluent group substantially increased its share of total income.

---

[1] In market studies they are called classes E, D, C, A and B, respectively. We preferred using more meaningful names.

[2] Using the median as a deflator makes it possible to adjust the limits of the income categories independently of the changes in the form of the distribution.

Figure 5.1. Changes in the Share of Each Group in Total Income, Venezuela 1981-1990

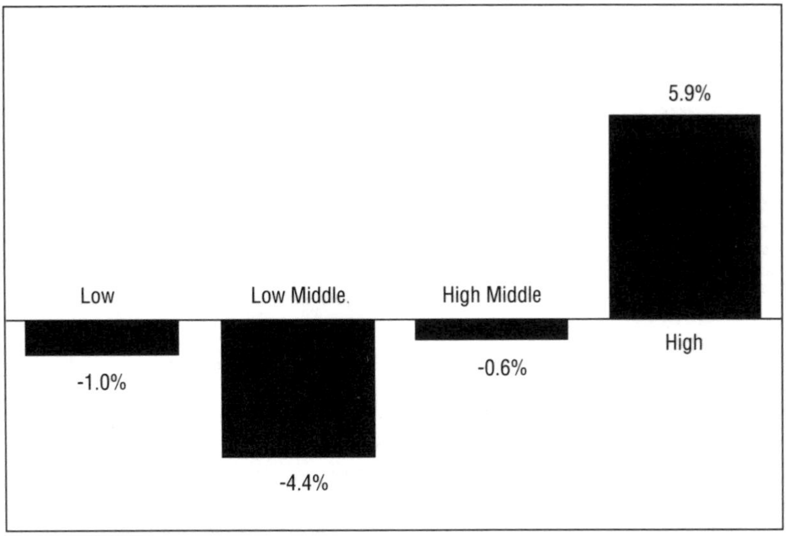

Source: Author's calculations.

Income Distribution in Venezuela

Measuring the characteristics of income distribution is essential in the formulation of economic and social policies. A basic objective of these policies in developing countries is to reduce the degree of distributive inequality. These measures are even more important in countries such as Venezuela, which are experiencing a process of macroeconomic adjustment with significant fiscal consequences. In this case, the figures on income distribution fulfill the function of identifying the impact on various groups of fiscal policy and, in general, public spending policy. Naturally, this permits improving the process of refocusing direct subsidies and allows shifting the burden of adjustment from one income group to another.

For the purpose of providing a comparative starting point, Table 5.1 gives an overall view of income distribution in Venezuela by quintile, with comparable figures from other Latin American countries. It should be noted that the figures for Venezuela, calculated on the basis of the OCEI household survey, are similar to the estimates developed by the

Table 5.1. Income Distribution by Quintile
(In percentages for the years indicated)

	Lowest	Second	Third	Fourth	Fifth
Brazil (1983)	2.4	5.7	10.7	18.6	62.6
Colombia (1988)	4.0	8.7	13.5	20.8	53.0
Costa Rica (1986)	3.3	8.3	13.2	20.7	54.5
Jamaica (1988)	5.4	9.9	14.4	21.2	49.2
Peru (1985)	4.4	8.5	13.7	21.5	51.9
Venezuela (1987)	4.9	9.7	14.3	21.9	49.3

Sources: Brazil, Colombia, Costa Rica, Jamaica and Peru: *World Development Report, 1990,* Table 30. Venezuela: authors' calculations, based on OCEI household survey.

World Bank using its International Comparison Program (ICP) methodology.[3] Consequently, the data for Venezuela are comparable to the data for the other countries included, which were prepared using the ICP methodology.

This comparison shows that the lowest quintile in Venezuela receives a larger proportion of income than does the same quintile in other Latin American countries, with the exception of Jamaica. Nevertheless, in a wider sense, income distribution in Venezuela exhibits a pattern of inequity very similar to that of the rest of the countries in Table 5.1.

Changes in Income Distribution in Venezuela

The following were used in the analysis of changes in income distribution: the coefficient variation of family income (i_1), the standard deviation of the logarithm of family income (i_2), the Gini coefficients (i_3), the Theil coefficients (i_4), the asymmetry (i_5) and the distribution kurtosis (1_6), standardized at the [0,1] interval. These coefficients were calculated for 1981, 1987, 1989, and 1990 using a subsample of household data from the OCEI household survey for the second half of the year in question. The size of the subsample in each of these years is indicated at the bottom of Table 5.2.

All indicators show an increase in the inequality of both income distributions between 1981 and 1990. Blackburn (1989) proposes an interesting interpretation linking the variations in the Gini coefficient (i_3) to the transfer of income necessary to achieve the most inequitable distribution of income based on the least inequitable distribution. According to this calculation, in 1981, a monthly transfer of 578 Bs. (1990 value) would have been necessary from families with a lower than av-

---

[3] The World Bank's ICP estimates are as follows: 4.7, 9.2, 21.5, and 50.6 percent from the first to the fourth quartile. (See *World Development Report, 1990,* Table 30).

Table 5.2. Indicators of Income Distribution Inequality in Venezuela, 1981, 1987, 1989, and 1990

Based on Total Household Income

	1981	1987	1989	1990
i_1	0.386291	0.430648	0.453037	0.433225
i_2	0.364292	0.382476	0.399708	0.393213
i_3	0.397860	0.410865	0.409872	0.417877
i_4	0.719227	0.759714	0.795819	0.795819
i_5	-0.125874	-0.163880	-0.313187	-0.198075
i_6	1.000000	0.726744	0.485201	0.610874

Based on the Per Capita Income of the Members of the Household

	1981	1987	1989	1990
i_1	0.386291	0.481044	0.580752	0.506577
i_2	0.364292	0.409062	0.435310	0.416578
i_3	0.397860	0.438620	0.463797	0.443995
i_4	0.719227	0.808556	0.885224	0.847317
i_5	-0.125874	-0.095841	-0.127400	-0.139415
i_6	1.000000	0.766871	0.522466	0.589971

Source: Authors' calculations based on data from the OCEI household survey. All indicators standardized at the interval (0...1).
Note: Size of the sample: 1981   3,217
                             1987   3,216
                             1989   3,768
                             1990   3,797

erage income to families with above average incomes, so that the Gini coefficient would equal the 1990 figure. The increase in distributive inequality during the 1981-1990 period was equivalent to the transfer of 4 percent of the average monthly income (14,461 Bs. in 1990) from the poorest families to families with larger incomes.

The standard deviation of the income log (i_2) is extremely sensitive to the increase in low-income households (type γ inequality), and exhibits a very smooth trend throughout the period: total income grew 0.8 percent per year and per capita income fell 0.2 percent per year. However, between 1987 and 1989, total income grew at 2.2 percent and per capita 3.2 percent, suggesting that the macroeconomic adjustment had negative consequences for the poorest families, substantially increasing the number of households with an extremely low income. Between 1989 and 1992 the i_2 value declined, suggesting an improvement in the situation of the poorest families, probably associated with the implementation of a massive program of direct, tightly focused transfers. The sign and variation of the asymmetry (i_5) suggest the same type of process in the lower income sectors.

With respect to the middle-income levels (type β inequality), the trend of the kurtosis (i_6) strongly suggests that income dispersion tends to contract near the values of central tendency of the distribution. This could be interpreted as a uniformization of the middle levels, possibly due to a reduction in the number of families in the middle-income levels.

Poverty in Venezuela

Poverty is the term used to describe the situation in which individuals, frequently a family, are unable to satisfy their basic essential needs. The ambiguity of the term is due precisely to the subjectivity of the definition of "basic essential needs." The inadequacy of methods based strictly on income (monetary and/or cash) in measuring so complex a state as poverty have been discussed at length.[4] Nevertheless, the criterion most frequently used to identify poverty is the comparison between per capita family income and the poverty line, usually defined as the cost of a basic basket of food necessary to provide adequate caloric and protein intake according to international standards.

Our standard of comparison is the Basic Consumer Food Basket, the cost of which is estimated by AGROPLAN, based on information provided by the National Nutrition Institute. The contents of this basket are determined annually on the basis of information about actual food consumption. Consequently, the cost of the basket incorporates the income and substitution effect on consumer food demand, thus avoiding the overvaluation that usually occurs when fixed-weight food baskets, adjusted for changes in the price of the contents, are used for long periods of time.[5]

The poverty line in Venezuela was calculated for 1981, 1987, 1989, and 1990 as twice the value of the minimal consumer food basket estimated by the National Nutrition Institute. The cost of the Basic Consumer Food Basket used in this study takes into account the existence of significant substitution effects in the consumption of food. These effects are particularly intense when inflation suddenly accelerates, as it did in the 1987-1989 period. This may partially explain the difference between our figures and the figures based on consumer baskets with fixed contents. Once the poverty line has been established, values can be assigned to the poverty indicators shown in Table 5.3.

A closer interpretation of the data shows that poverty has increased not only in extent but also in severity. The count index shows that the percentage of the population below the poverty line has increased from 24 percent in 1981 to 60 percent in 1990. These results coincide with earlier

---

[4] The series of volumes entitled *The Political Economy of Poverty, Equity, and Growth* edited by D. Lal and H. Myint for the World Bank contains interesting material on this subject.

[5] It should be noted, however, that we made no corrections for understated income. Consequently, our results are not strictly comparable to those obtained by ECLAC (1990). Our figures are higher even though the trend of the size of the problem is similar.

Table 5.3. Poverty Indicators in Venezuela, 1981-1990

	1981	1987	1989	1990
Count index	0.240	0.446	0.600	0.592
Income gap index	0.360	0.443	0.469	0.467
Sen index	0.115	0.262	0.366	0.356
Foster-Green-Thorbecke I	0.086	0.201	0.282	0.277
Foster-Green-Thorbecke II	0.042	0.111	0.168	0.166

Source: Author's calculations based on OCEI household survey

studies of the situation in Venezuela (González et al., 1988), which indicate similar increases in the percentage of the population living in poverty.

The severity of poverty has increased just as dramatically. The income gap index can be interpreted as the amount of the transfer that would be needed to raise the income of each poor family to the poverty line. According to the results shown in Table 5.3, the average transfer necessary to accomplish this went from 36 percent of the poverty line in 1981 to 47 percent in 1990. Given that there has been an increase in both the nominal value of the poverty line and the number of recipients of transfers, it is clear that the total transfer required has become much larger. An approximate calculation indicates that in 1990 the total transfer involved was on the order of 200 billion Bs., or about a fourth of that year's fiscal budget.

The results of the Sen, FGT I and FGT II indices are consistent with this interpretation. Since these indicators are more sensitive to changes in the regressivity of income distribution, they give an account not only of the increase in the severity of poverty, but also of substantial changes in the relative position of poor families among themselves.

Nevertheless, the situation appears to have stopped deteriorating in 1990. It is still too early to know for certain whether this is a reversal of the trend or merely a partial recovery after the 1989 downturn.

Conclusion

The analysis presented in this section shows that the 1980s in Venezuela were characterized by an increase in distributive inequality and a considerable intensification of poverty. Both processes are manifestations of a particularly serious phenomenon in a country such as Venezuela, which represents a substantial setback in the economic development process. At a time when per capita GDP was falling steadily, and the labor market was showing signs of weakness, fiscal policy was not adjusted to better maintain and accumulate human capital.

In 1989 fundamental changes were made in the economic policy of Venezuela, prompted by the development of a basic stabilization model and a shift of emphasis in public spending toward direct subsidies to the poor. Since the process is still in the early stages, it is very difficult to predict whether these changes in fiscal policy will help to stop the deterioration of the social situation. Yet there are some encouraging signs. The downward trend of the poverty indicators seems to have halted in 1990, probably as a result of the increase in direct transfers to the poor. However, the stabilization program has created tension in some basic institutions, the reform of which will be discussed. The subjects chosen for the four sections of program analysis (electricity subsidies, social insurance, education, and gasoline) are currently—and for the first time—at the center of a major public debate in Venezuela.

The Electricity Subsidy and its Distributive Effects

Several years ago a heated debate erupted in Venezuela, calling into question the country's comparative advantage in the production of aluminum. Some argued that what made this industry profitable was the huge subsidy that companies such as Venezolana de Aluminio (VENALUM) were receiving in their consumption of electricity. More recently, the Central Coordination and Planning Office of the Presidency of the Republic and the Inter-American Development Bank prepared an estimate of shadow price ratios for project evaluations by the public sector (CORDIPLAN-IDB, 1990). In this study, a shadow price ratio of 3.184 was estimated for electricity, which, together with that of natural gas, diesel fuel, and drinking water, turned out to be one of the highest.

This information suggests that electricity has been highly subsidized by the state, which is responsible for the generation of 85 percent of the energy produced as well as the distribution of electricity in most of the national territory. But does the electricity subsidy really amount to anything?

Electricity is recognized as a superior good, i.e, its consumption increases with income. It might be supposed, then, that an electricity subsidy will be regressive, that it will essentially benefit the high-income sectors of the population. However, there are certain extenuating circumstances in Venezuela: first, a so-called social rate is charged for low levels of consumption; second, the service is actually provided free of charge to the poorest sectors of the population through what are known as losses through theft. The question then is which of these effects prevails; or, what is the distributive impact of a subsidy to electricity consumers?

The objective of this section is, first, to accurately estimate the amount of the subsidy granted to consumers of electricity. Then, an attempt is made to determine how the subsidy is distributed among the different sectors of Venezuelan society and if this distribution is equitable.

Organization of the Venezuelan Electrical Sector

The Venezuelan electrical sector comprises a total of 11 companies, which are listed below:

Public companies:

- Compañía Anónima Nacional de Desarrollo y Fomento Eléctrico (CADAFE)
- C.V.G. Electrificación de Caroní, C.A. (EDELCA)
- Energía Eléctrica de Venezuela (ENELVEN)
- Energía Eléctrica de Barquisimeto (ENELBAR)

Private companies:

- Electricidad de Caracas (ELECAR)
- C.A. Luz Eléctrica de Venezuela (CALEV); Electricidad de Guatire y Guarenas (ELEGGUA)—private subsidiaries of ELECAR.
- The other four are small companies with specific regional markets: C.A. La Electricidad de Valencia (ELEVAL), C.A. Luz Eléctrica de Yaracuy (CALEY), C.A. Luz y Fuerza Eléctrica de Puerto Cabello (CALIFE) and C.A. Electricidad de Ciudad Bolívar (ELEBOL).

Three of the companies—CADAFE, EDELCA and ELECAR—generate 90 percent of the system's total energy and account for 79 percent of the sales. Approximately 60 percent of the power generated is hydroelectric, while the remainder is produced in plants that use some type of petroleum-based fuel.

The Ministry of Energy and Mines (MEM) is responsible for formulating national energy policy and regulating the activities of the electric companies. Nevertheless, some of its activities overlap with the Venezuelan Investment Fund (FIV), an organization which as majority shareholder has all public companies under its authority. EDELCA is also under the authority of the Corporación Venezolana de Guayana (CVG), the parent of all public companies in the southeast region of the country.

History

Until recently, electricity was produced in Venezuela in thermal plants fueled with hydrocarbons. With the construction and start-up of the Guri Complex in 1986, a process of replacing thermoelectric energy with hydroelectric energy was initiated. This was the result of abundant hydraulic resources capable of generating low-cost energy, combined with the high fuel prices in the international market.

Despite the significant change in the technology utilized, the prices of the service were not adjusted to reflect the new structure of cost of production. This does not mean that there were no changes made in the rates, which have increased substantially in nominal terms since 1986, but rather that such changes were part of a strategy to compensate for the inflation in the Venezuelan economy. In fact, if the trend of electrical rates in the 1980-1990 period is examined in both nominal and real terms, it is clear that in the commercial and industrial sectors, inflation practically eliminated the effect of the increases, resulting in a few small increases in real terms between 1989 and 1990. In the residential sector, the rate increases did not offset inflation, causing a rate reduction in real terms in 1986.

It was not until the macroadjustment plan was implemented in 1989 that a decision was made to adopt a new rate policy based on the marginal, long-term cost of electricity. This was why the National Electrical Rates Committee was established as an autonomous agency with responsibilities to:

- Define the criteria for designing the rate structure;
- Define operations profitability of enterprises in the sector;
- Evaluate the rate adjustments requested by the enterprises;
- Recommend appropriate rate adjustments to the government.

The Committee consists of representatives from the Ministries of Development and of Energy and Mines, the Central Coordination and Planning Office (CORDIPLAN), the FIV, the CVG and the Venezuelan Chamber of the Electrical Industry (CAVEINEL).

This change of orientation was prompted by recognition of distortions caused by the existing rate structure. This exacerbated the financial problems of the electrical companies by making them increasingly dependent on government assistance while encouraging excessive use and waste by consumers. The first step toward correcting this situation was the nominal rate increase ordered in March 1989, when residential rates were raised 30 percent and industrial rates 50 percent, with monthly adjustments of 3 percent and 5 percent, respectively, in the following 20 months. These increases were instituted in all public and private electric companies, with the sole exception of EDELCA, which negotiates rates directly with consumers in Guayana or establishes them in interconnection contracts with distributing companies.

The Electricity Subsidy

The electricity subsidy in Venezuela is not a quantity that can be determined by examining accounting records; it is an implicit subsidy defined by the difference between the rates charged for the service by the electric companies and the opportunity cost, i.e., the shadow price of electricity. This difference, multiplied by the consumption of energy, gives the total amount of the subsidy.

The subsidy to electricity consumers can thus be expressed by the following formula:

$$S = [(PSe - Te) Ce]$$

where:

S = net subsidy to consumers
PSe = shadow price of electricity
Te = nominal electrical rate
Ce = consumption of electricity

The Shadow Price of Electricity

As indicated above, it was not until 1989, with the creation of the National Electrical Rates Committee, that the long-term marginal cost of electricity was accepted in Venezuela as the best approximation of the shadow or efficiency price of electricity. It was then decided to take the first steps toward calculating the marginal costs of the Venezuelan electrical system. In 1990 an agreement was signed with CORDIPLAN and the World Bank to conduct the required study. The study is divided into two phases: a short, simplified stage, designed to provide a rough approximation of the marginal costs of the Venezuelan electrical system, and another, more detailed phase, in which all of the necessary information will be assembled and the estimates fine-tuned.[6]

Several characteristics of the first phase of the study (which has already been completed) will be highlighted. First, the estimates are based on a single, aggregate marginal cost at the generation/transmission level (equal to 21 US mills/Kwh). This cost takes into account the marginal cost of the hydroelectric power generated by EDELCA and the marginal cost of the thermoelectric power generated by some of the distributing companies. Each company's marginal distribution costs are then added to this figure.

Second, this part of the study focuses on four of the distributing companies: CADAFE, ELECAR,[7] ENELBAR and ENELVEN, which sell 59 percent of the energy (EDELCA sells 37.26 percent). For the time being, the smaller regional companies will be excluded.

The results of the first phase of the "Study of the Marginal Costs of the Venezuelan Electrical System" are shown in Table 5.4.

---

[6] The marginal cost of the power generated by EDELCA was estimated at $15 million (75.55 cents/Kwh at the average 1990 exchange rate of 50.38 Bs./$). This calculation is based on the company's expansion plans, which include the construction and start-up of the Macagua II hydroelectric plant in 1994.

[7] Including its subsidiaries, CALEV and ELEGGUA.

Calculation of the Subsidy

The subsidy to electricity consumers is calculated as the difference between the marginal cost rates and the electric rates charged by the companies. If this difference is positive, a subsidy to electricity consumers exists in that sector; if, on the other hand, the figure is negative, there is a consumption tax.

Table 5.5 summarizes the results obtained for EDELCA. Since this company directly negotiates the rates applicable to each customer, the rates vary considerably from customer to customer, requiring calculations for each one. Table 5.6 shows the results obtained for each electrical distributing company included in the marginal costs study.

Although at first glance the resulting subsidies seem not to be offset by the tax on industrial energy consumption, there is a kind of cross-subsidy, with one sector financing—at least partially—the consumption of others.

However, the data available give no idea of the transfers involved; to gain a complete picture of the situation, the subsidies (taxes) calculated per unit of consumption must be multiplied by the quantities of energy sold by the companies in 1990. These calculations are shown in Tables 5.7 and 5.8.

These figures enable us to calculate the transfers between the participants in the system. With respect to EDELCA, there is a substantial subsidy to the industrial concerns in Guayana (33.5 percent of the total), but in relative terms most of the subsidy is received by the electrical distributing companies that buy hydroelectric power from EDELCA (66.5 percent of the total, including GURI and CADAFE Regional).

For distributors, the results show that the implicit tax on consumers in the industrial sector is not enough to cover the subsidies received by other sectors. It should be noted that in relative terms, there

Table 5.4. Rates According to Marginal Costs
(Cents/Kwh)

	CADAFE	ELECAR	ENELBAR	ENELVEN
Residential	282.22	337.00	180.15	166.80
Commercial LV	360.65	339.00	236.25	144.70
Commercial MV	266.80	205.50	170.35	118.90
Industrial LV	291.85	335.50	228.10	142.50
Industrial MV	228.25	212.30	0.00	0.00
Industrial HV	102.10	103.90	104.25	109.45
Government	174.20	261.25	123.30	0.00
Agriculture	0.00	0.00	0.00	0.00
Average rate	269.49	312.38	198.25	148.04

Source: CORDIPLAN-MEM-World Bank-National Electrical Rates Committee, "Study of the Marginal Costs of the Venezuelan Electrical System, Caracas," 1991.
Note: LV, low voltage; MV, medium voltage; HV, high voltage.

Table 5.5. EDELCA. Difference Between Marginal and the Average Rate Charged in 1990

	Invoicing total (billions of Bs.)	(Kwh) (%)	Revenue total (billions of Bs.)	Average (Bs.) %	Rate (cents/Kwh)	Subsidy (cents/Kwh)
Guayana subtotal	17.7	53.19	7.7	77.25	43.76	31.81
Interconnection subtotal	15.6	46.81	2.2	22.75	14.65	60.92
Total	33.3	100.00	10.0	100.00	30.13	45.44

Sources: C.V.G. EDELCA, January-December 1990 statistics and author's calculations.

Table 5.6. CADAFE - ELECAR - ENELBAR - ENELVEN. Difference Between Marginal Cost Rate and the Average Rate Charged in 1990
(Cents/Kwh)

Subsidy (Tax)	CADAFE	ELECAR	ENELBAR	ENELVEN
Residential	186.39	253.23	107.93	112.34
Commercial	8.22	23.80	75.10	19.83
Industrial	(81.34)	(138.37)	(15.03)	20.19
Government	19.39	29.96	(30.31)	0.00

Sources: CORDIPLAN-MEM-World Bank, "Study of the Marginal Costs of the Venezuelan Electrical System," Caracas, 1991 and author's calculations.

Table 5.7. Subsidy to EDELCA Customers

	Invoicing (Kwh) (billions of Bs.)	1990 %	Subsidy (cents/Kwh)	Total subsidy (billions of Bs.)
Guyana subtotal	17.7	53.19	31,81	5.6
Interconnection subtotal	15.6	46.81	60,92	9.5
Total	33.2	100.00	45,44	15.1

Sources: C.V.G. Edelca, January-December 1990 statistics and author's calculations.

Table 5.8. Subsidy (Tax) to Customers of the Distributing Companies
(In billions of Bs.)

Total subsidy (Tax) (Bs)	Residential sector	Commercial sector	Industrial sector	Government sector
CADAFE	6.2	0.1	(3.30)	0.80
ELECAR [1]	6.8	0.6	(3.10)	0.09
ENELBAR	.5	0.2	0.40	(0.03)
ENELVEN	2.4	0.1	.24	0.00
Total	15.9	1.0	6.56	0.92

Sources: CAVEINEL statistics, 1990 and author's calculations.
[1] Includes its subsidiaries CALEV and ELEGGUA.

is a significant difference between the subsidy granted to the residential sector and the subsidy granted to the commercial and public sectors. In the latter instance the rates charged by the distributing companies are close to the marginal cost; it is possible that, because of the monthly adjustments ordered, current commercial rates exceed marginal cost.[8]

An Additional Transfer Implicit in the Theft of Energy

Electricity users are also subsidized when they simply take the energy without paying for it; in this case, the transfer can be estimated as the value of the "stolen" energy at its marginal cost. To calculate the subsidy implicit in losses through theft, a few assumptions must be made:

- Losses through theft are estimated as a third of the total system losses;[9]
- The subsidy implicit in losses through theft is received by the residential sector.[10]

Both of these assumptions were used in calculating the total system losses, the losses through theft, and their marginal cost value (Table 5.9). The marginal cost residential rate was used for the latter calculation.

Distribution of the Subsidy

Once information has been obtained about the origin and destination of transfers involved in the subsidies (taxes) to electricity consumers, a more detailed description of the route of the transfers must be given in the same sequence as the electricity is produced. Thus, we find that the first subsidy is granted when the hydroelectric power is generated

---

[8] At the same time, the implicit tax on the industrial consumption of energy must have increased.

[9] According to experts, the losses sustained in the Venezuelan electrical system are of three types:
  • One third can be attributed to the system's technical losses (defined as the minimum level at which electrical companies operate since the costs of operating at a lower level would outweigh the benefits);
  • One third can be attributed to billing problems (due both to incorrect billing by the companies and the "tricks" consumers play to pay less, such as tampering with meters);
  • One third can be attributed to "thefts" of energy.

[10] The basis for this assumption is that thefts of power occur primarily in the barrios, and although there may be some small businesses, they are usually attached to a house or, in any case, are supplied low voltage power similar to that received by nearby residences.

Table 5.9. Subsidy Implicit in Losses Through Theft

Company	System losses		Losses through theft		Marginal cost residential rate (Bs/Kwh)	Subsidy (millions of Bs.)
	Total (Mwh)	% (of lost energy)	Total (Mwh)	%(of lost energy)		
CADAFE	6,246,171	32.02	2,082,057	10.67	2.82	5,875
CALEY	17,205	11.72	5,735	3.91		
CALIFE	85,400	26.19	28,467	8.73		
ELEBOL	128,912	32.49	42,971	10.83		
ELECAR [1]	1,514,401	16.02	504,800	5.34	3.37	1,701
ELEVAL	369,481	37.81	123,160	12.60		
ENELBAR	149,946	12.64	49,982	4.21	1.80	90
ENELVEN	1,052,104	19.76	350,701	6.59	1.67	585
Subtotal	9,563,620	25.63	3,187,873	8.54		8,252
EDELCA	1,311,049	7.37				
Total	10,874,669	19.73				

Source: Author's calculations.
[1] Includes the subsidiaries CALEV and ELEGGUA.

by EDELCA. As mentioned above, 33.5 percent of this subsidy is received by industrial customers in Guayana and the remaining 66.5 percent by the electric distributing companies.

What happens with the subsidy to industrial customers? If we assume that all these companies produce tradable goods, the price of which is determined by the international market, then the subsidy remains in the companies and is passed on to shareholders in the form of larger dividends (if the companies earn a profit). However, since many of these industrial customers are state enterprises, not all of which are profitable, there are two possible uses for the electricity subsidy: to compensate for inefficiency or to be converted back into government funds.

What happens when the subsidy is received by distributing companies? It could be considered additional income and then added to the profits; however, the subsidy usually does not remain in the companies but is passed on to customers in the commercial, public, and residential sectors. This occurs either through the subsidy implicit in the rates or in the form of loss through theft. The amount of the subsidy received from EDELCA by the distributing companies and the tax on electrical consumption in the industrial sector is not sufficient to cover the transfers to customers; the net result is a system-wide deficit of more than 10 billion bolivars.

Distribution of the Subsidy to the Residential Sector Among the Various Income Categories

Once the extent of the problem has been determined and assuming that it is concentrated primarily in the residential sector—where rates

Table 5.10. Electricity Expenditures of Families Grouped According to Income Level

	Level 1	Level 2	Level 3	Level 4	Total
Expenditures in millions of Bs.	278	354	421	603	1,656
Percentage	16.80	21.37	25.43	36.40	100.00

Source: Central Bank of Venezuela. Survey of Family Budgets in the Caracas Metropolitan Area, 1986.

are farthest from the marginal cost and losses through theft occur—the question must be asked whether there is any justification for maintaining the electrical system operating deficit. Looking at the figures, only a distributive type criterion could be used to justify such a deficit; consequently, this section examines the distributive impact of the subsidy to the residential sector to determine whether an argument of this type has any validity.

Breaking down the subsidy to residential consumers of electricity is not easy because information on the consumption patterns of families grouped according to income level is scarce in Venezuela. The only source available is the Survey of Family Budgets in the Caracas Metropolitan Area, conducted by the Central Bank of Venezuela in 1986. Table 5.10 shows the pattern of electricity expenditures of families grouped by income level according to the above survey.

Analysis of the statistics of the Ministry of Energy and Mines for the same year (1986) in the Caracas metropolitan area reveal that receipts from residential sales of electricity are less than the figure mentioned in the Central Bank survey.[11]

Table 5.11, prepared for verification purposes, tallies the total receipts from the sale of electricity in 1986—equal to household electricity expenditures—and distributes the expenditure percentages among income levels calculated in Table 5.10. These figures are divided by the average residential electric rate to obtain the consumption (in Kwh) for the level; next, this figure is divided by the number of families in each level to calculate per family consumption. The purpose of these calculations is to determine whether it makes sense to use an average rate to calculate the consumption in Kwh of each level. Doubt arises because a social rate is applied to consumption below a certain level, which, if substantial, would lower the rate applicable to Level I.[12]

---

[11] This is understandable since the household survey takes the average consumption of a family in each income level and multiplies it by the total number of families in that level. This procedure tends to overestimate total consumption per income level.

[12] Assuming that electricity is a superior good, which means its consumption increases with income.

Table 5.11. Distribution of Electricity Expenditures per Family in Each Income Level

	Level 1	Level 2	Level 3	Level 4	Total
Expenditures					
(millions of Bs.)	222	283	337	482	1,324
Rate (Bs./Kwh)	0.56	0.56	0.56	0.56	0.56
Energy (Kwh)	398,260	506,639	603,123	862,976	2,370,998
Kwh/Family	196	249	297	424	

Source: Author's calculations.

Nevertheless, the results obtained support the initial result that the social rate applies to a level of consumption so low that it is difficult to qualify for it.[13] If the rate for Level I were below the average rate, per family consumption—which is close to consumption per subscriber—would increase, violating the premise that electricity is a superior good and contradicting ELECAR experts' opinions on consumption in the Caracas metropolitan area.

The data in Table 5.11 imply an income elasticity for residential electricity of less than one, contradicting what has been found concerning characteristics of electrical consumption in Venezuela;[14] nevertheless, as mentioned above, the Survey of Family Budgets in the Caracas Metropolitan Area is the only available source that links family electricity expenditures to income level—an essential requirement for our analysis.

The following assumptions are also made:

- The pattern of electricity expenditure observed in 1986 holds true for 1990;
- The pattern of electricity expenditure observed in the Caracas metropolitan area holds true for the rest of the country.

These assumptions are used to calculate the distribution of the electricity subsidy among families who pay for the service.

The results shown in Table 5.12 indicate a regressive subsidy since, in absolute terms, the most affluent families receive more than twice the subsidy granted the poorest; the regressivity is even more pronounced in the case of the per capita subsidy, since individuals in

---

[13] In the case of ELECAR, for example, to qualify for the social rate, consumption must not exceed 50 consecutive bimonthly kilowatt hours or 100 Kwh in any bimonthly period. As soon as either of these levels is exceeded, the rate for residential service is permanently applied. (Official Gazette No. 4,080. Special Edition of March 29, 1989).

[14] EDELCA's most recent estimates, which are currently being reviewed by the World Bank, indicate that the income-elasticity of residential consumption is 0.88.

Table 5.12. Distribution of the Subsidy Implicit in the Rates, by Income Level

	Level I	Level II	Level III	Level IV	Total
Expenditure					
(millions of Bs.)	1,255	1,596	1,900	2,719	7,471
Expenditure (%)	16.80	21.37	25.44	36.40	100.00
Rate (Bs./Kwh)	0.82	0.82	0.82	0.82	0.82
Energy (Kwh)	1,532,182	1,949,136	2,320,330	3,320,031	9,121,679
Subsidy (Bs./Kwh)	1.75	1.75	1.75	1.75	1.75
Total subsidy					
(millions of Bs.)	2,675	3,403	4,051	5,796	15,925
Subsidy (%)	16.80	21.37	25.44	36.40	100.00
Per cap. subsidy (Bs.)	451.07	626.26	799.41	1,721.34	804.35
Subsidy per					
household (Bs.)	2,939.16	3,732.84	4,421.21	6,322.54	4,357.38
% household income	4.42	3.07	2.28	2.03	2.51

Source: Author's calculations.

Level IV receive more than three times the subsidy granted those in the poorest group. Nevertheless, it should be noted that given the degree of inequality of income distribution in Venezuela, and calculating the per family subsidy as a percentage of income, the distribution of the subsidy implicit in the electrical rates is less regressive than the distribution of income.

To evaluate the distributive impact of the subsidy on those who "steal" power, and following the same line of reasoning, the following assumptions were made:

- That the subsidy implicit in losses through theft is distributed among the income levels in the same way as families who live in poor dwellings are distributed in these same levels;
- In 1990 the distribution by income level of families who live in poor dwellings is the same as it was in 1986;
- In the rest of the country, the distribution by income level of families who live in poor dwellings is the same as that observed in the Caracas metropolitan area.

Table 5.13 shows that the distribution of the subsidy implicit in losses through theft is different from the subsidy implicit in the rates, since it is a type of transfer received primarily by the poorest sectors of the population.

Conclusions and Policy Recommendations

There is little justification for the subsidy implicit in the residential electrical rates since, in addition to the distortions it causes in consumption, its distributive impact is completely regressive, primarily

Table 5.13. Distribution by Income Level of the Subsidy Implicit in Losses Through Theft *(In thousands of Bs.)*

	Level I	Level II	Level III	Level IV	Total
No. of families living in poor dwellings[1]	20,699	7,173	4,124	0	31,996
% of total	64.69	22.42	12.89	0.00	100.00
Total subsidy (millions of Bs.)	5,338	1,850	1,063	0	8,251
Subsidy (%)	64.69	22.42	12.89	0.00	100.00
Per capita subsidy (Bs.)	900.15	340.45	209.88	0.00	416.77
Subsidy per household (Bs.)	5,865.34	2,029.22	1,160.76	0.00	2,257.76
% household income	8.83	1.67	0.60	0.00	1.30

[1] According to the Central Bank of Venezuela, Survey of Family Budgets in the Caracas Metropolitan Area, 1986
Source: Author's calculations.

benefiting the population with the highest incomes. If, in addition, it is agreed that the income elasticity of residential electrical consumption is higher than the elasticity implicit in the findings of the Survey of Family Budgets in the Caracas Metropolitan Area, then the regressivity of the subsidy is even greater.

In the case of the subsidy implicit in losses through theft, although it is a more distributive transfer than that received by the poorest segment of the population, it is an inefficient and unconventional mechanism.

It might be helpful to reflect on the processes that brought these subsidies into existence. The conclusion concerning the subsidy implicit in losses through theft would be that this is a case of resignation to a billing and collection process that is both complex and futile. The basic assumption is that the costs of performing these functions in the barrios, which is essentially where this phenomenon occurs, outweigh the probable receipts; however, there seems to be no empirical evidence to support this attitude, since there is virtually no precedent—either successful or unsuccessful—showing that any effort of this type was ever made.[15]

Concerning the subsidy implicit in the rates, the problem seems to be one of political negotiation and expediency. Although the rates applicable to all sectors have remained more or less constant for years, when external and internal pressures to modify the rate structure increase, the tendency is to raise commercial and industrial rates while minimizing conflict with residential consumers; the result—as the research shows—is a tendency toward cross-subsidization between sectors.

This discussion is intended to emphasize that while a distributive argument might be a good ex post justification, it may not be the reason

---

[15] Some authors suggest legalizing this situation by installing collective meters in the barrios and making collections with the cooperation of community leaders.

why these programs exist. Nevertheless the question arises whether a policy of indulgence toward the theft of electricity—since, as concluded above, the subsidy in the rates is unjustifiable—is a good distributive tool. Perhaps it is nothing more than an ineffective substitute for taxation (Lecaros, 1983) and it would be better to think of a "realistic" social rate for a specific sector of the population. Although the subsidy implicit in thefts benefits the poor, a number of equity problems are involved. What determines access to the subsidy is not the income level of the individuals concerned but rather the possibility of making a secret connection.

One option would be to institute a subsidized rate—lower than the marginal cost—for consumption up to a certain level,while other levels of consumption cover the cost. This would be a direct subsidy to the poor, financed with government funds.

If the subsidy is not going to be financed with government funds, a cross-subsidy could be used, provided that it is kept within the same residential sector (so that the richest subsidize the consumption of the poorest). The National Electrical Rates Committee is currently evaluating some options of this type.

In addition to designing the rate structure applicable to end users, another important issue is the subsidy EDELCA grants to the distributing companies. As long as this transfer exists, the distributing companies will have little or no incentive to solve problems such as losses through theft (since the subsidy they receive is large enough to cover them). If the subsidy in the residential rates is covered by taxes in other sectors, then the companies will have found an "inefficient" way out of their problems, but still a solution from their point of view.

Finally, the subsidy that EDELCA grants for the consumption of electricity by major industrial clients in Guayana does not seem logical either, especially in the case of public enterprises. As for companies with profitability problems, there is no justification for using the electricity subsidy to hide inefficiency. If the companies are profitable, the subsidy is converted back into new funds for the government, so why not utilize these funds directly from the start?

The Social Insurance System in Venezuela

This section analyzes the distributive impact of the programs of the Venezuelan Social Insurance Institute (IVSS). The IVSS administers social insurance programs providing old-age, medical care, and disability coverage for its affiliates and, in some cases, their families. The differences between social security and social insurance programs have been clearly delineated in the literature and consist basically of three issues: type of risks covered, universality of coverage, and method of financing.

There are no distinct boundaries that define a system and make it possible to classify it unequivocally as one type or another. The IVSS provides services for its affiliates that are typical of more extensive social security systems and obtains some of its financing from the national budget. However, the method of financing and the limited capacity to provide services to its affiliates makes the IVSS part of a social insurance system and not a social security system.

Coverage of the Social Insurance System

The social insurance system covers about a third of the economically active population of Venezuela. Officially, social insurance coverage is obligatory and universal for all workers under contract or in a labor relationship. This includes all private employees (except workers at home, temporary, and occasional workers) regardless of the size of the company where they work. Also included are public employees whose employment relationship is subject to the provisions of labor law.

The actual coverage of the social insurance system, based on the number of insured individuals who contribute to the IVSS, includes little more than 30 percent of the economically active population as well as about 60 percent of those employed in the modern sector of the economy. This level of coverage has remained relatively constant since the early 1970s and shows no clear signs of climbing any higher. Since the social insurance system provides medical coverage for affiliates of the general system and their families, the number and percentage of the population covered by the benefits of the system are much larger. Slightly over 30 percent of the Venezuelan population as a whole is entitled to medical care through the social insurance system.

The coverage of the social insurance system is determined by a labor market structure that excludes certain population groups from the system. Indeed, access to the social insurance system involves considerable expense. Given the lack of controls, it is reasonable to assume[16] that only employees in the modern private sector and the public sector are potential contributors to the system (not all of them are actual contributors, as the figures concerning IVSS contributors show). This excludes employees of microenterprises in the informal sector and self-employed workers.[17]

The analysis of the occupational status of employed workers by decile in the distribution of family income clearly shows that the labor market is an important factor in determining the affiliates of the system. If it is assumed that only employees under contract or in a labor relationship in the public sector and the modern private sector are po-

---

[16] The assumption implies that the informal sector as a whole is excluded from the system. The work of Mesa-Lago as well as studies concerning the "legality costs" of informal companies suggest that this is actually the case. In a group of informal companies in Caracas, Cartaya (1988) estimates that obligations to the IVSS account for more than a third of the costs of regularizing the companies' legal status.

[17] As of the date of this study, IVSS authorities had decided to regulate the access of self-employed workers. Nevertheless, given the productivity and income of self-employed workers in the informal sector, it is unlikely that such regulation will produce any significant increase in the number of covered workers.

tential affiliates, the percentage of eligible workers increases significantly as income increases. It is important to note that this is the result of the occupational status of workers at various family income levels and not of any rule governing affiliation or exclusion. The low potential coverage for low-income workers is the result of (1) evasion practices in the case of employees of microenterprises, or (2) the lack of regulations for self-employed workers. In both cases the real problem is whether these types of businesses can afford a 14 percent increase in their labor costs, especially when it is clear that their main comparative advantage is the low cost of labor. The response from the labor market is negative: these companies do not participate in the system.[18] Moreover, the percentage of families eligible to obtain coverage from the social insurance system under the current rules of affiliation clearly increases with income.

Financing The Social Insurance System

The Venezuelan social insurance system is financed chiefly by employee and employer contributions, calculated as a percentage of individual wages. In addition, the state (not in its role of employer) helps to finance the system through contributions made to cover the administrative costs of the system. The system also receives income from investments (financial investments in particular). The receipts of the social insurance system are between 1.2 and 1.6 percent of GDP, whereas expenditures are from 1.1 to 1.3 percent of GDP. This places Venezuela among the countries with the lowest social insurance costs in Latin America and the Caribbean (Mesa-Lago, 1989).

Revenues from Contributions

The social insurance system obtains 70 percent of its total financing from employer and employee contributions. The social insurance contributions are a direct, regressive payroll tax. They are calculated as a percentage of the worker's reference wage, based on the degree of risk the IVSS assigns the company. Taxable wages are limited to a maximum of 15,000 Bs. a month and are calculated by deducting legal profit-sharing payments and sporadic bonuses (year-end bonus and irregular overtime pay, for example) from the total amount received by the worker. The state contributes 1.5 percent of the taxable wages to cover the administrative costs of the Venezuelan Social Insurance Institute.

Since the marginal contribution rate is zero for the portion of wages in excess of the taxable wage limit, the taxable percentages of total

---

[18] It is noted that even in government credit programs for microenterprises, access to credit is not conditional upon fulfillment of the company's obligations to the IVSS.

income drops sharply for workers with incomes above this ceiling, creating a substantial regressive bias. Since the taxable wage limit is defined in nominal terms, in times of inflation the actual percentage of the contribution tends to fall as a result of the displacement of workers with wages above the taxable wage limit.

Both factors have made adequate financing of the social insurance system difficult in recent years. First, the maximum taxable wage has remained the same, in real terms, since 1967, despite the acceleration of inflation in the 70s and 80s. Second, in 1980 the average wage was above the taxable wage limit. Even though the legal taxable percentage (the marginal rate for wages below the taxable wage limit) remained the same until 1988, the fact that wages are above the ceiling means that the average contribution rate (measured as a percentage of total wages) has fallen steadily since 1980.

Revenues from Investment

The other important component of revenues from the social insurance system is investment returns. These depend on: (1) the composition of the system's assets, which determines the total funds available for investment, (2) the composition of the system's financial investments by type of instrument, which determines the mobility of the investments and the possibility of maximizing returns, and (3) the return on the funds as compared to inflation and the performance of the financial system, which determines whether and how quickly the reserves for long-term contingencies are deteriorating in real terms.

With respect to the composition of the system's assets, the situation is disturbing. In 1989 only 35 percent of the total assets (excluding suspense accounts) was invested in financial instruments. Of the remainder, 25 percent was invested in operations (mostly hospitals and insurance administrative buildings) and other assets, and 35 percent was tied up in receivables (late contributions). The high percentage of assets in receivables is a direct result of employer evasion and delays in paying the contributions withheld from workers. Curiously, the private sector is not alone in evading payment. Of the system's accounts receivable in 1989, 42 percent were government entities.

As far as the system's financial investments are concerned, in 1989, 56.6 percent of the funds were invested in government securities (mostly long-term, low interest bonds issued by public corporations), and 43 percent in commercial securities (many of which are long-term mortgage bonds bearing interest far below the market rate). This means that the third element in the equation, the return on the system's investments, is negative in real terms, lower even than the return obtained by commercial banks in operations subject to interest rate controls.

The Financial Equilibrium of the Social Insurance System

The IVSS has accumulated a substantial surplus in recent years, totaling approximately 0.2 percent of GDP. Assuming a national savings rate/GDP of 20 percent, the IVSS is a significant saver in the Venezuelan economy. Nevertheless, the accounting of insurance companies requires the establishment and maintenance of contingency reserves to cover the equally contingent liabilities inherent in the promise to provide medical care and pensions.

The accounting of the IVSS is presented as though it were that of a commercial company with no contingency reserves for actuarial coverage of future services. Although it has never been formally acknowledged, the impression is that, from a technical viewpoint, the social insurance system has gone out of control; what was once a fully financed system has become a system dependent on instant financing. This is due not to specific policy decisions, but rather to the indecision concerning factors that jeopardized the system's viability.

A look at the system's current surplus reveals that it has been declining as a percentage of GDP since 1978. Nevertheless, the question to be answered is what would have happened if the IVSS had been required to establish financial reserves to cover the old-age pension contingency? From this perspective, the situation is completely different. Not only do the accounting practices correctly describe the actual practices of the IVSS, but also, given the low yield of its financial investments, they show that the IVSS pension fund has constantly been losing value in real terms. For 1989, the loss of value of the pension fund, taking 1978 as a reference, was a little more than 25 billion 1989 bolivars, or approximately 2 percent of that year's GDP. Despite the limitations of an exercise such as this without the support of actuarial data, the analysis gives a completely different picture of the financial position of the IVSS. In 1985 the IVSS began experiencing substantial and growing capitalization deficits, which totaled 2 percent of GDP in 1989. In 1989, replenishment of the pension fund would have required a disbursement of 25.55 billion bolivars, or approximately 5 percent of that year's fiscal budget. Thus, it is clear that reestablishment of the pension fund is scarcely feasible without large public sector surpluses.

The Distributive Impact of IVSS Programs

One of the basic limitations encountered in this analysis is the lack of information about users grouped by income level. However, if we consider the IVSS as the nucleus of an insurance system, we can analyze the impact of the system through the costs of coverage for various population groups. To arrive at an estimate of the distributive impact, we designed a statistical experiment that would enable us to assign contributors to the IVSS to various deciles in the distribution of family income.

Analysis of the data from the household survey, arranged according to occupational status, shows that of the total number of public employees, only 49.3 percent contribute to the IVSS partial system, while employees in the modern private sector contribute 67.6 percent to the IVSS general system. The remaining employees in the modern private sector evade payment of IVSS contributions, while the reason for nonparticipation by public employees is the existence of special medical and retirement plans that replace social insurance.

The household survey also contains data concerning occupational status, income of employed workers, and personal data about the employed worker and his family. Using the data on occupational status and income of employed workers, a random number from a uniform distribution was assigned to each public employee and to each modern private sector employee. This random number was used to arbitrarily assign potential contributors to the group of current contributors or noncontributors. The percentages used for this apportionment were those mentioned in the above paragraph for the public and modern private sectors.

This apportionment procedure is random with respect to the level of family income, even though it takes into account the probabilities for each worker in each income decile of being employed either as a public employee or a modern private sector employee. The procedure accurately reflects the exclusion of certain groups (the informal sector, for example) which, because of their occupational status in the labor market, are excluded from social insurance coverage. However, it makes no distinction within potentially covered groups between the various sectors or occupations. This can represent a substantial bias if, for example, workers from poorer families are less educated and are discriminated against with respect to coverage, unlike more educated workers who are better informed about their rights.[19] With due acknowledgment of the qualifications involved, the distribution of workers by decile is presented in Table 5.14.

Based on this distribution experiment, we can describe several characteristics of coverage offered to families in differing income levels. First, it is clear that as the level of family income rises, the number of IVSS contributors increases more rapidly than does the total number of workers. It is important to note that this occurs in the lower income groups where a large proportion of informal sector workers are legally excluded from IVSS coverage. Second, only affiliates of the IVSS general system enjoy medical insurance benefits and extend those benefits to their families. Given the structure of the labor market, the percentage of families covered by IVSS medical insurance also increases for the higher income deciles.

Table 5.15 shows the results of this experiment in terms of the burden of IVSS contributions on workers and families in different income levels. Since average IVSS contribution rates decrease as total

---

[19] The literature on domestic labor markets suggests that this may be a serious problem even in modern companies, which discriminate against certain occupations and less-educated workers in complying with this type of obligation.

Table 5.14. Contributors to and Beneficiaries of the Venezuelan Social Insurance
Institute in 1990
(By decile of income distribution)

				% Households covered	
Decile	No. of Workers/ household	No. of Contributors/ household	% Workers who contribute	Partial system	General system
1	1.5	0.3	19.3	4.9	26.5
2	1.6	0.4	26.2	9.9	28.3
3	1.6	0.4	27.9	12.1	32.4
4	1.8	0.5	27.6	11.3	28.8
5	2.1	0.7	32.3	13.0	28.7
6	2.3	0.8	33.5	12.7	29.0
7	2.2	0.9	39.9	17.4	36.6
8	2.3	0.9	37.0	14.9	36.7
9	2.2	0.9	40.5	19.5	29.9
10	2.0	0.8	37.7	10.3	27.4
All	2.0	0.7	33.1	12.9	30.5

Source: Demographic data on income distribution and related data, OCEI household survey. The data on IVSS
contributions and coverage are experimental.

wages increase,[20] the first column of the table is not surprising. However, given the structure of employment in different deciles, the second column (which indicates the percentage of family income
represented by the IVSS contribution) shows that some regressivity of
the contribution is compensated for and the burden of the contribution as a percentage of family income increases for families with higher
incomes.

The second panel of the table shows the share of each decile in the
financing of the IVSS and in total family income.[21] The picture that
emerges is that of a regressive tax, since the share of the first and last
deciles in financing the IVSS is smaller than their share of the total
income. In other words, the population as a whole finances the coverage of the poorest and richest groups.

One of the issues of the distributive impact of financing the IVSS
is defining the effect of the parameters that change relative financing
burden. In practical terms, there are two basic parameters available
to IVSS administrators: the taxable wage limit and the contribution
rate. It should be noted that above the taxable wage limit, the mar-

---

[20] This is because the marginal contribution rate is zero for wages above the taxable
wage limit.

[21] In reality, this is income from the labor market. Assuming the distribution of
physical and financial assets is still more skewed than that of human capital, it is
clear that we are underestimating the degree of inequality in income distribution.

Table 5.15. Contributors to and Beneficiaries of the Venezuelan Social Insurance Institute in 1990 by Workers and Families
(By decile of income distribution)

Decile	Contribution rate		Total decile share in	
	% Salary	%Family income	IVSS financing	Total income
1	13.5	3.5	2.1	2.5
2	13.1	4.1	4.5	4.6
3	12.9	4.9	6.4	5.4
4	13.4	4.8	7.5	6.5
5	12.5	4.2	8.2	8.1
6	12.5	4.7	11.7	10.2
7	11.9	5.4	15.0	11.6
8	11.9	4.3	13.4	12.9
9	11.4	4.4	15.8	15.0
10	10.6	2.7	15.2	23.2
All	12.2	4.1	100.0	100.0

Source: Demographic data on income distribution and related data, OCEI household survey.The data on IVSS contributions and coverage are experimental.

ginal contribution rate is zero; therefore the average contribution rate declines. In Table 5.16 this question is examined from the perspective of a controlled reform of the rules of financing the system. The point of departure is the situation prior to 1989, when the taxable wage limit was 3,000 Bs. a month and the total contribution rate was 12 percent. In 1989, a reform was introduced whereby (1) the taxable wage limit was increased to 15,000 Bs. a month and (2) the total contribution rate was changed to 14 percent.

First, the change in the taxable wage limit has a greater impact on overall IVSS financing than the change in the contribution rate. According to our calculations, changing only the wage limit increased receipts by 152 percent, while changing the contribution rate and leaving the taxable wage limit alone increased them 20 percent.

The distributive impact of the two policies is completely different. The average contribution rates on wages tend to "flatten out" when the taxable wage limit is exceeded, while they maintain their regressive bias when only the contribution rate is increased. This is natural since an increase in the taxable wage limit raises the marginal contribution rate of the portion of wages below the new ceiling. Changing the taxable wage limit in our experiment put it near the modern economy's average wage; consequently, the average contribution rates are not exactly equal.

With respect to the share of each decile in the total financing of the system, changing the contribution rates has no significant effect

Table 5.16. A Policy Experiment with the Contribution Rates and Taxable Wage Ceilings of the Venezuelan Social Insurance Institute, 1990

Decile	Base scenario (1)			Change taxable wage limit (2)			Change contribution rate (3)		
	% wages	% total financing	% family income	% wages	% total financing	% family income	% wages	% total financing	% family income
1	9.2	3.8	2.1	11.5	2.1	2.9	10.8	3.8	2.4
2	7.1	6.5	1.9	11.0	4.6	3.4	8.5	6.5	2.3
3	5.9	7.9	2.0	10.8	6.4	4.1	7.0	7.9	2.4
4	6.3	9.0	1.9	11.4	7.6	4.1	7.4	8.9	2.2
5	5.5	9.7	1.6	10.5	8.2	3.5	6.6	9.7	2.0
6	4.9	12.1	1.6	10.4	11.7	3.9	5.8	12.1	1.9
7	4.3	14.3	1.7	9.8	15.0	4.4	5.2	14.4	2.0
8	4.2	12.5	1.3	9.9	13.4	3.6	5.1	12.6	1.6
9	3.9	13.5	1.2	9.4	15.7	3.6	4.7	13.6	1.5
10	2.8	10.5	0.6	8.8	15.1	2.2	3.4	10.6	0.7
All	4.9	100.0	1.4	10.1	100.0	3.4	5.9	100.0	1.6

Source: Author's Calculations based on OCEI data

Notes: (1) Base scenario keeps the contribution rate at 12 percent and the taxable wage limit at 3,000 Bs.

(2) Change taxable wage limit to 15,000 Bs.

(3) Change contribution rate to 14 percent. Changes in total contributions to social isurance by scenario (as a percentage of the base scenario)

(2) 151.9 percent.

(3) 20.1 percent.

on the original (regressive) situation. However, changing the taxable wage limit substantially increases the share of the upper deciles in total financing while decreasing the share of the lower deciles. In terms of the burden on family income, the result is the same: changing the taxable wage limit tends to smooth out the burden on family income for each decile, whereas changing the contribution rates has no significant effect.

The lesson to be learned is that in terms of its financial and distributive impact, the most appropriate policy is to keep updating the taxable wage limit. In fact, in the historical tradition of the system before the 1980s, taxable wage limits were much higher than the average wage of the modern segment of the economy, resulting in the average contribution rates being similar for all levels of income distribution.

The Distributive Impact of Old-Age Pension Programs

It is generally believed that old-age pension programs such as those of the IVSS represent a large transfer of resources to the beneficiaries of the system, typical of defined benefit systems.[22] The force of this argument is that in the rules governing the financing and services of the system, there is no relationship between the employee's contributions and the benefits he receives through old-age pensions.

Financially, the problem becomes a question of defining a time limit for financing the system or, how long can the system pay the pensions promised in the benefits formula without changing the amounts paid in by current contributors.

Ideally, a fully financed pension system should have an infinite financing capability, with the present expected value of the contributions equaling the benefits promised over an infinite period of time. If the administrators of the system, for any reason, increase the benefits or reduce the contributions, the pension system moves toward a partially financed system, shortening the length of time during which the present expected value of contributions is equal to benefits. In this type of system, contributions and benefits are periodically adjusted to restore its financial equilibrium. Ultimately, the period in which contributions vary becomes infinitely short, and we find ourselves in a system with instant financing, with contributions and benefits varying constantly in order to reestablish the instantaneous financial equilibrium. This allows the system administrators to offer benefits that are not actuarially financed, in the sense that the temporary surpluses

---

[22] The terms "defined benefit" and "defined contribution" refer to two old-age pension systems. In the former, pensions are defined as some fraction of the final wage and do not necessarily have any relationship to the contributions made by the beneficiary. In the latter, pensions are defined as the net present value of the contributions made by the beneficiary. Obviously, under the "defined benefits" system the possibility exists of defining pensions that destroy the financial and actuarial equilibrium of the system, whereas in the "defined contributions" system this possibility is more remote (although not impossible).

(those occurring in early stages when the number of contributors is greater than the number of beneficiaries) can be used to grant pension plans that will require additional contributions from future affiliates. It is often said that the liberal granting of unfinanced pensions in the early stages of the system's development is what causes pension systems to become instantly financed (where the contributions of current affiliates finance the pensions of current beneficiaries).

In a defined benefits system, calculating the actuarial balance of the pension system depends on (1) demographic trends, (2) the contribution rate, (3) the benefits formula and (4) the policy governing the investment of reserve funds accumulated by the system. Concerning the first point, Venezuela is a typical Latin American country, in that its population is beginning to show signs of aging. However, if we compare this data with the demographic situation of mature Latin American pension systems, it is obvious that Venezuela's situation is hardly desperate, especially when compared to the 2.04 maintenance rate in Argentina in 1983 (Isuani, 1988). Venezuela still has not experienced a crisis in terms of the demography of its pension system, and it would be best to take corrective measures before a crisis occurs.

Concerning the contribution rates, Venezuela's problem in the past was the failure of administrators to prevent the decline that occurred in the contribution rates of the 1980s, as explained above. Apparently, a policy that keeps the taxable wage limit above the average wage is not only more efficient in terms of increases in the overall financing of the system, but is also more equitable in distributive terms.

As far as the definition of benefits goes, pensions are granted and calculated in nominal terms, which reduces the real value of the benefits when inflation accelerates. Despite periodic adjustments of the pension value, generally concomitant with wage increases, the average value of old-age pensions has fallen constantly in real terms since 1976. In fact, the growth rate of the average pension is much lower than that of the modern sector average wage. In this sense especially, the problems of the IVSS old-age pension system did not necessarily originate in the excessive generosity of system administrators in granting pensions.

For a worker who has contributed for the minimum period of 750 weeks, the internal rate of return of his pension plan is a function of the growth of real wages and inflation. The analysis of three alternative rates of real wage growth (1 percent, 0 percent, and -1 percent per annum) yields internal rates of return, from the worker's perspective, that are lower than inflation in high-inflation scenarios and higher than inflation in low-inflation scenarios. The extreme sensitivity of the internal rate of return to inflation is due specifically to the decline of the real value of pensions defined in nominal terms.

If demographic variables and the contributions and benefits rules are causing the dissolution of the pension system, which is precisely what is happening, it is clear that the IVSS investment policy is to blame. In fact, if we refer to Table 5.17, an analysis of investment policy, it becomes clear that the actuarial imbalance of the system stems in part from the decline in the real value of its contingency reserves. The important thing from the distributive viewpoint is that this decline did not benefit current retirees (who obtain internal rates of return from the pension plan very similar to the rate of inflation), but rather the state and state enterprises that used these funds to finance their operating deficits.

In terms of policy, it is clear that current proposals to reestablish the pension fund by increasing contributions are good but do not go far enough. So long as the state has the power and the resolve to finance its current deficits with pension system funds invested at extremely negative real interest rates, there is no real chance of restoring the contingency reserve funds. The difference between a public and a private system is precisely this: in a private system the state's ability to plunder pension funds is greatly diminished. It is this point, and not issues about the greater intrinsic efficiency of the private sector, that must influence any discussion about changing the pension system.

Subsidies in the Medical Insurance System

Calculating subsidies in the medical insurance system is complicated by a lack of information about the users of the system. The most reasonable method of proceeding, therefore, is to compare coverage costs for various income levels with the costs of purchasing equivalent coverage from a private insurance company. This method does not reveal the direct and indirect subsidies granted through the provision of medical services, but it does indicate those implicit in obtaining coverage from insurance providers.

There is a great difference between the premiums paid by contributors to the IVSS for medical insurance and the premiums paid for private medical insurance covering a similar level of services calculated for an equivalent risk pool. In fact, given the distribution of wages and contributions in 1990, an individual insured by the IVSS paid an average of 8,624.40 Bs. a year. The same individual would have had to pay a premium of about 35,000 Bs. a year to obtain similar coverage from a private company.[23]

The distributive impact of paying medical insurance premiums is neutral. In fact, as a percentage of family income, the premiums actually paid

---

[23] This calculation is based on interviews with private insurers who offer medical insurance policies with coverage similar to that of the IVSS, including coverage for catastrophic illness. Currently, given the negative selection problems plaguing the individual health insurance market, these premiums are about 90,000 Bs. The compulsory aspect of social insurance eliminates the negative selection problem while creating a sufficiently large and diverse pool of insured people to permit lowering the premiums to the level mentioned in the text. In addition, the policy of private insurance companies is to use investment returns to finance part of the cost of illnesses. This is another area in which the IVSS has shown great weakness (see the section on revenues from investments).

Table 5.17. Internal Rates of Return of the IVSS Pension Plan

Rate of real wage growth	30% inflation	10% inflation
1.0	26.2	12.4
0.0	25.6	11.7
-1.0	24.9	10.9

Source: Author's Calculations

Table 5.18. Subsidies Implicit in Medical Coverage—Venezuelan Social Insurance Institute, 1990
(By decile of income distribution)

	Medical Insurance Total Cost		Subsidy[1]	
Decile	Bs./year	% family income	Bs./year	% family income
1	2,276	5.2	32,723	74.1
2	4,512	5.7	30,487	38.5
3	5,440	5.8	29,559	31.6
4	7,642	6.8	27,358	24.5
5	7,613	5.4	27,386	19.4
6	10,929	6.1	24,070	13.5
7	10,644	5.3	24,355	12.1
8	9,482	4.2	25,517	11.4
9	13,217	5.1	21,782	8.4
10	13,821	3.4	21,178	5.3
All	8,624	5.0	26,375	15.2

Source: Author's Calculations
[1]Shown as the difference between the cost of similar private insurance for an equivalent risk pool (35,000 Bs./year) and the IVSS price for medical coverage.

to the IVSS medical insurance system in the various deciles are similar. Nevertheless, if (as in Table 5.18) we calculate the amount of the implicit subsidy as a percentage of family income, the picture changes completely. The subsidy has an extremely progressive distribution and is highly sensitive to changes in the family's position in the distribution of income.

From this perspective, all beneficiaries of the system receive a subsidy, regardless of income level. In one sense, this means that the deficit of the medical insurance system is linked to the low premiums charged (which are actuarially unfair to the IVSS). However, it should be noted, first, that in the insurance system, part of the cost of illness is covered by investment returns, an area in which we have repeatedly seen the IVSS fail. Second, the IVSS medical insurance system has become a rationing system characterized by low quality services and lengthy waits, which discourages use of the medical care facilities by high-income groups. Thus, our estimate of the subsidies implicit in the purchase of medical coverage undervalues the total subsidy received by users of the medical care system, in particular those in the lower deciles of income distribution.

A serious problem of the medical insurance system is the existence of a considerable financial deficit, which threatens the viability of the care provided. As seen above in the discussion of the financial position of the social insurance system, the expenses of the medical care subsystem are the largest component of the total expenses of the IVSS. Secondary information also suggests that the per patient cost of medical care is extremely high.[24] The common perception of the IVSS as an inefficient provider of medical services is of little use in terms of developing policy alternatives. The conclusion is that the IVSS medical insurance system, inefficient as it is, is an important means of distributing resources to the poor. The basic question is how to make the system more efficient?

The answer to this question is twofold: first, there is a need to infuse the system with additional resources. This option, however, is unpopular because of the system's proven inefficiency. The second, of an organizational nature, concerns the need to make changes in the risk coverage and basic health care system. As an insurance company, the IVSS has no comparative advantage in owning and operating hospitals. In fact, placing risk coverage and the health care system under the same authority diminishes and distorts the incentives to control costs that exist in systems where the insurer is institutionally different from the provider. The separation of these two functions of the IVSS—specifically, its division into two different institutions—could create beneficial pressures that would increase the efficiency of the system.

Nevertheless, it is important that the monopolistic power of the IVSS as an insurer be preserved—in the sense of preserving the obligation to purchase coverage for all workers eligible under the rules of affiliation—as a means of counterbalancing the monopolistic power of the medical profession. The experience of the United States, where excessive fragmentation of the market share of insurance companies has led to loss of control over health care costs, is relevant to reforms to the Venezuelan health care subsystem of the social insurance system. In fact, the medical profession develops standards of care, which, by their very nature, cannot be subjected to market restrictions and which function as de facto monopolistic power. Eliminating the monopolistic power of the social insurance system might remove all public control over the growth of health care costs.

Conclusion

The picture that emerges from this study is that of an insurance system beset with serious operating and financial problems, but which fulfills and has fulfilled an important function by providing one segment

---

[24] According to analyses of the per patient costs of medical care, it is estimated that the costs per bed per day of IVSS hospitals are the highest in the national medical system, and are even higher than those of private clinics.

of the population with risk coverage. However, the IVSS was not designed to function institutionally as a redistributive mechanism. The distributive role it plays in the provision of medical coverage is a byproduct of the rationing system adopted by the medical care subsystem to avoid financial collapse. For those who actually utilize the system, this means a nightmare of long lines, delays, and inadequate care.

One of the most surprising aspects of our analysis is the limited distributive impact of the pension system (at least in the direction indicated, from contributors to beneficiaries). The state has been the primary beneficiary of the transfers generated by the pension system. The pension system, despite its formal designation as a defined benefits system, has not brought about a transfer of resources to its beneficiaries. Thus, privatization of the pension system might be very beneficial for current contributors, provided that the state restores the resources of the IVSS pension fund.

With respect to the system of medical coverage, the basic problem seems to be institutional. An effective program of cost controls and incentives to improve the efficiency of the system requires the separation of two IVSS functions: one as an insurance company and the other as a provider of medical services. Without such a separation, the only way to control costs, if it is done at all, is to ration user services. This does not seem to be a reasonable method of controlling costs and, moreover, it creates no incentive to improve the efficiency of the service. Institutional separation would allow the insurance system to have more impact on costs and would give care providers incentives to streamline and improve the efficiency of their service. The example of the interaction between medical clinics and private insurance companies can shed some light on the type of reform needed.

Finally, the analysis illustrates a fundamental weakness of the social insurance system in Venezuela— its method of financing which excludes large, low-income groups from protection under the system. Any discussion of enlarging the redistributive role of the IVSS cannot overlook the basic issue of public financing needed to expand coverage. The Venezuelan government's proposals to reform and expand the system sidestep this issue and are limited to promises of expanded coverage and services. These promises have done little more than further erode the credibility of the IVSS as an institution and to complicate the urgent tasks that its transformation will require. Instead of simply promising more services and greater coverage, it is important that the government first determine the final goal of the proposed reform (e.g., a social security system) and second, determine the extent to which the state is prepared to finance the expansion of services and coverage.

The Impact of Public Education Spending in Venezuela

This section analyzes the distributive impact of public education spending. Its objective is to determine what percentage of government spending on education is received by the population, as grouped by income level and, more generally, by standard of living. Given certain limitations of the data used, which are explained below, this should not be considered an impact study per se.

Education spending programs are justified on the basis of efficiency and equity. In terms of efficiency, the government must invest in education because of the externalities in universal education. The government should also invest to correct deficiencies in the capital market that make it difficult to find financing for projects involving investments in human capital (Jiménez, 1987). However, the main justification for public aid to education is the distributive effects of the private financing of education. There is universal belief that an individual's success in life should not depend on the parents' ability to pay for higher education (Stiglits, 1988: 372). This justification of the government's educational activities has always carried weight in the public debate in Venezuela. It is assumed that this type of intervention has a positive effect on the intergenerational distribution of wealth and social mobility. The concept of equality of educational opportunities is, therefore, the most common meaning of the term equity in education.

It is pertinent to ask, who are the actual beneficiaries of the subsidy inherent in public education spending? It should be assumed that a reasonable objective of such spending is to help those whose ability to pay is sufficiently limited to prevent their attending school, while those who are able are usually willing to pay for their education. By focusing public education spending on individuals in the economically least advantaged groups of society, a progressive effect on income distribution results, even excluding intergenerational effects. However, it is not enough to merely hope that education expenditures will guarantee the attainment of such a goal. There are many examples of education expenditures with regressive results regarding distributive equity, despite the fact that their objectives lay in precisely the opposite direction. This study focuses on the regressive results of public education spending.

The Criteria for Judging the Equity of a Spending Program

Within the scope of this study there are divergent opinions about the equity of government education spending. The literature reveals that there are many criteria for forming opinions about equity, which, although they have much in common, can lead to different conclusions when applied to different situations.

Fields (1975) has proposed that a distinction be made between:

a) Equal opportunity criteria: a spending program is equitable if population groups have access to the program in proportion to their importance in the total population;

b) Cost-benefit criteria: a program is equitable if the costs paid by population groups are proportional to the benefits each receives, regardless of implications this has on access to the program;

c) Ability-to-pay criteria: assuming a decreasing marginal utility of income, a program is equitable if its cost-benefit ratio increases as a function of income.

A thorough comparison of these criteria is beyond the scope of this study. It will suffice to say that Fields' definition (a), with modifications, is the one used most often in the following analysis. The reason for choosing it is that there is insufficient information available on the tax burden of the Venezuelan public to provide a basis for opinion required by definitions (b) and (c).[25] The most important modification is that instead of proportionality of access, we refer to proportionality of expenditure. Specifically, we call a spending program equitable if the level of spending that the population groups receive is proportional to their share in the total population.

Methodological Aspects

The study follows the methodology utilized by Le Grand (1982), which is based on the question, who uses the educational services financed by the government? If a distribution of users by socioeconomic level is available, the share of each of these groups in expenditures can be determined for each educational level.
    More specifically, the study will proceed in accordance with the following steps:

• Determination of the socioeconomic distribution of the public education system users.
• Determination of education spending by level (preschool, elementary, secondary and higher education).
• Calculation of the percentage of the education budget received by users in each socioeconomic level and in each educational level.
• Calculation of indices and review of complementary aspects (calculation of the average subsidy and socioeconomic level per household, comparison of the socioeconomic composition of public and private sector users, and comparison of the subsidy with education expenditures made directly by each household).

Data

The most complete source of the data required to determine who uses the educational services financed by the government is provided by FUNDACREDESA, a government foundation created to study

---

[25] The only study of this kind to which we have had access asserts that the tax burden in Venezuela, taken as a whole, falls most heavily on the poorest households (Escobar, 1990).

Table 5.19 Venezuela, 1986. Distribution of the Population by Socioeconomic Level

Level	%
High and high-middle	5.48
Low-middle	14.10
Laborer	42.37
Marginal	38.05
Total	100.00

Source: FUNDACREDESA, 1989.

the physical and psychological development of the Venezuelan population. FUNDACREDESA has published data from representative samplings of the Venezuelan population. This is especially useful since they reveal the percentage of students of differing ages grouped according to whether they attend a public or private school and according to the socioeconomic level of their families. The population is thus divided into five levels: high, high-middle, low-middle, laborer, and marginal, the latter group comprising, according to FUNDACREDESA, the population living in extreme poverty. Given the relatively small quantitative significance of the high level, FUNDACREDESA adds data on subjects in this category to that of the next lower category—high-middle—for the purposes of presenting information about the educational variables in its study. We have done the same. Table 5.19 shows the distribution of the population in 1986 according to this classification by levels.

The advantages discussed make it advisable to utilize this source for the study, although a few comments are in order.

The main difficulty posed by this information is that socioeconomic levels are not defined according to the usual scale of monthly or annual household income, but rather are based on a scale which determines the socioeconomic level to which each household belongs. This is based on several factors: the primary source of income, the type of housing, the mother's educational level and the profession of the head of the household.[26] Although this calculation is of considerable value, it creates insoluble problems when attempting to compare it with other sources of important data such as the household survey or the Family Consumption Survey of the Central Bank of Venezuela. In the follow-

---

[26] The social stratification scale used by FUNDACREDESA divides each variable into five items and each of these is assigned a decreasing weight according to the quality of the five. The total of the items determines the level to which each family belongs. The sample included 24,640 families from around the country (FUNDACREDESA, 1989).

Table 5.20. Venezuela, 1986. Use of Public Education by Socioeconomic and Educational Level
(Percentage)

| | Educational level | | | |
Socioeconomic level	Preschool	Primary	Secondary	Higher
High and high-middle	21.4	19.9	40.9	59.9
Low-middle	62.4	52.4	78.5	76.1
Laborer	79.9	92.3	96.8	88.2
Marginal	85.4	97.2	98.6	97.2

Source: FUNDACREDESA, 1989.

ing analyses a few simple but reasonable assumptions are made which help overcome this obstacle.

The information concerning the university level refers only to the socioeconomic composition of students in the National Pre-Enrollment System of the Office of University Sector Planning (OPSU). Although the data use the same scale developed for the FUNDACREDESA survey, using the data assumes that the composition by socioeconomic origin of the students who enter the university is the same as the composition of the student body as a whole.

The information concerning the education budget and its distribution by program was obtained from the Ministry of Education of Venezuela in the Ministerial Annual Report.

The Users of Public Education in Venezuela

Four-fifths of the student enrollment at all levels is in public sector institutions, with minor variations within each educational level.

An essential step in determining the actual purpose of education spending is to determine to what extent the differing socioeconomic levels attend public or private educational institutions.[27]

According to FUNDACREDESA, the socioeconomic levels differ considerably in their use of public education for their children, as can be seen in Table 5.20. This shows the percentage of all enrolled children in each socioeconomic level who attend public educational institutions.

---

[27] Many private educational institutions—for example, those belonging to Fe y Alegría, an organization affiliated with the Catholic church—receive a substantial economic subsidy from the government. In this study, however, we assume that the only students benefiting from public education spending are those enrolled in public institutions.

Table 5.21. Venezuela, 1986. Distribution of Public Education Spending by Educational Level

Level	%
Preschool	6
Primary	23
Secondary	24
Higher	47
Total	100

Source: Annual Report of the Ministry of Education, 1986.

With few exceptions, it can be determined that the use of public education increases as the socioeconomic level decreases and the educational level increases. If a student is from a lower socioeconomic level, it is more likely that he or she will be in a public educational institution, a probability that increases as one moves up the scale from the preschool level to higher education.

The Distribution of Public Spending by Educational Level

In 1986, education spending allocated to specific educational levels totaled 13,376 billion Bs. at current prices[28] and was distributed among the educational levels as shown in Table 5.21.

A discernible pattern emerges[29] that is not unusual for Venezuelan public education, where the predominance of higher education over the other levels is considerable. It may have become even more pronounced in recent decades. Márquez (1990) presents figures indicating that in the 1984-1989 period, public spending on each educational level decreased in real terms, but the average rate of average annual growth for higher education was -1 percent, while the rate of the other levels was about -10 percent. In the same period, the share of

---

[28] According to the Annual Report of the Ministry of Education for 1987, this figure reflects the total budget allocations made directly to preschool, basic, middle and diversified and higher education, plus the expenditures budgeted by state and municipal governments. The latter figure was not exact for 1987 but was estimated on the basis of the analysis conducted for 1989 by González (1991). The central government's budget allocations for the general administrative expenses of the Ministry of Education were not included, given the difficulty of linking them to specific educational levels. Finally, the expenditures of state and municipal governments were assigned in their entirety to the preschool, elementary, and middle school levels, given that contributions of local governments to higher education institutions are rare and insignificant in terms of the total budget for the post-secondary level.

[29] The figures presented assume an elementary cycle of six years and a secondary cycle of five, following the pattern common in many countries and in effect in Venezuela since the 1970s. This clarification is necessary since, as a result of the

spending on higher education in total public education spending remained the same with minor variations. Spending on other levels was cut almost in half to pay for the Education Ministry's assistance, planning, and administration expenses.[30]

The Distributive Impact of Public Spending

Comparing the information presented thus far makes it possible to form an opinion about the distribution of public education spending between each of the socioeconomic levels defined. Table 5.22 shows this distribution by educational level and in comparison with the distribution of the population.

Public education spending can be considered progressive for all levels, with the exception of higher education, in which case it is distinctly regressive. We used equity criterion as the equivalency between the percentage of the population in a given level and the percentage of public spending that individuals in that level receive (i.e., equity as defined in Fields' criterion (a), as explained above). The result is that for preschool, elementary and middle levels, the percentage of public spending received by children from the two lowest levels is greater than the relative weight of these groups in the population. In higher education, the highest level receives a large proportion of the spending—as much as five times its weight in the total population—and, in terms of spending, the lowest receives the equivalent of about one-twentieth its relative weight in the total population. The comparison is even more striking between the proportion of the population represented by the two highest groups—a fifth of the total—and the 70 percent of higher education spending they receive.

1978 reform of the Venezuelan educational system, the expense items by level now refer to basic education. This is understood as that which extends through six years of the traditional elementary cycle plus the first three years of the old *bachillerato* (high school), with the name middle and diversified being given to the last two years of conventional secondary school. Since FUNDACREDESA groups students into age groups that coincide with the traditional division of the study cycle, we estimated the relative share of the last three years of basic education based on the historical series of expenditures prior to changing the definition of the items. We then subtracted it from the total basic education item and added it to the figure for middle and diversified education, applying various consistency tests to maximize the probability that the estimate is within an accurate range. Consequently, in the remainder of this analysis, secondary or middle education refers to the equivalent of five years of the traditional *bachillerato*, with respect both to budget figures and enrollment.

[30] Reimers (1991), selecting a longer period, provides data indicating that the average annual rate of growth in public spending on higher education in real terms was the only positive one—approximately 3.87 percent between 1970 and 1986—while the rates of elementary and secondary education are -2.16 and -7.91, respectively. Thus, there seems to be no reason to think that the year selected for our analysis is unusual.

Table 5.22. Venezuela, 1986. Distribution of Public Education Spending by Level
(Percentage)

Socioeconomic/educational level	Preschool	Primary	Middle	Higher	Population
High and high-middle	1.94	2.65	2.20	27.37	5.48
Low-middle	9.69	8.29	8.87	42.91	14.10
Laborer	44.51	35.52	40.43	27.13	42.37
Marginal	43.86	53.54	48.50	2.41	38.05
Total	100.00	100.00	100.00	100.00	100.00

Source: Author's calculations based on FUNDACREDESA, 1980.

Table 5.23. Venezuela, 1986. Distribution of Public Education Spending by Socioeconomic
Level
(Percentage)

Level	Expenditure	Population
High and high-middle	13.08	5.48
Low-middle	23.35	14.10
Laborer	33.69	42.37
Marginal	29.88	38.05
Total	100.00	100.00

Source: Author's calculations based on FUNDACREDESA, 1980.

What is the balance with respect to the distributive impact of education spending as a whole? Table 5.23, shows the distribution of the population by level, but compares it instead with the distribution of aggregate public education spending, without distinguishing between educational levels.

The balance is unfavorable to the progressivity of spending. Although the first three levels of expenditure are received more than proportionately by students in the two lowest socioeconomic levels, the relative weight of higher education in the expenditure is large enough to render this fact meaningless. Therefore, since public education spending for higher education is received primarily by the two highest levels, the net effect of education spending as a whole seems to be regressive. Education spending at the higher level is so large in relative terms, as compared to public spending on other levels, that it only requires the distribution of spending at this level to be distinctly regressive for spending as a whole to be regressive.

Another way of looking at the subject is to compare the cumulative subsidy received by a student from the marginal level who stays in public schools from preschool through the end of the bachillerato (Bs. 31,847) with what a student from the highest level receives, even if he

Table 5.24. Venezuela, 1986. Absolute and per Student Total of the Education Subsidy by Socioeconomic Level

Level	Absolute total of the subsidy (millions of Bs.)	Subsidy per student (Bs.)
High and high-middle	1,750	9,253
Low-middle	3,123	6,662
Laborer	4,506	3,054
Marginal	3,996	2,144
Total	13,375	3,324

Source: Author's calculations based on FUNDACREDESA, 1980.

Table 5.25. Venezuela, 1986. Indices of Inequality in Education Spending

	Index
P High and high-middle	2.38
P Low-middle	1.65
P Laborer	0.79
P Marginal	0.78
Gini	0.16

Source: Author's calculations based on FUNDACREDESA, 1980.

only attends a public university, having completed the rest of his studies in private schools (Bs. 79,918).

Table 5.24, which provides a comprehensive view, shows the absolute amount of the subsidies by level, together with the subsidy per student enrolled in public institutions.

On average, a student from the highest socioeconomic level receives more than four times the amount received by a student in the least advantaged level.

Table 5.25, on the other hand, shows two indices normally used to measure the regressivity of spending programs. The first is simply the quotient of the percentage of spending received by one level and the percentage of the total population in that level, and the second is the Gini coefficient, which compares the distribution of spending with the theoretical, perfectly egalitarian distribution (Sen, 1981).

The first four rows (P index) indicate that while the two highest levels receive a more than proportionate share of public education spending, the two lowest receive a less than proportionate share. The Gini coefficient in the fifth row indicates a degree of inequity in education spending less than that shown by the same coefficient calculated for income distribution in Venezuela, estimated at 0.41 for total income in 1987. According to these indices, public education spending as a whole is far from equitably distributed (20 percent of the population in the highest level receives almost 40 percent of the spending) although its distribution is less regressive than the distribution of income.

The apparent, most direct cause of the inequality in spending is the financial arrangement in public higher education whereby the only way of providing financial aid to students is to waive tuition for all who register, regardless of their socioeconomic background. Thus, there is no possibility of directing aid to where it is needed most and, quite literally, a situation is created in which numerous students who are able to pay are subsidized, providing them with an incentive to do something they would do anyway, such as attending a university. One way of comprehending the magnitude of this problem is to simulate the variations in the above indices if students from at least the highest level were made to pay the cost of their higher education. Such a measure would be enough to bring the Gini coefficient of public education spending to near zero, i.e., absolute equality.

Other related causes concern the political economy of public spending and of education spending in particular. The fact that higher education withstood the fiscal crisis better than other educational levels suggests that its ability to exert political pressure is greater than that of the other levels. A detailed study of such factors is beyond the scope of this study.

Alternative Sources

To corroborate the above conclusions, we examined the OCEI household survey and extracted information concerning the number of children in each age group who attend school in each quartile of per capita income. This information was not used initially because, unlike the FUNDACREDESA data, it is impossible to distinguish between children who attend a public school and those who attend a private school. Nevertheless, assuming that each quartile uses public education in the same proportion as the corresponding level of the above classification provides the set of inequality indices shown in Table 5.26, together with an estimate, based on the same assumptions, of the weight of the education subsidy per household per quartile as a percentage of the average income per household per quartile.

These indices, although based on the above assumption, have an advantage over previous indices because they compare the distribution of students who receive public education spending with the quartile distribution of students in each age group (instead of the quartile distribution of the general population). These indices take into account the fact that low-income families tend to have more children. Clearly, the general patterns of the above data still hold: the richest 25 percent receives a more than proportionate share of public education spending, while the poorest 75 percent receives a less than proportionate share. The most drastic changes have to do with the difference between the P coefficient for the top group in Table 5.25 (2.38), and the same coefficient for the highest quartile in Table 5.26 (1.77). If we are to be-

Table 5.26. Venezuela, 1987. Indices of Inequality in Education Spending and Relative Weight of the Subsidy

	Index	Percentage of income
P Quartile IV	1.77	5.0
P Quartile III	0.85	5.0
P Quartile II	0.77	7.0
P Quartile I	0.78	14.0

Source: Author's calculations based on FUNDACREDESA, 1980.

lieve this second calculation, the inequity in spending is somewhat less significant than it originally appeared to be. Nevertheless, the principal characteristics of the overall situation remain unchanged and the inequality of public education spending is conclusively demonstrated, despite the fact that education expenditures represent a subsidy of increasing importance as the level of household income decreases.

Public Education Spending and Household Education Expenditures

To complete the picture of the distributive impact of public education spending, it is interesting to note how public education spending received by various households compares with education expenditures these same households make from their own funds. Although there is no consistent information on the subject, and assuming that the quartiles of income distribution in the household survey are comparable to those in which the Central Bank of Venezuela presents in its survey, we can make an estimate.

Table 5.27 shows the results of this approximation.[31] As can be seen, if an opinion about the progressivity of public education spending in Venezuela were to be based on this information, it would be correct to say that redistributive objectives are being fulfilled. Public spending represents a larger percentage of the total education expenditure per household in the lowest quartile of per capita income, and varies uniformly until reaching the highest quartile, where the percentage is lowest. In other words, public education spending, as a percentage of the education expenditures per household, benefits the poorest households more.

The main reason for this is that even though most of the spending goes to higher education and is used much more extensively by the highest quartiles, the lowest quartiles tend to have more children.

---

[31] The following analyses include as household education expenses all expenditures in the categories "Education and others," "Tuition," "Monthly fees," "Textbooks," and "Educational supplies" in the Survey of Family Budgets in the Caracas Metropolitan Area.

Table 5.27. Venezuela, 1986. Percentage of Household Education Expenditures Financed by the Government

Quartile	Subsidy	Private expenditures	Total
IV	77.46	22.54	100.00
III	54.82	45.18	100.00
II	41.32	58.68	100.00
I	32.54	67.46	100.00

Source: Author's calculations based on FUNDACREDESA, 1980.

Table 5.28. Venezuela, 1986: Comparison of the Education Subsidy and Private Education Expenditures per Household, by Quartile (Bs.)

Quartile	Subsidy	Private expenditures	Total
IV	4,755.33	9,859.12	14,614.45
III	4,805.44	6,823.68	11,629.12
II	5,686.19	4,686.31	10,372.50
I	5,742.44	1,671.31	7,413.45

Source: Author's calculations based on FUNDACREDESA, 1980.

This conclusion, however, must be corrected by the information in Table 5.28, which shows that the government's contribution per household is very similar in absolute terms in all quartiles.

It is not so much a question of the government helping the lowest income quartiles with a larger subsidy but rather that private expenditures are much greater—six times greater—in the highest quartile than in the lowest. This creates the peculiar aspect observed in the relative weights of private and government spending in each quartile. It should be noted that because of public spending, differences in household education expenditures are overall much smaller than if said expenditures depended entirely on direct disbursements by the families.

Conclusions

According to Fields' definition (a), a spending program can be considered equitable if each of the different population groups receives a share of projected spending in proportion to its relative weight in the total population. The analysis in the preceding pages shows conclusively that public education spending in Venezuela cannot be considered equitable.

In fact, according to the analysis based on the FUNDACREDESA classification, students from the highest 20 percent socioeconomic level of the population receive about 40 percent of the spending, while those from the 40 percent socioeconomically least advantaged receive less than 30 percent. The results obtained using information from the household survey and assumptions explained above are basically similar, although they indicate a somewhat less extreme regressivity.

These conclusions are even clearer when based on the percentage of the public education budget that goes to students in each level who attend public institutions, a percentage that drops sharply in the higher socioeconomic levels. The verdict is clearly against the equity of education spending, despite the fact that most children and young people in the higher levels do not use public education.

This general conclusion must be qualified, since it is not true for each of the education levels taken separately, but only for the highest level. The preschool, elementary and secondary levels are the ones where the spending pattern can unequivocally be termed equitable. But the fact is that this situation, which involves the vast majority of public school students, may be counterbalanced by the opposite effect of higher education spending. This result does not seem unusual within a comparative framework (Psacharopoulos and Tilak, 1991), although it is no less important in terms of the distributive impact of public education spending in Venezuela.

This is the basis for the clearest and most important policy recommendation of this study: the key to reversing the regressive character of education spending is adjusting the focus of higher education spending. In the present circumstances, the only way to provide financial aid to post-secondary students in Venezuela is to waive tuition for all students who enroll in a public higher education institution. A tuition system based on ability to pay or a student loan program would achieve similar results, while permitting recovery of a considerable percentage of costs. This tuition system will redirect a large proportion of public education spending to the lowest levels, a measure that will be not only more equitable but more efficient. This is not a policy change that would be easy to implement (Navarro, 1991).

Another aspect of the main conclusion, which may seem contradictory, is that because the subsidy is distributed inequitably does not mean that it does nothing to alleviate the inequality. This is seen in sections of this study which show that the dispersion of total education spending by quartiles (i.e., the total public spending received by each household plus disbursements from their own funds) is less than the dispersion of private spending in the same quartiles, and also that the education subsidy is much larger for poor households as a percentage of income. The explanation for this is that although it is not equitable, the distribution of public education spending is less inequitable than income distribution. The fact that so regressive a subsidy can appear to have a beneficial impact on distribution, however, leads not so much to an appreciation of the so-called benefits of the subsidy as to an awareness of the extreme inequality of income distribution in Venezuela.

The Indirect Gasoline Subsidy

The goal of this section is to determine whether an implicit gasoline subsidy exists, how large it is, and how it affects income distribution.

Our results show that in 1991 the subsidy exceeded 6 bolivars per liter and totaled more than 75 billion bolivars. This represented 10 percent of the national budget and 2.25 percent of the gross domestic product. The subsidy was received largely by the higher income levels—for every bolivar received by the lowest level, the highest level received 4.99. The resources did not go to the neediest sectors and, as a result, did not improve distribution.

These results raise questions about the continued existence of this subsidy and provide an opportunity for the development of policies aimed at improving this situation. A concrete policy proposal is advanced, which requires an understanding of why the subsidy has persisted and what arguments have been made for maintaining it:

• "It is a subsidy that is received very inefficiently by the low income sectors, but it is received." This argument has been used frequently. It denotes a lack of confidence in the social policy of the Venezuelan government, a topic not discussed in this section since it would not be feasible to propose a solution without including the state. Consequently, it will be assumed that the entire subsidy is returned to society through public spending or some other distributive mechanism.

• "The gasoline is our's and so it should be cheap. If Venezuela is a producer of oil, why should we have to pay the international price?" In this argument, political reasoning is used to keep prices low. The questions we must ask are: What does "international price" mean? Is it the price in London or at a Venezuelan port? In this study it is shown that the domestic price of gasoline should be higher than the current price, which is closely related to the export price of gasoline, and that the domestic price of gasoline is lower than prices in other countries.

• Venezuelans have become accustomed to low fuel prices,[32] which has created resistance to change and makes price adjustments difficult. In 1991 monthly price adjustments of 15 and 25 centavos were made, with the current price being Bs. 4.60. These increases represent 3.3 and 5.4 percent of the price, respectively, and although they are relatively small, demonstrations were organized against the increases.[33]

---

[32] As demonstrated in a survey conducted by CORPOVEN (a subsidiary of the petroleum industry), 52 percent of the population opposes an increase in the price of gasoline, despite the fact that the additional resources generated would go to education, health care, and safety.

[33] Inflation in Venezuela in 1991 was 31 percent, and the total price adjustment was 35.9 percent. Even so, one of the main topics of discussion was the excessive (disproportional) increase in fuel prices.

• "Keep public transportation prices relatively low." This argument is based on the premise that increasing the price of gasoline will increase the price of public transportation, "directly affecting the resources of Venezuelans, which are already greatly depleted." This argument justifies some governmental action in the transportation sector. In this study we propose a direct subsidy to public transportation, since it is progressive.

The remainder of this study is organized as follows: first, the implicit gasoline subsidy is calculated for 1986, 1989, 1990, and 1991. Second, its effect on income distribution is studied. Finally, the results are summarized and policy proposals are made.

Calculation of the Subsidy

In this section the implicit gasoline subsidy for 1986, 1989, 1990, and 1991 is calculated. The subsidy is defined as the difference between the average sales price to the public and the opportunity cost. The opportunity cost is the alternative use of the product. In this case, since gasoline is a tradable good, it has an obvious alternative use: export. The opportunity cost is the sales price at the port (the frontier price), adjusted for distribution and transportation costs.

Intuitively, it can be said that the shadow price (or opportunity cost) is what it costs society to manufacture an additional unit of this product, or what society is not collecting as a result of not reserving it for better alternative use.

Export gasoline and gasoline consumed internally differ in lead content and octane. These differences involve additional refining processes. Nevertheless, the additional cost necessary to produce gasoline for export represents less than 1 percent of its sales price. For this reason, this cost is not taken into account in calculating the subsidy. For the purposes of this study we assume that the costs are the same and that the refinery must sell the different gasolines at the same price.

We define the sales price at the refinery as P_{gr}; hence the sales price at the pump is the addition of the refinery-to-pump transportation cost to P_{gr}. The sales price at the port will be the same as the refinery price plus the cost of transporting the gasoline from the refinery to the port. These costs include transportation, administration, and sales expenses associated with exporting gasoline.

Methodology and Calculation of the Subsidy

The implicit gasoline subsidy is determined by estimating the price of gasoline at the pump, based on the frontier price and adjusted for transportation costs. Below, the subsidy is calculated as the difference between the opportunity cost and the real sales price. Finally, the subsidy will be determined per year, per capita, and per day in both nominal and real terms.

Price of Gasoline at the Pump

As indicated above, gasoline is a tradable good and its domestic price should equal the frontier price adjusted for transportation costs. The pump price of gasoline (the price at service stations) is defined as:

$$P_{gs} = P_{gf} - CT_{rp} + CT_{rs} \tag{1}$$

where P_{gs} is the price of gasoline at the pump,
P_{gf} is the frontier price of gasoline (FOB),[34]
CT_{rp} is the cost of transportation between the refinery and the port, and
CT_{rs} is the cost of transportation between the refinery and the pump.

Transportation Cost

Transportation cost is defined as the costs incurred by the petroleum industry to ensure that a liter of gasoline arrives at the point of sale. From this perspective, the sales, advertising, and marketing expenses are also part of the transportation costs.

It should be noted that the transportation costs between the refinery and the pump depend on the local sales price of gasoline, since part of the distribution is via land transportation. Consequently, the local transportation cost must be adjusted by adding gasoline price increments to it. The land transportation cost can be defined as follows: expenditure on gasoline and other factors not related to gasoline such as the driver's wages, depreciation of trucks, etc.

$$P_{gs} = P_{gr} + CTT_{rs} (a (1+p_{gs}) + (1-a)) + CC_{rs} \tag{2}$$

where "a" is the proportion of the expenditure on gasoline in the total cost of land transportation,

P_{gs} is the increment in the price of gasoline,
CTT is the cost of land transportation, and
CC are the marketing costs.

---

[34] The frontier price is the average export price throughout the year.

Calculation

With information on exports and local sales, the implicit gasoline subsidy is determined using formulas (1) and (2). In Table 5.29 six factors were considered in determining the subsidy: the export price (Bs./l), the cost of refinery-to-port transportation, the cost of refinery-to-pump transportation, the shadow price, and the subsidy in nominal and real terms. Each of these is explained below.

1. The export price per liter of gasoline is determined, in bolivars, based on the average export price, the exchange rate, the foreign currency implicit price factor,[35] and the liters in each barrel.

The foreign currency implicit price factor is used to adjust distortions in the nominal exchange rate when the latter does not reflect its opportunity cost. For example, in 1986 there was an official exchange rate and a free exchange rate, and the difference between the two (the premium) was more than 200 percent. Consequently, its opportunity cost was somewhere between the two rates.

2. To determine the refinery-to-port transportation cost, the total expenditure for this activity must be calculated. This consists of the direct transportation cost and the administrative and sales expenses that make the export possible.

The transportation cost can be found by dividing total expenditures by total liters exported. This cost is relatively low, less than 10 centavos for all years, representing less than 1 percent of the sales price.

Subtracting the refinery-to-port transportation cost from the frontier cost gives the refinery price.

3. The refinery-to-pump transportation costs were adjusted and the pump price was calculated using formula (2).

In this case, the cost is substantial compared to the refinery price, representing 66, 42, 32, and 33 percent of the refinery price for 1986, 1989, 1990, and 1991, respectively. Adding the refinery-to-pump transportation cost to the refinery price gives the pump price, which will be compared to the real sales price to determine the subsidy.

4. The subsidy per liter is the difference between the pump price and the average sales price for the year. As Table 5.29 shows, the average sales price is always lower than the pump price, which proves the existence of an implicit subsidy.

---

[35] The implicit price of foreign exchange is used to determine its shadow price. It is assumed that in 1989, 1990, and 1991, this factor was 1, since there was a flexible exchange rate.

Figure 5.2. Comparison of the Subsidies in Real Terms

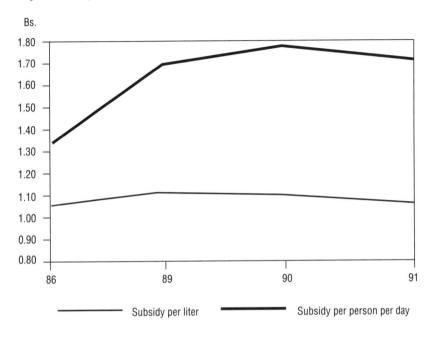

Bs.

Source: Author's calculations.

In 1986 the subsidy was relatively low due to a negative oil shock, not to local price adjustments. In 1989 and 1991 price adjustments were made that did not compensate for devaluation, and for this reason the subsidy increased in nominal terms.

5. The total subsidy is obtained by multiplying the subsidy per liter by the total liters sold locally. This amount is expressed in billions of bolivars and ranges from 8 billion in 1986 to 75 billion in 1991. For example, in 1991 the subsidy represented 10 percent of the national budget and 2.25 percent of the gross domestic product. Each inhabitant received, on average, a little less than 3,700 bolivars a year, 10 bolivars a day.

6. To calculate the subsidy in real terms, the consumer price index was used and both the subsidy per liter and the subsidy per capita per day were deflated. Figure 5.2 shows the trend of the subsidy over time.

Table 5.29. Calculation of the Subsidy

	1986 $	Bs.	1989 $	Bs.	1990 $	Bs/	1991 $	Bs.
Export price (/barrel)	15.80		19.20		21.00		22.00	
Contents of each barrel	157.50							
Average exchange rate		7.50		34.70		50.40		59.80
Pricing factor		2.13		1.00		1.00		1.00
Export price								
per barrel		252.00		665.00		1,059.50		1315.60
per liter		1.60		4.22		6.73		8.35
Transport cost: refinery-to-port								
Total (millions)		256.00		410.00		533.00		693.00
Liters of gasoline sold (millions)		7,551.00		8,558.00		8,986.00		9,435.00
Expenditure per liter		0.034		0.048		0.059		0.073
Gasoline price at refinery		1.57		4.17		6.67		8.28
Transport cost: refinery-to-pump								
TOTAL (millions)		7,163.00		11,462.00		14,900.00		19,370.00
Adjustment for new gasoline price		7,991.00		15,218.00		18,684.00		24,807.00
Liters of gasoline sold (millions)		8,908.00		10,368.00		11,325.00		11,891.00
Expenditure per liter		0.90		1.47		1.65		2.09
Price of gasoline at the pump		2.46		5.64		8.32		10.37
Sales price (Average)		1.50		2.00		3.45		4.05
Amount of subsidy per liter		0.96		3.64		4.87		6.32
Total subsidy (millions of Bs.)		8,577.00		37,763.00		55,123.00		75,102.00
Population (millions of people)		17.80		19.20		19.80		20.40
Total subsidy per resident		482.00		1,962.00		2,781.00		3,678.00
Total subsidy per resident per day		1.34		5.45		7.72		10.22
Price index		100.00		326.00		440.00		594.00
Subsidy per liter (1986 prices)		0.96		1.12		1.11		1.06
Subsidy per person (1986 prices)		1.34		1.67		1.75		1.72

Source: Author's calculations.

Distribution of the Subsidy by Social Level

Once the per-liter gasoline subsidy is determined, the question is who receives it? How is it distributed? To answer these questions, the Central Bank of Venezuela's 1986 Survey of Family Budgets in the Caracas Metropolitan Area was used to study the different ways in which consumers receive the subsidy.

Three mechanisms through which consumers receive the subsidy are examined below. First, people who buy gasoline at service stations receive a per-liter subsidy. Determination of this subsidy requires that the gasoline consumption of each social level be known. This subsidy will be called the direct subsidy.

Second, people who use public transportation or other means of paid transportation (for example, school buses, taxis, etc.) receive an indirect subsidy, which is reflected in a lower fare. To simplify calculations,[36] it is assumed that carriers and/or drivers do not appropriate the subsidy but pass it along to the consumer in the form of lower fares. This assumption allows us to determine how much subsidy each bolivar spent on public transportation buys.

Third, the gasoline subsidy also affects the cost of the goods transported. Cheaper gasoline lowers the final price of these goods. Consequently, the direct consumption of goods also has an indirect subsidy. In this case the same assumption will be made as for the indirect transportation subsidy.

The information for the following sections on these three mechanisms is arranged in quartiles. We make the assumption that families in the rest of the country behave like the families in the quartiles of the metropolitan area.

Direct subsidy (gasoline purchase)

Consumers receive a direct subsidy when they buy gasoline at service stations. The budget survey indicates the amount spent by level to purchase gasoline for vehicles. In addition, expenditures for items related to what we have called public transportation are shown in Table 5.30.

Gasoline expenditures increase with social level, while the opposite occurs with transportation expenditures, especially for trips on buses and collective taxis. Total gasoline expenditures are 2 billion bolivars, while transportation expenditures are nearly 2.3 billion bolivars. These findings have interesting distributive effects and are analyzed below.

The direct subsidy per level is obtained by multiplying the total liters consumed by the per-liter subsidy determined in the preceding section. The results of this calculation are shown in Table 5.31. The total number of people in each level is approximately 796,000. The average subsidy for all levels is 404 bolivars per person. Nevertheless, the highest level receives nearly eight times more than the lower levels.

Public Transportation

The indirect subsidy obtained through public transportation will be determined as follows: first, the number of liters consumed by

---

[36] If this assumption cannot be made and if part of the subsidy is appropriated by the carrier, an adjustment of the expenditure must be made. This would complicate the study. In the final part of the report an analysis is given of what would happen in such cases.

Table 5.30. Expenditure on Gasoline and Public Transportation. Entire Metropolitan Area, 1986
(Billions of Bs.)

| | Levels | | | | |
	1	2	3	4	Total
Gasoline for vehicles	136	329	543	995	2,003
Public transportation					
Bus trips	54	61	36	19	170
Collective taxi trips	471	465	367	160	1,462
Domestic bus trips	21	21	14	21	78
School buses and taxis	63	134	182	180	559
Foreign bus trips	0	1	0	0	1
Domestic coll. taxi trips	0	1	0	0	1
Total	609	682	600	380	2,271

Source: Author's calculations based on consumption survey, Central Bank of Venezuela.

Table 5.31. Direct Gasoline Subsidy, per Person, per Year, 1986

| | Levels | | | | |
	1	2	3	4	Average
Expenditure on gasoline (Bs.)	171	413	682	1,250	629
Average price of gasoline	1.50				
Gasoline consumption (liters)	114	276	455	833	419
Subsidy per liter	0.96				
Subsidy per level (Bs.)	110	265	438	802	404

Source: Author's calculations based on consumption survey, Central Bank of Venezuela.

carriers throughout the country are calculated. Then, the consumption of gasoline for public transportation in the metropolitan area is estimated. Third, with the total liters consumed by carriers and the total expenditure on transportation per level, the subsidy and its share of total expenditures on transportation are calculated. In this way, the subsidy per bolivar invested in transportation is determined.

Table 5.32 shows the percentage of the subsidy that each bolivar invested in transportation buys. The total number of liters consumed in the metropolitan area is 155 million, which, when multiplied by the subsidy per liter, gives the total indirect subsidy.

If the subsidy were eliminated, the price of transportation would increase 6.6 percent (for 1986). This means that each bolivar invested in transportation is purchasing part of this subsidy. Table 5.33 shows

Table 5.32. Percentage of Subsidy on Expenditures for Public Transportation and Freight, 1986

	Per person	Country (billions)	Metropolitan area (billions)
Public transportation (liters/year)	49	869	155
Subsidy per liter	0.96		
Total subsidy (Bs.)	47	837	149
Expenditure on public transportation			2,271
% subsidy/public trans. expenditures			6.6
Freight (liters/year)	33	579	103
Subsidy per liter	0.96		
Total subsidy (Bs.)	31	558	100
Total expenditure			102,902
% subsidy/total expenditure			0.1

Source: Author's calculations based on consumption survey, Central Bank of Venezuela.

the subsidy per level and, as can be seen, higher levels receive less subsidy per person (31 as opposed to 50) than lower levels, which leads to the conclusion that this part of the subsidy is progressive.

Transport of Goods

The total liters consumed in the transport of goods is 33 liters per person per year. We make the assumption that all consumer goods are transported and that the gasoline consumed in the process is proportional to the price of the good transported. This assumption is necessary since the only way to distribute the liters of gasoline is through the total consumption of each level.

Table 5.32 shows the consumption of gasoline for the transport of goods (freight) in the metropolitan area, as well as the subsidy. Assuming the freight component of the baskets of goods purchased by each level is the same, then each bolivar spent on the consumption of goods purchases the same amount of subsidy. This assumption is the basis for the calculations in Table 5.32, which shows that 0.10 percent of consumption is subsidized.

The figures indicating consumption by level were obtained from the budget survey conducted by the Central Bank of Venezuela and are shown in Table 5.33. The per capita subsidy reveals that the average is 31 bolivars per person per year and that higher levels receive a larger proportion. This makes sense, since the higher levels consume more than lower levels and the subsidy was distributed through consumption.

Table 5.33. Indirect Subsidy per Level and per Person. Public Transportation and Freight, 1986

	Levels				
	1	2	3	4	Total
Public transportation (millions of Bs.)	609	682	600	380	2,271
Percentage of subsidy	6.6				
Total subsidy per level (millions of Bs.)	40	45	39	25	149
Persons per level (thousands)	796	796	796	796	3,185
Subsidy per person (Bs.)	50	56	50	31	47
Total expenditure (millions of Bs.)	14,128	20,904	24,806	43,064	102,902
Percentage of subsidy	0.10				
Total subsidy per level (millions of Bs.)	14	20	24	42	100
Persons per level (thousands)	796	796	796	796	3,185
Subsidy per person	17	25	30	52	31

Source: Author's calculations based on consumption survey, Central Bank of Venezuela.

Table 5.34. Total Subsidy, 1986
(Bs.)

	Levels				
	1	2	3	4	Average
Total subsidy per person	177	347	517	886	482
Direct	110	265	438	802	404
Indirect	67	82	80	84	78
Public transportation	50	56	50	31	47
Freight	17	25	30	52	31
Total subsidized (Bs.)	177	347	517	886	482
Average per capita income	10,193	19,047	30,391	77,433	34,209
% subsidy on income	1.7	1.8	1.7	1.1	1.4

Source: Author's calculations based on consumption survey, Central Bank of Venezuela.

Results and Conclusions

Table 5.34 summarizes the results by type of subsidy and by level, and the graph shows the composition of the subsidy in each level. First, the results are summarized. Second, the effects of dropping the assumptions made throughout the study are analyzed in terms of their impact on the subsidy. Third, the impact that the free price of gasoline would have on the economy is studied and the arguments on which the gasoline subsidy is based are questioned.

It should be noted that the direct subsidy is regressive and the public transportation subsidy is progressive. Nevertheless, the net result is that for every bolivar received by the lower class, the upper class receives almost five bolivars (Bs. 4.99). This proves that the subsidy as a whole is regressive.

Conclusions

This study demonstrates the existence of an indirect gasoline subsidy due to the domestic sales price being lower than the opportunity cost of gasoline, adjusted for transportation costs. This subsidy represented 2.25 points of GDP and 10 percent of the national budget in 1991. The subsidy is regressive as a whole and, consequently, there is no justification for continuing it.

Although the indirect subsidy through public transportation is progressive, it is considerably smaller than the direct subsidy, which is extremely regressive, making the overall effect regressive.

It is important to analyze how the final results are affected by eliminating the assumptions made in the study. First, since the exported gasoline and the gasoline sold locally are different, approximately 1 percent would have to be deducted from the frontier price,[37] which would reduce the subsidy for 1991 by 8 centavos. Whether or not this adjustment is made, the final conclusions of the study remain unchanged.

Second, if the cost of transporting goods were calculated according to the type of goods consumed in each level and not on the basis of the total consumed, income distribution would be changed by an amount equivalent to 15 percent of the subsidy,[38] which would not change its regressive character.

Finally, it is interesting to compare the opportunity cost of gasoline with the sales prices in other countries. Table 5.35 shows the sales price of gasoline in the United States, the United Kingdom, France, Switzerland, Venezuela (real price) and Venezuela (shadow price). The price per liter is shown in both dollars and bolivars. The last column of the table contains an index indicating how much larger or smaller this price is than the "shadow price" in Venezuela.

Comparison of prices reveals that they are all higher than the shadow price in Venezuela. In particular, the price in the United States is 85 percent higher and the price in European countries is 300 percent higher. Currently, the average sales price is less than half of what the price of gasoline should be.

---

[37] It should be remembered that the difference in the cost of refining the two grades of gasoline is less than 1 percent of the price of gasoline produced for export.

[38] The indirect subsidy distributed through the transport of goods represents 15 percent of the total subsidy granted. Adjusting these calculations would not change the final results.

Table 5.35. Comparison of Gasoline Prices in Different Countries

| | Price of gasoline per liter | | |
	$	Bs.	Index
United States	0.32	19.20	85.1
Switzerland	0.71	42.60	310.8
United Kingdom	0.83	49.80	380.2
France	0.92	55.20	432.3
Venezuela	0.07	4.05	-60.9
Venezuela (shadow price)	0.17	10.37	0.0

Source: Author's calculations based on consumption survey, Central Bank of Venezuela.

If we ask whether Venezuela should have cheaper gasoline than other countries, the answer is yes. But if we ask whether Venezuela should have a gasoline sales price that is half its opportunity cost, the answer is not so clear, and this study has shown not only that a subsidized gasoline price makes no sense but also that society would be better off if the subsidy did not exist.

In conclusion, the gasoline subsidy has three components, two of which are regressive and only one of which, the indirect public transportation subsidy, is progressive. Consequently, there is no reason for the continued existence of this subsidy.

Elimination of the Subsidy

Table 5.34 shows the amount of the subsidy as a percentage of family income. In the lower levels the subsidy represents between 1.7 and 1.8 percent of income and in the highest level 1.1 percent. In other words, lower levels receive a subsidy that is larger in real terms than that received by upper levels. This means that eliminating the subsidy without implementing some alternative measure would have a proportionately larger impact on the lower levels.

As the study demonstrates, a progressive subsidy could be granted for public transportation. Abolishing the gasoline subsidy would provide the necessary funds.

The Cost of Uncertainty

As a final point, the overall effect of using the shadow price of gasoline as a means of eliminating the subsidy will be studied. The first conclusion is that the price of gasoline should be raised to its shadow price and that each time the export price changes, the local price should be changed to eliminate any subsidy, since it is extremely regressive. This would cause the local price of gasoline to fluctuate with the international price of a barrel of gasoline.

Developed countries have had to pay for instability caused by the price of gasoline. The mobilization of economic resources with price changes results in adjustment costs for society. Hausmann (1990) estimated the adjustment costs generated by the instability of oil prices at 8 percent of GDP when the shock was 9.5 percent.

In addition to the adjustment costs generated by instability of oil prices, the adjustment cost generated by fluctuating gasoline prices must also be paid. We envision two situations, one in which the price remains constant and another in which the price varies with international fluctuations. In the first, there is the risk of granting an implicit subsidy to the upper classes, which would adversely affect distribution. However, there is no uncertainty in such a system and, consequently, no adjustment costs are incurred. In the second, there is no possibility of any subsidy being granted, but some uncertainty exists and adjustment costs may be involved.

Clearly, none of the situations are desirable and probably none are optimal. An intermediate point might be interesting. Future studies might include a design for a stabilization fund for the oil industry that would lower total costs through subsidies granted by setting the price of gasoline as opposed to adjustment costs generated by the uncertainty of gasoline prices.

Figure 5.3. Comparison of the Subsidies Received

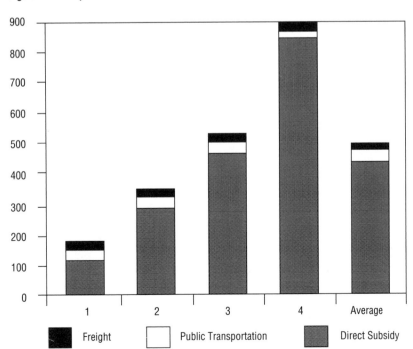

Bibliography

Acedo Machado, Clementina. 1982. *La implementación de los derechos sociales en un estado populista benefactor: El caso del seguro social en Venezuela.* Caracas: Universidad Católica Andrés Bello.

Ahmad, Ehtisham, and Yan Wang. 1989. Inequality and poverty in China: Institutional change and public policy, 1978-1988. Background paper, *World Development Report 1990.* New York: Oxford University Press.

Ahmad, Ehtisham, J. Dreze, J. Hills, and A. Sen. 1990. *Social security and welfare in developing countries.* New York: Oxford University Press.

Altimir, Oscar. 1982. *The extent of poverty in Latin America.* World Bank Staff Working Paper no. 522. Washington DC: The World Bank.

Atkinson, A.B. 1987. Income maintenance and social insurance. In *Handbook of public economics*, Vol. 2, eds. Alan Auerbach and Martin Feldstein. Amsterdam: North-Holland.

_____. 1989. *Poverty and social security.* New York: Wheatsheaf Press.

Atkinson, A.B., and J.E. Stiglitz. 1980. *Lectures on public economics.* Maidenhead, U.K.: McGraw-Hill.

Azpurua, R., R.A. González, and G. Machado. 1988. Evaluación social de la inversión del estado venezolano en las empresas de Guayana. Paper prepared toward master's in administration, IESA, Caracas. Mimeo.

Beodo Curras, M. 1985. *Manual teórico-práctico de la ley del seguro social.* Caracas: Vadell Hermanos Editores.

Birdsall, N., and E. James. 1990. *Efficiency and equity in social spending: How and why governments misbehave.* PRE Working Papers. Washington, DC: The World Bank.

Blackburn, M. 1989. Interpreting the magnitude of changes in measures of income inequality. *Journal of Econometrics* 42:21-25.

Champernowne, D.G. 1974. A comparison of measures of inequality of income distribution. *The Economic Journal* 84:787-816.

Compendio estadístico del sector eléctrico: edición 1987-1988. 1990. Caracas: Ministry of Energy and Mines.

Consideraciones sobre el consumo de electricidad en Venezuela. 1989. Caracas: Corporación Venezolana de Guayana.

CORDIPLAN. 1991. *El gran viraje.* Caracas: CORDIPLAN.

CORDIPLAN. 1986. *Informe social 3.* Caracas: CORDIPLAN.

Cornia, G., R. Jolly, and F. Stewart. 1987. *Adjustment with a human face.* Vol. 1. Oxford: Clarendon Press.

Davies, James B., and Ian Wooton. 1989. Payroll taxes in Brazil: An analysis of the major efficiency and equity issues. Department of Economics, University of Western Ontario, London, Canada.

De Oliveira, Francisco E.B., K. Beltrao, and T. LeGrand. 1989. The effects of new, proposed and provisional reforms on the financial solvency of the Brazilian national social security system: 1988-2010. Latin America and Caribbean Technical Department, The World Bank. Mimeo.

Di Lodovico, Amadeo T. 1991. *Pobreza: Una breve síntesis de sus conceptos y formas de medición.* Papeles de Trabajo IESA. Caracas: IESA.

El financiamiento de la educación en los países en desarrollo: Opciones de política. 1986. Washington, DC: The World Bank.

Encuesta de hogares por muestreo. n.d. Caracas: Oficina Central de Estadística e Información.

Encuesta sobre presupuestos familiares del área metropolitana de Caracas. 1986. Caracas: Banco Central de Venezuela.

Encuesta sobre presupuestos familiares del área metropolitana de Caracas. 1989. Caracas: Central Bank of Venezuela.

Escobar, G. 1990. *Equilibrio y justicia: El impacto del gasto público en Venezuela.* IESC Working Papers. Caracas: Ediciones IESA.

Estadísticas de EDELCA, Enero-Diciembre 1990. 1990. Caracas: Corporación Venezolana de Guayana.

Estadísticas del Sector Eléctrico. 1990. Caracas: CAVEINEL

Estudio de los costos marginales del sistema eléctrico venezolano. 1991. Caracas: CORDIPLAN.

Estudios laborales. 1986. In *Ensayos sobre derecho del trabajo y disciplinas afines en homenaje al Profesor Rafael Alfonso Guzmán.* Caracas: Universidad Central de Venezuela.

Fields, G. 1975. *Higher education and income distribution in a less developed country.* Oxford Economic Papers (June).

Foster, J., Joel Greer, and Erik Thorbecke. 1984. A class of decomposable poverty measures. *Econométrica*:761-766.

Foxley, Alejandro, E. Aninat, and J.P. Arellano. 1979. *Redistributive effects of government programmes: The Chilean case.* Surrey: Pergamen Press.

Frey, B.S. 1978. A politico-economic model of the United Kingdom. *Economic Journal* 88:243-253.

FUNDACREDESA. 1989. *El proceso educativo venezolano.* Caracas: Ministerio de la Secretaría de la Presidencia.

FUNDACREDESA. 1990. *Proyecto Venezuela: Estudio nacional de crecimiento y desarrollo humanos de la república de Venezuela.* Caracas: Ministerio de la Secretaría de la Presidencia.

Garay, J. n.d. Legislación del seguro social. 4th ed. Caracas: Librería Ciafré.

Glewwe, P., and D. de Tray. 1989. *The poor in Latin America during adjustment: A case study of Peru.* World Bank LSMS Working Paper no. 56. Washington, DC: The World Bank.

Golbert, Laura, and Lo Vuolo, Ruben. n.d. Aporte para un debate sobre previsión social. Proyectos ARG/86/035 y RLA/86/004, Ministerio de Salud y Acción Social, U.N. Development Program.

González, Bernando B., Juan Luis Hernández M., Arturo Araujo M., and Gabriele Merz. 1988. *Consumo de alimentos entre los estratos mas pobres.* Caracas: ILDIS.

González, R.A. 1991. Educación: aspecto financiero. Diagnóstico de la distribución de competencias. Estudio de Transferencia de Competencias COPRE-PNUD, Caracas. Mimeo.

Iduani, Ernesto A. 1988. *Seguridad social en Argentina.*

International Monetary Fund. 1986. *Fund-supported programs, fiscal policy and income distribution.* Paper no. 46 (September). Washington, DC: IMF.

Jallade, Jean-Pierre. 1989. *Public expenditure and income distribution in Colombia.* World Bank Staff Paper no. 44. Baltimore: Johns Hopkins University Press.

Jimenez, E. 1987. *Pricing policy in the social sectors: Cost recovery for education and health in developing countries.* Washington, DC: Johns Hopkins University Press for the World Bank.

Le Grand, J. 1982. *The strategy of equality: Redistribution and the social services.* London: George Allen & Unwin.

Lecaros, F. 1983. El sistema eléctrico interconectado de Venezuela. In *Análisis de costos marginales y diseño de tarifas de electricidad y agua,* ed. Ives Albouy. Washington, DC: Inter-American Development Bank.

Marquez, G. 1990. The recent evolution of public expenditure in education, health and housing in Venezuela. Caracas. Mimeo.

McGreevey, William. 1990. *Social security in Latin America: Issues and options for the World Bank.* Latin America and Caribbean Regional Office, the World Bank, Washington, D.C.

Meerman, J. 1979. *Public expenditure in Malaysia: Who benefits and why.* New York: Oxford University Press.

Meldau, Elke C. 1980. *Benefit-incidence of public health expenditure and income distribution: A case study of Colombia.* North Qunicy, MA: Christopher Publishing House.

Méndez, P. 1980. *Manual práctico para el seguro social.* Caracas: Centro Asesor del Seguro Social.

Mesa-Lago, Carmelo. 1989. Aspectos económico-financieros de la seguridad social en América Latina y el Caribe: Tendencias, problemas y alternativas para el año 2000. Study commissioned for the World Bank, Latin American Technical Department.

_____. 1990. *Investment portfolio of social insurance/pension funds in Latin America and the Caribbean: Significance, composition and performance.* Internal Discussion Paper, the World Bank.

Ministerio de Educación. 1987. *Memoria y cuenta, 1986*. Caracas: Ministerio de Educación.

Navarro, J.C. 1991. Educación: Aspecto organizativo funcional. Diagnóstico de la distribución de competencias. Estudio de Transferencia de Competencias COPRE-PNUD, Caracas. Mimeo.

_____. 1991. Venezuelan higher education in perspective. *Higher Education* 21.

Parot, R.. 1990. *Estimación de precios de cuenta para Venezuela*. Internal Working Paper, Inter-American Development Bank, Washington, D.C.

Peacock, A.T., and J. Wiseman. 1961. *The growth of public expenditure in the United Kingdom*. London: Allen and Unwin.

Peltzman, S. 1980. The growth of government. *Journal of Law and Economics*:209-287.

Petrei, Humberto, et al. 1987. *El gasto público y sus efectos distributivos: Un examen comparativo de cinco países de América Latina*. Río de Janeiro: ECIEL.

Política de precios de la energía eléctrica a largo plazo. 1991. Caracas: Corporación Venezolana de Guayana.

Psacharopoulos, G., and J.B.G. Tilak. 1991. Schooling and equity. In *Essays on poverty, equity and growth*, comps. Deepak Lal and Hla Myint. Washington, DC: Pergamon Press-The World Bank.

Puffert, Douglas J., and Emmanuel Y. Jimenez. 1988. The macroeconomics of social security in Brazil: fiscal and finnancial considerations. Brazil. Mimeo.

Ravaillon, Martin, and Monika Huppi. 1989. Measuring changes in poverty: A methodological case study of Indonesia during an adjustment period. *The World Bank Economic Review* 3:37-82.

Reimers, F. 1991. *Educación para todos en América Latina en el siglo XXI: Los desafíos de la estabilización y el ajuste para la planificación educativa*. Caracas: CINTERPLAN.

Republica de Venezuela. 1989. Decreto 393. *Reforma parcial de reglamento general de la ley del seguro social*. Gaceta Legal Ramirez & Garay no. 736 (August 31).

Rodríguez-Grossi, Jorge. 1989. *Public spending on social programs: Issues and options.*

Samuelson, P. 1954. The pure theory of public expenditures. *Review of Economics and Statistics* 36:377-389.

Selowsky, Marcelo. 1979. *Who benefits from government expenditure? A case study of Colombia.* London: Oxford University Press.

Sen, Amartya. 1976. Poverty: An ordinal approach to measurement. *Econométrica*: 219-231.

_____. 1979. *Sobre la desigualdad económica.* Barcelona: Editorial Crítica.

Stiglitz, J.E. 1988. *Economics of the public sector.* New York: W.W. Norton & Company.

Urrutia, M., and C. de Sandoval. 1979. *Politica fiscal y distribución del ingreso en Colombia.* London: Oxford University Press.

The World Bank. 1988. *World Development Report.* New York: Oxford University Press.

The World Bank. 1991. *Venezuela poverty study: From generalized subsidies to targeted programs.* Washington, DC: The World Bank.

The World Bank. 1990. *World Development Report.* New York: Oxford University Press.

Zuckerman, Elaine. 1989. *Adjustment program and social welfare.* World Bank Discussion Paper no. 44. Washington, DC: The World Bank.

INDEX